Shouting at Amen Corner

*Dispatches from the Masters—
The World's Greatest
Golf Tournament*

by
Ron Green

compiled by
Scott Martin

a **SPORTS**MASTERS book

a division of Sports Publishing Inc.
www.SportsPublishingInc.com

Director of Production: Susan M. McKinney
Cover design:Todd Lauer, Terry N. Hayden

ISBN: 1-58382-018-3

A SportsMasters Book
SPORTS PUBLISHING INC.
804 N. Neil
Champaign, IL 61820
www.sportspublishinginc.com

Printed in the United States.

For Arnie and Jack and Billy Joe,
and all the others who have won and lost
in golf's grandest theater.

Contents

Acknowledgments

Scott Martin would like to thank Greg and Mary Frye, Paul Haag, Mike Persinger, Gary Schwab, Stewart Spencer, and John Luby.

Preface

Ron Green has written columns for *The Charlotte News* and *The Charlotte Observer* four times a week for over 40 years. He has interviewed legendary athletes like Joe DiMaggio, Michael Jordan, and Wilt Chamberlain. He has been to four Olympics, 22 Super Bowls, and covered 46 seasons of ACC basketball. And in all the years and all those columns, he has loved nothing more in his job than writing about golf.

Ron has been to Augusta to cover the Masters 45 times while becoming one of the best golf writers in the country. In 1958, he had breakfast with Arnold Palmer on the morning when Palmer went out and won his first Masters. Ron has watched the glorious shots and felt the heartbreaks—and has written them by heart.

It has been my privilege to be his sports editor for the past 14 years. It is a privilege to read his words and thoughts once again about golf's great tournament, the Masters.

Gary Schwab
Charlotte Observer Executive Sports Editor

Introduction

Asked to evaluate the course on which the Masters is played each spring, famed golf architect Robert Trent Jones said, "Augusta National is overexposed but not overrated. There are courses around the country as good, but they don't get the same exposure. That's because the Masters is Scarborough Fair, the gathering of eagles.

"Everyone wants to make the trip to Mecca."

I made that trip 45 times as a sports writer and columnist for *The Charlotte News* and later *The Charlotte Observer*, and I never failed to be thrilled. I usually arrived on Monday or Tuesday, and those were the best days of the week, because you had it all ahead of you. The eagles had gathered, the vast green emptiness of the fairways lay waiting, and the trees and shrubs were in bloom. There was time to anticipate, speculate, to chat with past greats who had come back to stand on the lawn under the trees like monuments, to walk around the place and be embraced by it.

It is the very sameness that Trent Jones mentioned that, to a great extent, makes the Masters one of our loveliest, most exciting, and more revered sporting events

Your first look at Augusta National is a breathtaking experience that you never forget. But you don't fully appreciate the course, the tournaments, the whole of this celebration of spring, until you've seen it several times. You build a storehouse of memories that give character to every hole and an appreciation of each hour and each situation of these four days in spring.

That is the purpose of this book, to take you from Ben Hogan to Tiger Woods and tell you about what happened and what they said and how they looked and how it sounded and felt and what became of them. These are the articles I wrote on the days these things happened. From them, you can watch the passing of Hogan and Snead and Nelson and the coming of

Palmer and Nicklaus and Player, and then their passing and the coming of Trevino and Watson and the dark-starred Weiskopf and Norman, and their passing and the coming of Love and Couples and then the wonder child Woods.

This is not a complete history. In many instances, you will find nothing about a certain day in a tournament. What this book is meant to do is let you go inside the locker room or out onto the course with the men who have made the Masters so intriguing. You can hear them talk about the course and about each other and about how it feels to be out there around Amen Corner—the 11th, 12th and 13th holes—trying to win on Sunday afternoon. You can get a feel for the times, the changing course, and equipment and attitudes, the times when you could buy a ticket whenever you wanted one and the times when you couldn't even get on the waiting list.

I wrote more than 250,000 words about the Masters, walked more than 1,000 miles around its fairways. I saw Hogan walking up the 18th fairway with that slight limp, a grimace on his face that resembled a smile. I saw Arnie's Army recruited and watched it storm the hills and valleys, whooping for the slashing hero.

I saw Nicklaus holing a long, curling putt on the 16th and then leaping around the green with putter raised, making what Tom Weiskopf, waiting on the tee to hit, later called "Bear tracks." I saw Miller make six birdies in a row, Weiskopf make a 13 on No. 12, and Norman and Watson and Palmer butcher the last hole when they might have won.

Moments of greatness, moments of dreadful failure.

Tradition hangs in the air, wanders invisibly but palpably around the course and through the clubhouse, itself a prop out of "Gone With The Wind," shaded by trees that have stood for 250 years.

Beauty is everywhere. Shots seem purer and more beautiful in flight against this backdrop.

The back nine is Eden with flagsticks, all pines and azaleas and dogwoods and rambling creeks and little ponds and memories and promises. This is where you go to feel the embrace of the Masters before the battle starts, to see the beauty, to know the peril, to look for ghosts, to listen for echoes.

This is where you find Amen Corner, so named by famed golf writer Herbert Warren Wind in 1958. He took the designation from an old spiritual song, "Shouting At Amen Corner."

I regret, for myself and for this book, that I can't tell you firsthand how it was before 1955. I missed the victories by Hogan and Snead, although I did see them play many times after that. I missed Gene Sarazen's double eagle on the 15th in 1935, of course, and Byron Nelson's playoff victory over Hogan in 1942.

And you won't find a lot here about the inner workings of the Masters. One reason I never lost my awe of the place and the event, is that I never looked under the carpet to see if there was dust there. I didn't want to know what made the Masters tick. Club politics, fusses over invitation lists, money—things like that I've avoided; they're not about golf shots and shining moments and green jackets.

Forty-five years. My fondest memory of the Masters? Nicklaus winning his sixth in '86 was one. Nicklaus beating Weiskopf and Miller in '75, the greatest Masters of them all, was another. Palmer beating Dow Finsterwald and Gary Player in a playoff in '62 makes the list. Hogan burning down the back nine in 30 shots long past his prime. Larry Mize's pitch-in to beat Norman. So many.

But the fondest had nothing to do with a shot or a score. It was the first time I drove down Magnolia Lane, back when they let the working people come in that way, parked, walked around the clubhouse and saw the golf course spread before me. That was the fondest.

1955

This was the first year I covered the Masters for The Charlotte News.

If Ben Hogan played in a tournament I was covering, I watched him play, and I always spent time listening to him in the locker room.

When I wrote about him in the 1955 Masters, he was still the best, but he was in the autumn of his career, and his putter was starting to desert him. The putting yips that eventually drove him out of tournament golf had taken root.

"I'm not afraid of missing the putt," he once said in a rare moment of candor. "I'm afraid I can't draw the putter back. When I look at the cup, it's filled with my blood."

He could still hit the shots. He had lost a playoff to Sam Snead in the 1954 Masters. He was second again, to Cary Middlecoff, in 1955, and a couple of months later lost his chance at a fifth U.S. Open title when little-known Jack Fleck beat him in a playoff at the Olympic Club in San Francisco. Hogan tied for second in the 1956 U.S. Open and won his last victory in the Colonial Invitational in 1959.

In one of his most remarkable performances, Hogan threatened to win the 1960 U.S. Open before going into the water twice on the last two holes. Arnold Palmer was the winner. And then, in one final curtain call for this great talent in 1967, Hogan shot 30 on the back nine at Augusta and 66 for the round.

No one in sports ever fascinated me the way Ben Hogan did, out there in his gray cardigan sweater and white snap-bill cap, a cigarette clenched in his teeth, a limp in his walk, his eyes staring. He was like a mythical figure to me. Still is.

Once the 12th green was rebuilt, and when the Masters rolled around, the green was as hard as Washington Road, which runs in front of the club. I heard the complaints from players and went out there and spent hours watching shots hit into that green. Every shot that landed on the green bounced over. Except one. Hogan's shot landed on the green, took a little hop and stopped three feet from the cup.

THEY CHEERED HOGAN,
EVEN IF HE DIDN'T WIN

The throng around the 18th green at Augusta National Golf Course yesterday gave the gaunt, limping Texan a tremendous ovation as he completed another Masters tournament. They knew he was second to Cary Middlecoff, but memories of bygone victories stirred them.

There was something electric in the air as the winner of every major championship in the world putted out in the gathering darkness and the rain.

A few minutes later, the grimness gone from his countenance, Hogan sat in the clubhouse and talked of the future. It was not heartening news for the millions who have cheered him. And yet, he was cheerful.

"I don't know what is to happen," Hogan said. "My knee has been giving me a lot of trouble recently. I have had to lay off because of it. If it doesn't get better, I may have to play even less."

The ailing knee is the result of Hogan's automobile collision that almost ended his career many years ago.

"And the concentration," he went on. "It's awful. It just isn't there. I try to figure out a shot and I can't. It's just awful."

It was strange, but he smiled as he said this. It was this one thing—concentration—that made Hogan one of the greatest players the world has ever known.

Asked about his tournament, Hogan frankly admitted that he had held little hope of catching Middlecoff on the final 18 holes after trailing by four strokes through 54.

"I knew I couldn't catch him if my putts didn't start falling, and I wasn't making any. I made only one putt of more than seven feet in the entire tournament.

"You have to be putting well to win here. It is hard for anybody to come here and learn to read the greens right away. One is slow, the next is fast, and all of them have a lot of undulation.

"I just haven't been playing enough," he continued. "I played 13 exhibitions after the National Open last year. After that, I didn't play any until I played in Florida a few weeks ago."

Hogan said he was pleased with his second-place finish but was not satisfied with the way he played.

"I wouldn't be satisfied," he said, "if I had shot 186 instead of 286."

He said he felt he had played better than last year, when he tied Sam Snead for the championship and lost by one stroke in a playoff.

And then he got back to the future.

"I don't have any plans right now," he said. "I am going home now, and I don't think I'll be playing any golf until the National Open.

"I plan to continue to play in the Masters, the Open and the Colonial Invitational until I can't play golf anymore. It won't make any difference if I can't win them. I'll play in them just to be playing."

NOTES AND OBSERVATIONS

BYRON PUTS NELSON HOLD ON CHAMPS DURING MASTERS PLAY

You would have thought Byron Nelson had won the Augusta Masters Championship, the way he was smiling.

"I just brought in my sixth winner," he beamed.

Lord Byron was Cary Middlecoff's playing partner in the final round yesterday. When Middlecoff won, it marked the sixth time (not counting By's two wins) that Nelson had played the last round with a winner.

He brought Sam Snead in twice and Ben Hogan, Herman Keiser, and Claude Harmon once each.

"I couldn't pick a man out of the field who would be better to have with you on that last round," Middlecoff said. "If I seemed to get into trouble or tighten up, he'd pat me on the back and say, 'Come on now, just play your game.' That helped a lot."

Incidental Intelligence: The champion got up at eight, had scrambled eggs and orange juice for breakfast, took his hay fever pill, didn't eat any lunch, and was very nervous until he teed off.

Bobby Jones called Middlecoff's second-round 65 "The greatest round in the history of the tournament." Lloyd Mangrum holds the record of 64.

Morganton's Billy Joe Patton, far out of the running this year because of "poor driving, awful second shots and bad putting," said, "The golf course is the master here now. When you have three such perfect scoring days as we had the last three and the scores are no lower than they are, then you know that the course has virtually mastered the Masters."

Jackie Burke had a quadruple-bogey nine on No. 13, but that was mild compared to what happened to Pinehurst's Dick Chapman. After turning in 36, Chapman had everything happen to him. He took an eight on the par-four 11th hole, thanks in part to an unplayable lie, then set what must be a record for No. 16. He took a 10 on the par-three hole and wound up being told he couldn't post a score because he had played the wrong ball. He hit three shots in a water hazard there and three-putted. The fans cheered him for playing it out.

Old-timer Billy Burke clung to tradition by wearing a dress shirt and tie while playing and he did okay, too . . . Gene Sarazen fell out in his usual attire—knickers . . . Al Besselink had 47 shots on the first nine yesterday, wound up with an 83 . . . Byron Nelson said Middlecoff's "big" shot was a six-foot sidehill putt on the fifth hole. "It was one of those sliders," said By. "When he made it, I knew he was in."

1956

An amateur has never won the Masters, and given the fact that almost all top-notch players turn pro early in their lives now, there may never be an amateur winner. Ken Venturi, who would later win the U.S. Open and become a longtime television commentator, almost did it.

He was cocky, which, while it may offend the senses of some, is an attribute in athletes. It's just self-confidence expressing itself. Venturi had a wealth of that until the final round. He was a three-round sensation, but on Sunday, he shot 80 and allowed Jackie Burke to slip on the green jacket.

As we've seen many times over the years, nobody— nobody—is immune to nerves on Sunday in Augusta.

NOTES AND OBSERVATIONS

PROS GIVE VENTURI MASTERS' VOTE OF CONFIDENCE

Ken Venturi, a San Francisco car salesman, got into the Masters tournament on the vote of the pros. The pros obviously knew whereof they were voting. He tore the Augusta National layout to shreds with his opening-round 68 yesterday.

He started with four straight birdies. When someone asked if this rapid beginning put the pressure on him, he answered, "No, it made me feel like I should get a couple more.

"I was shooting for 69, and I was already one stroke under that, so I didn't feel any pressure at all."

Venturi is a student of Byron Nelson, the aging great who has won two of these titles. "I owe this round to Nelson," said Venturi.

Tommy Bolt, who put himself into a good position with a 68, couldn't get away without one complaint.

"I had a bad lie on the 18th," he snorted. "It didn't upset me, but the gigglers did. There were some kids standing there giggling because I had a bad lie. They thought it was funny."

"SATISFIED?" answered Ben Hogan, who had a neat 69, "I'm never satisfied. When you get satisfied, you're in a helluva shape."

Hogan intentionally played for the sand trap in front of the green on the second hole, a par five.

"That's the safest place to put it," he explained. "Hit it anywhere else, and you don't know where it is going. Put it in the bunker, and you've got an easy shot for the par." Hogan recalled that he didn't three-putt a green and said, "That's a record." Asked how long it's been since he putted well, Hogan answered, "1939. I was a good putter then."

VENTURI MAKES BIG MOVE TODAY FOR MASTERS TITLE

AMATEUR FOOLS EXPERTS, BUT CARY IS CLOSE

"I'LL OPEN UP FOR BIRDIES"

Ken Venturi, a dead-sure young amateur who has already done what others before him couldn't, has not yet begun to fight.

The 24-year-old San Francisco sensation fooled the experts yesterday, gaining ground instead of folding as they expected, and went into today's third round of the Augusta Masters with a four-stroke lead and a heart full of fire.

He tacked a 69, only sub-70 round of the day, onto his first-round 65 to post 135, tying the 36-hole record. Not only was he the first amateur ever to lead the tournament, he had done it two days in a row. He plans to make it four.

"I'm planning to make my move tomorrow," said Venturi, sipping ice tea in the clubhouse after he had whipped high winds and the rugged Augusta National Course yesterday.

"I'll either win it or lose it tomorrow. I don't mean I'll play it silly. I played conservatively today. Tomorrow, I'll open up a little and go for my birdies where they're supposed to come and play it safe on the other holes. I won't go hog wild. Do that and this course will eat you alive. But I'm going to try to make my move in the third round."

There is no longer any doubt that the dark-haired confident Ken is capable of a move.

Yesterday, when he was supposed to fold, he tacked three more strokes onto his lead over second-place Cary Middlecoff, the defending champion.

When someone mentioned folding, Venturi answered, "If anyone's going to fold, I don't think it will be Middlecoff and I don't think it will necessarily be me."

He figured two more 69s would make him the first amateur in history to take the prized championship, if he could score them.

NOTES AND OBSERVATIONS

WARD: "VENTURI WON'T LOSE LEAD"

BOLT BLOWS TO DOUBLE-BOGEY; SOUCHAK SOUR AFTER WEAK 73

"I'm hot as a $2 stove," snorted Tommy Bolt, who is known as an even-tempered man because he is seemingly always mad.

He had just taken a fat double-bogey six on the 18th hole to finish at 74 in the second round of the Augusta Masters instead of 72 as he had expected to do. Cause of this, according to Bolt, was a galleryite.

"I hit a bad shot out of the sand trap," he said, "and some so-and-so yelled, 'Break it, go ahead and break the club.' It was one of those idiots who is too lazy to go out on the course.

"What kind of game is this when it starts getting so a guy yells like he's at a baseball game?"

Bob Rosburg slapped a four-iron on No. 12 far over the green and out of bounds. "I'm the only man who ever hit one out of bounds there," he laughed. He allowed too much for the wind, which died as he hit.

Ben Hogan thought over his hope-killing 79 and said simply, "I was just putting badly." He rolled off one short putt after another that didn't drop, including an 18-incher at 18.

Biggest thing Venturi's won is the California State Amateur. Harvie Ward, Venturi's closest friend and the present National Amateur champion (he was also low amateur here last year), said, "I don't think there's a chance Ken will blow up. The only way he can lose it now is through bad judgment. He won't beat himself with his game."

"DOOR HIT ME ON WAY OUT"—VENTURI

Ken Venturi, amateur sensation whose brassy shell finally cracked yesterday and let Jackie Burke don the green coat of the Augusta Masters champion, summoned just the right words to describe the stunning finish.

"I was running away from Cary Middlecoff," he sighed, "and the door hit me on the way out."

The door, as the "Frisco Kid" so aptly put it, was Jackie Burke, one of golf's nicest guys. Burke steamed home with a 71, a truly great round under the windy conditions, to make up an eight-shot deficit and capture the coveted Masters crown.

Venturi, leader for the first three days, appeared to have the title wrapped up when Middlecoff, the closest man to him at four strokes back, hit a run of three double-bogeys. Ken knew of Middlecoff's progress and said he was "playing Cary."

Suddenly, Burke was up out of the pack and home two shots ahead of Middlecoff. Venturi, last of the trio to finish, was never aware of Jackie's challenge until he reached the 18th green and was told he needed a birdie three to tie. Needless to say, he took a four, his 30-foot putt for a tie rolling agonizingly toward the hole as thousands held their breaths, then slipping off line.

Venturi, who commanded the favor of most of the tremendous gallery—for no amateur has ever won the Masters—used 80 strokes on the final round. He got only two pars and no birdies on the last nine.

"I didn't blow up," he insisted. "I just couldn't hole a putt. I missed four straight six-footers from the eighth through the 11th, putts I had been making. If I had made them, or even three of them, even Houdini couldn't have caught me. That's not blowing."

Burke, a baby-faced veteran who hadn't won a tournament since 1953 but was second so many times in 1954 that he finished second in money won, said he was simply trying to be low pro and had no thoughts of beating Venturi.

"I was trying to be low pro," he explained. "I thought at the 17th hole I had a chance to beat Middlecoff. I knew I couldn't beat Ken. I didn't know how he stood, and I figured him for no worse than a 76."

Burke said he was hoping for a 72 when he teed off in the playoff round. "I figured that would get me in the top four," the curly haired, 33-year-old Texan smiled.

It was a bit ironic that Burke's 289 total was identical to the scores Ben Hogan and Sam Snead posted in 1954 when they edged Billy Joe Patton—another rambunctious amateur—by one stroke, and Venturi's 290 was like Patton's score.

Like they say, an amateur never wins here.

NOTES AND OBSERVATIONS

Jackie Burke's big play in his dramatic drive to a Masters degree yesterday was the 17th hole. After he had hit the par-four green in two, stopping five feet from the pin, his playing partner, Mike Souchak, said, "Two fours will get you a tie."

Burke stroked the tricky putt, and as it crawled tantalizingly toward the hole, Burke said, "How about a three-four?"

It dropped.

Many of the pros called the Masters a "putting contest" this year because of the difficult pin placements, and Burke's win aided their arguments. He three-putted only one green in 72 holes, used only 29 taps his last round.

Burke's wife, Ilene, wept openly and shook violently as she waited for Venturi to putt on the final hole. Even after Venturi had missed his chance to tie, she wouldn't believe her husband had won. Mrs. Cary Middlecoff finally convinced her, and she broke down and sobbed loudly.

Bobby Jones, president of the Augusta Masters, said the windy conditions were the worst ever for the tournament. Some thoughtless guy asked Venturi how he felt when he didn't win. Venturi answered by asking, "How would you like to win the Masters?" "The Kid," as Ken became known, took his failure terribly hard. Only a phone call to his wife could console him in the least.

Prize money was upped from $20,000 plus $200 for all pros outside the top 24 to $30,000 and $300 for the non-collecting pros. It represented the largest output in history for the Masters, $42,300.

AUGUSTA MASTERS LEFTOVERS

Sam Snead has a caddy named O'Brien. Sam fired O'Brien after the 1953 Masters. "I don't want you to caddy for me ever again," related Snead.

"This year," said Snead, "I drove up and O'Brien came up and stood around. I asked him what he wanted, and he said he was my caddy.

"I asked him if he didn't remember I had fired him last year, and he said, 'Mister Snead, you can't get rid of me that easy.'

"He has no judgment about clubbing me. I finally told him to say, 'I don't know,' if I ever asked him what club to use.

"The other day, I was playing a practice round, and I asked O'Brien which way the wind was blowing on that hole the day before. He wouldn't answer me.

"I kept asking him, and finally he said, 'Mister Snead, I can't answer you. I don't want you chewin' me out.'"

Richard Tufts of Pinehurst, president of the USGA, was asked at Augusta what reactions the USGA had received from the new rule permitting players to leave the flag in the hole while putting.

"Very favorable," he said. "One pleasing aspect we didn't anticipate was the fact that the new rule cuts down on walking around the pin and leaves the greens in better shape for late players."

1957

Masters officials introduced the 36-hole cut in 1957, and it was a deep one. Only the low 40 and ties after two rounds qualified. Among the victims were Ben Hogan, Tommy Bolt, Cary Middlecoff, Art Wall, and Julius Boros, while Doug Ford, who was far from being the stylist they were, ended up winning the tournament.

Among those who did make the cut were five amateurs— Harvie Ward, who finished fourth, Frank Taylor, Rex Baxter, Don Cherry, and Hillman Robbins. Cherry was a famous singer whose biggest hit was "Band of Gold."

"RESURRECTED" BEN HOGAN LABELED MAN TO BEAT IN MASTERS PLAY

Ben Hogan, who has been pronounced dead as a contender for major championships many times, was back in his old familiar position of favorite today as a record field of 103 of the greatest golfers of this and other nations teed off in the first round of the 31st Augusta Masters Golf Tournament.

The graying Texas hawk, looking hard as nails, scored 69, 70, and 72 in his last three practice rounds here. With two months of concentrated preparation for the Masters behind him, and with his scores speaking out for his form, how can you go any way but with him?

Three others who, like Hogan, have been among the foremost players of the era—Sam Snead, Cary Middlecoff, and Jimmy Demaret—are rated as Ben's chief competitors.

Strangely absent in the speculation has been the name of defending champion Jack Burke Jr., who also won the PGA championship last year. This may be a mistake, for Burke's exceptional long iron play and steady putting certainly are worthy of consideration when championships are discussed.

The name of a Tar Heel has cropped up among the possible victors—that of two-time National Amateur champion Harvie Ward Jr., a Tarboro native now living in San Francisco.

Ward wrapped up preparations for today's opening with two consecutive 69s in practice.

"He's my darkhorse," commented Byron Nelson. "He's a fine player, and he's on top of his game. He may be an amateur, but you can't discredit his chances of winning."

Nelson played two warm-up rounds with Hogan and had this to say about Ben's game:

"He's playing well, but you get the feeling that he's still not playing as well as he thinks he should be."

Top choices among the younger players are Arnold Palmer, winner of the Azalea Open at Wilmington last week, Dow Finsterwald, Ken Venturi, and Mike Souchak.

Venturi, who missed tying for the championship here last year by one stroke after leading for three rounds, feels ready for another strong bid.

"I feel fine, physically and mentally," he said. "I can't say what my chances are. It depends. If you get it to roll in for you and get a couple of breaks, you've got a chance to win—anybody has. Right now, I can think of at least 10 players with good chances."

NOTES AND OBSERVATIONS

THOMSON OFF—HE MISSED 30-FOOTER

Peter Thomson of Australia, one of the top foreign threats in the Masters, was full of ginger after using only 29 putts in putting together a 72 yesterday.

"How long has it been since you putted that well?" someone asked him.

"Yesterday," he answered.

After rattling off the length of the putts he dropped, he added, "I missed one on the 18th."

"How long?"

"Thirty feet," he grinned.

HOGAN: "DESERVED TO BE CUT"
MIDDLECOFF: "TRIED MY HARDEST"

WHAT MAKES SAMMY RUN? "HOT PUTTING"

Ben Hogan, wearing the famed grin that has become his trademark through many years of championship golf, admitted, "I deserved to be cut," yesterday after he failed to qualify for the final 36 holes of the Augusta Masters.

Cary Middlecoff, another of the game's all-time greats, fell by the wayside as the Masters' new ruling backfired and became some of the most notable surgery ever performed.

"I tried harder to qualify for those last 36 holes," the stunned Middlecoff said, "than I could have tried if I had been going for the National Open championship."

The cutoff point was 150. Ben had 151, Cary 152. The knifing of these two sparkling names took the spotlight away from the masterful play of the second-round leader.

Sam Snead, the West Virginia slammer, won his coveted position with a 68 to go with his first-day 72 for a 140 total. Trailing closely behind as the Masters moved into the third round today were three-time winner Jimmy Demaret at 72-70-142; defending champion Jack Burke Jr. at 71-72-143; lame-armed Ed Furgol and National Amateur champion Harvie Ward at 73-71-144 apiece; leading money winner Doug Ford and three-time British Open king Peter Thomson at 72-73-145.

Snead's scores held the attention of the big galleries spread across the rain-soaked fairways only for a short while. When it began to appear that Hogan and Middlecoff might not survive the cut, Sambo was no longer a conversation piece.

With those two, and other such notables as Mike Souchak (152), Julius Boros (158), Art Wall Jr., and Gene Littler, being pared, the general opinion is that the rule will be revised next year to permit the low 50 or perhaps the low 60 to play the last two days.

Snead credited his excellent iron play and an equally new putting stroke.

"I'm more relaxed in this tournament than I have been since I don't know when," he beamed. Always a good drawing room storyteller, he was in rare form after shooting that 68.

"I won't attempt to explain my new putting stroke," he said. "I'll just say that I'm hitting the ball more solidly now on my putts."

Sam, a two-time winner here, cruised out in 34, two under par, but ran into water trouble at the par-three 12th and took a five.

Burke played remarkably steady golf, scoring 16 pars, one bogey, and one birdie. His bird came on the 14th, where he rolled in a 40-foot putt from the fringe of the green.

There is considerable speculation here that Ward may be poised for the third big splash by an amateur here in four years. Billy Joe Patton almost won it in 1954, and Ken Venturi came within a shot last year.

Ward is playing unspectacular but very steady golf — the kind that has won many a Masters.

NOTES AND OBSERVATIONS

SNEAD WANTS PRESTIGE, THEN MONEY

Sam Snead wants more than anything to win the National Open, the big one that has always gotten away from him, but if he ever won it, he says, then his next consideration would be those tomato cans he reportedly filled with money and buried in his backyard.

"If I had ever won the Open," he said, "then I would much rather win the world championship. This prestige stuff is nice, and as I say, I want the Open more than any now. But I'll take that $100,000 at Tam O'Shanter rather than another Open."

Snead tossed a little dart at Hogan, who has been tuning up for the Masters at Seminole for two months. "Can't all of us be like some people," he said. "Can't all of us play one course for two months and concentrate on sharpening our game."

CHAMP FORD: "I'M A GORILLA GOLFER"
SNEAD: "HE LOOKS AWFUL"

A "gorilla golfer," self-described, yesterday won the 21st annual Augusta Masters golf tournament with one of the most brilliant rounds and one of the most spectacular finishes in the history of the event.

Doug Ford of Yonkers, N.Y., caught third-round leader Sam Snead on the 11th hole of the final round, passed him on the 12th, and raced in with a 66, too much for the West Virginia Slammer's brilliant rally to equal.

In one of the week's great moments, Ford blasted out of a sand trap in front of the 18th green into the cup, some 35 feet, for a closing birdie that erased all doubt about the outcome.

Ford calls himself "a gorilla golfer."

"I'm not pretty to look at out there," he explained. "My swing is far from a picture swing. I have to fight the ball and fight the course all the way around, sort of the way a gorilla would go at it."

Snead, a far more graceful loser than he has been on occasion, added this:

"Around the greens, I'll take Ford. That's where he won it today, with his chipping and putting. His mechanics look something awful, but he's like Bobby Locke. He does the same thing every time. Ford beats that ol' ball into the ground and don't give a durn whether it gets up into the air or rolls on the ground, just so long as it goes toward the hole."

Ford started three strokes off Snead's 214 pace. Sandwiched between them were National Amateur champion Harvie Ward, Arnold Palmer, and Stan Leonard.

When the warm, sunshiny day's combat was done and the last of the many thousand spectators had tramped the final hole, Ford stood at the head with 283, Snead had 286, Jimmy Demaret 287, and Ward 288. Peter Thomson, Ed Furgol, and other challengers with excellent chances were brushed aside in Ford's rush to the title.

Ford, 34 years old and the fastest player on the golfing tour, went all out, even after he appeared to have the coveted crown cinched.

"I've never been a very good safe player," he said. "I make more bogeys trying to play safe than I do when I'm bold."

Hence the shot that Doug felt won the tournament for him. It came at the par-five 15th. This green is guarded in front by a creek that invites disaster.

Doug's caddy pleaded with him to lay up to the edge of the creek and chip over, but Ford shrugged off the advice. He pulled out a four-wood and lashed at the ball.

It came down on the far bank of the creek and bounded up onto the green, 10 feet from the hole. The champion two-putted for his birdie.

Then followed the brilliant shot on 18, described by Ford as "the greatest shot I ever hit."

The throng around the 18th went mad when Ford's trap shot plunked down onto the edge of the green and trickled into the hole.

Snead's chances were destroyed when he bogied five of six holes, beginning at the ninth. But even though he knew he could not win, the Slammer birdied three of the last four holes in the fashion of the all-time great he is.

1958

In 1958, Arnold Palmer won the first of four he would win. I had drinks with Arnie and his wife, Winnie, at the Bull Bat Lounge in the old Richmond Hotel and then had breakfast with them on the Sunday he won.

He said he couldn't understand why Ken Venturi had been made such a huge favorite. On Sunday, he was paired with Venturi and beat him, Doug Ford, and Fred Hawkins by a shot.

Although such things are difficult to pin down, this victory may have been the one that started the world's love affair with Arnie. It was not his most dramatic win by any measure, but his slashing, gambling style captivated the crowd and signaled what was to come.

NOTES AND OBSERVATIONS

Are new stars like Howie Johnson, Dave Ragan, J.C. Goosie, et al., making the tour tougher this year than in the past?

Dow Finsterwald, who gets his cash regardless of who is entered, thinks not.

"There are plenty of fine new players every year," he observed, "but they are offset by those who are playing less such as Sam Snead and Cary Middlecoff.

"This Venturi, though, would still be winning if Snead and Middlecoff and all the rest were playing."

VENTURI: A STEP TOWARD THAT PROMISE

Ken Venturi has vowed that he will someday win the Augusta Masters championship.

The 27-year-old "Frisco Kid," the hottest thing to hit professional golf in many years, yesterday laid the cornerstone for the possible fulfillment of that promise.

On a day when many of the world's greatest players were taking advantage of the Augusta National golf course in one of its least cantankerous moods ever, it was Venturi out in front with a four-under-par 68.

PATTON COMES UP WITH ANOTHER CHUCKLE

Billy Joe Patton gave the gallery a chuckle on the second hole. Delayed on the tee by the twosome ahead of him, he sprawled on the ground and said, "Holler when they get out of the way."

NOTES AND OBSERVATIONS

HOGAN: "GLAD I DON'T HAVE TO MAKE A LIVING AT GOLF"

A year ago yesterday, Sam Snead led the Masters with 140, and Doug Ford, the eventual winner, had 145. Yesterday, Ken Venturi led the tournament with 140, and Ford had 145.

Venturi came out of his miracle round of 72 overjoyed.

"The way I made that 72," he said, meaning, of course, 40-32, "it was good for my morale. I feel like I'm going downhill again."

He called his five-birdie 32 on the back the best nine holes he has ever played in competition. It was not necessary for him to say it. Everything considered, it was one of the best nines ever played in this tournament.

Ben Hogan, as forgotten as Hogan can be after shooting 77 yesterday, smiled a little and said, "I'm glad I don't have to make a living playing golf" . . . He plans to make his usual appearances this year in the Colonial Invitational and the National Open. This Masters is Ben's first tournament, excepting a two-day event at Seminole, since the Palm Beach tournament early last summer.

PALMER SCOFFED AT VENTURI'S ODDS, RODE KEN'S PACE TO MASTERS TITLE

OTHERS DROWN IN MISTAKES; ARNIE STEADY

Arnold Palmer sat at the breakfast board in the Richmond Hotel Saturday morning with his wife, Winnie, and some writer friends and unsuspectingly tipped off his listeners on the eventual winner of the 22nd Masters championship.

No one, however, recognized Palmer's words as the left-handed prophecy that they were. It was only after the strong, bronzed Latrobe, Pennsylvania, son of a golfing professional got home ahead of a stumbling field with a 284 total yesterday that his observation took on its proper perspective.

As he munched his cornflakes Saturday morning, Arnold said, "I don't see how they can make a fellow like Ken Venturi such a heavy favorite in this tournament. There are too many good players here to pick out one and say he is going to win."

Ironically, Palmer used Venturi as his pacer yesterday in winning the title after getting into position Saturday with a four-under-par 68—good enough to tie Sam Snead for the 54-hole lead at 211. Arnie was paired with hotshot Venturi for the final 18.

"I decided to try to shoot what Ken shot," Palmer recalled. "I figured he was three strokes behind and was going to be charging at it, going all out to try to catch up. I felt that if I could stay even with him on those final 18, I would shoot well enough to win."

After 17 holes, the quiet 28-year-old had accomplished his aim.

On the 18th, Palmer three-putted from some 50 feet to shoot 73, one stroke more than Venturi scored. This one-stroke difference left the gate open for defending champion Doug Ford and veteran campaigner Fred Hawkins, playing in the same twosome, to tie.

But both missed 10-foot putts on the last green by inches, and Arnold had the symbolic green jacket that he had dreamed of since childhood.

What may go down as one of the most memorable shots of the Masters proved to be the margin of victory for Palmer. It occurred on the 13th hole and was preceded by an upsetting incident on the 12th. Arnie's tee shot on the par-three 12th buried in rough ground behind the green. The rules permitted relief from a buried ball, but there was considerable discussion about whether the rules covered the particular area in which Palmer's ball had stuck up.

Palmer played the buried ball and scored a double-bogey five with it, then played a provisional ball, taking relief from the buried ball, and scored a three. He said he knew he was entitled to the three but was taking no chances.

With the confusion still fresh at the 13th, Palmer sent a tee shot long and straight down the fairway of the par-five hole that has been the Waterloo of so many.

Some might have played safely, short of the creek fronting the green, but Palmer elected to go for the flag with his second. He sent a three-wood sailing across the yawning hazard, onto the green some 18 feet from the hole. He then sank the putt for an eagle three.

Palmer got $11,500 for his win. Ford and Hawkins tied for second at 285. Venturi, who had promised to win the Masters someday, missed his chance to do it this year when he three-putted three greens in a row, beginning at the 14th, and wound up tied with Stan Leonard for fourth.

NOTES AND OBSERVATIONS

TREES HONOR PATTON

Scattered around the back nine of the Augusta National Golf Club are several bridges named for some of the great stars who have performed in the Masters during the past 22 years.

After a recent dedication of overpasses honoring Byron Nelson and Ben Hogan, Bobby Jones' wife commented to the greatest of them all, "Bob, I think we should dedicate something to Billy Joe Patton."

"I told her," Jones recalled at the presentation ceremony yesterday, "that Billy Joe didn't like anything that spanned water.

"I remember the first time I ever saw Patton. It was in the woods to the right of the 14th fairway. I think it would be a fitting tribute to him to name those woods the 'Patton Woods,' and I'm going to suggest it to the board of governors."

Patton shot the works in an all-out effort to win the title yesterday, but inconsistency told on him. He felt he might be heading in when, after bogeying the first, he birdied the next two, but too many bogies dotted his final round of 74.

Champion Arnold Palmer apparently felt no qualms about taking the tee for the showdown round. After tying Sam Snead for the 54-hole lead Saturday, Arnold and his wife, Winnie, had dinner at the club.

"After dinner," Winnie recalled, "we went back to the hotel. I went in to take a shower, and when I came out, Arnold was asleep.

"I said, 'He must not be too worried about it if he can sleep like that.'

"This morning, he didn't appear nervous at all. He said nothing about his chances, but then, he never does."

There is a possibility Palmer will be asked to play with President Eisenhower this weekend. He may also appear on TV's *Ed Sullivan Show.*

Arnold has snatched the tab of "hottest thing in golf" away from Ken Venturi. In the last six weeks, he has finished second at Baton Rouge, third at New Orleans, 12th at Pensacola, first at St. Petersburg, second after a playoff at Wilmington, and first at Augusta.

1959

As Art Wall prepared to tee off on the 15th hole of the final round in 1959, I walked right past him. Our eyes met, and there was an unstated acknowledgment that we had seen each other. I had gotten to know Wall a bit, become friends with him, which was not easy. He was a quiet, withdrawn man.

Little did I know I was walking past the winner of the tournament while on my way out to see some other player whom I thought would win. Wall snuck up on us, scoring birdies on five of the last six holes for a closing 66, a wonderful round on a day when only one other player (Dick Mayer with a 68) broke 70. He came from 13th place. He didn't usually smile a lot, but he did that day.

HOGAN TAKES LESSONS, TOO

Even the great ones take lessons.

Ben Hogan, one of the premier players of all time, had veteran Johnny Revolta working with his putting yesterday. The Texas Hawk spent about an hour on the practice green with Revolta, noted as one of the game's best technicians, watching and advising.

Hogan's major trouble here in recent years has been on the big, faster greens.

Sights and sounds of the Masters: Defending champion Arnold Palmer, testing a new driver, blasting tee shots out of the practice range into an adjoining highway. Tommy Bolt, U.S. Open king, playing like a machine—to perfection; Lew Hoad, tennis ace in town for a show last night, watching fellow Australian Peter Thomson practice putting; Ken Venturi, reporting that fellow San Franciscan Harvie Ward, two-time National Amateur champion, couldn't make it because of business commitments.

ANYBODY CAN WIN AT AUGUSTA

Sam Snead, who almost became one of the few men in history to be hanged underwater, may become the only man ever to win four Augusta Masters championships this week.

The Slammer, who revealed yesterday that his fishing boat capsized and he became entangled in an anchor line on a recent fishing trip, teed off in the opening round of the Masters today as a 5-1 favorite.

It was one of the greatest votes of confidence ever given anyone in this talent-laden event, approaching the record 4-1 accorded young Ken Venturi last year.

A three-time winner here along with Jimmy Demaret, Snead said he was almost not around to try for that fourth championship. His boat capsized on a recent fishing excursion off Boca Raton, Florida. He carried a companion to shallow water, but a loop in an anchor line slipped around his neck. The undertow took his feet from beneath him and left him hanging below water. Some quick thinking and some fancy scrambling spared the West Virginia wonder for another crack at the title.

"For a second there," grinned Sam, "I thought sure I was gonna be hung right there in the surf."

BEFORE THE MASTERS

The Augusta Masters opened today. Yesterday, the eve of the opening round, was a day for practicing and looking and talking, the calm before the storm. This was the picture and the soundtrack of the day:

The 10th hole, one of the most beautiful things in golf, lying like a green cathedral under scudding white clouds, bordered by the pink of the flourishing redbuds.

Lord Byron Nelson, who won it in 1937, holding court on a hillside in front of the clubhouse, telling writers, "I haven't played too well in recent years here, but I have gotten around with some pretty good scores on the knowledge of the course that I have picked up over the years.

"It takes at least three or four years to learn the course, and you keep on learning something new every time you play it.

"They call it a putting course. That's not true. It is a course which demands thought and placement of every shot."

Snead thrilling the gallery with a wedge shot on the seventh that danced within two feet of the cup, then leaving his birdie putt short . . . Ben Hogan searching for an hour on the practice green for the putting touch that has escaped him in recent years . . . Movie cameras grinding as Ken Venturi lashes long four-wood shots out across the practice fairway . . . Hogan, who says he wants to throw up when he hits a hook, being kidded about hooking his tee shot into a bunker on the fifth hole. "He hasn't been on the left side of that fairway since 1942," Cary Middlecoff says.

Jackie Burke paying Middlecoff a $5 bet and chirping, "Well, I did real well this year. I only lost $5 to you this time. You ought to play well this year. Your conscience won't be hurting you about taking all of my money like it has in the past." . . . Middlecoff noting his 11:30 starting time and saying, "Well, I've been yelling for an early starting time for three years. Now that I've finally got one, it'll probably rain like hell in the morning . . . Hogan sitting back sipping a drink and enjoying the exchange of patter between Burke and Middlecoff.

The spectators racing for cover as heavy rain begins to fall but dashing back when the rain stops to see the driving contest . . . "Ohs" as big George Bayer screams one 321 yards up the first fairway to win the contest . . . The sound of half a hundred typewriters clattering in the press tent as day nears its end . . . Night falling quietly, the course deserted, resting for the on-slaught to come.

NOTES AND OBSERVATIONS

BEN: OTHERS NOT MY STANDARD

A touch of the quiet tiger that lurks inside Ben Hogan and has made him one of the great golfers of all time flashed itself yesterday after the Texas Hawk had shot an opening round of 73 in the Masters.

Reminded that his score was only four strokes off the pace and outdistanced most of the rest of the field, Hogan turned his steely eyes toward the speaker and said, "What other people shoot is not my standard.

"My standard is hitting every shot right. Today I hit four bad shots. I expected to hit every shot right, and therefore I was below my standard. To me, the score is incidental. It is how you play that matters.

"They are talking about trouble in the wind. You are supposed to be able to cope with those conditions. Although I think the course played three or four shots harder today than it has earlier this week because of the wind, I do not blame the wind for preventing me from shooting better. I blame four bad shots."

NATIONAL RELENTS FOR ART

WALL RESPECTED OL' BEAR, WON MASTERS

CHAMPION'S FINISH ONE OF
CLASSIC'S GREATEST

Wise old Sam Snead, the slamming sage from West Virginia, once advised golf's young 'uns, "This Augusta National golf course is like an ol' bear.

"You can play with it kinda soft, but if you ain't careful, it'll reach up with one of its paws and cuff you a good one."

The old bear, lying with a false look of contentment under sunny skies and a faint breeze, growled and smote down all but one here yesterday in the final round of the Augusta Masters.

Only Art Wall Jr., who had thoughtfully demonstrated his respect for the capricious nature of the course through the early rounds, was allowed to play rough the final day.

The Pennsylvania pro, whose lean, hungry countenance and bowed shoulders cloak the tiger lurking in him, was rewarded with the green jacket symbolic of the Masters championship.

After lying cautiously back through the first two rounds to assure himself one of the exclusive invitations to play the last two, Wall turned the handle on the steam gauge Saturday but nothing happened. He shot 71 and lay obscurely in 13th position.

Pressing harder, he etched his name forever on the drama-steeped pages of Masters history with one of the classic's greatest finishes. He fired five birdies in the last six holes for a six-under-par 66 to post a total of 284. This was one stroke better than 1955 champion Cary Middlecoff could muster and two shots lower than defending champion Arnold Palmer could achieve.

Wheeling freely with a 70 and its accompanying large chunk of money as his target, businessman Wall had little idea of winning when he passed the 12th hole only one under par yesterday. Then things began to happen. Going boldly for everything, he two-putted for birdie on the par-five 13th, holed a 20-footer for his bird on the 14th, and two-putted for another birdie on the par-five 15th. Only after getting his par three on the 16th did Wall realize that he could win.

His playing partner, Julius Boros, told him at this point, "If you make one more birdie, you may take it all."

With the pressure suddenly on him, Wall made monkeys of the so-called experts who said he lacked the aggressiveness, the game, and the finishing kick to ever win a big one. He dropped a 15-footer for a birdie on the 17th, then hit his biggest and best drive up the canyon formed by thousands of sun-pinked spectators lining the 18th. His second shot, a nine iron, came to rest only 10 feet from the hole.

He later related, "As I walked up to the 18th green, I heard that thunder roll up from the 13th hole. I was fairly certain that meant Middlecoff had scored an eagle. I knew then what I had to do. I felt I needed a birdie on the last one.

"The putt looked like it might break either way, so I decided to hit it straight. As soon as I hit it, I felt it was in."

It was.

1960

I was standing with some other writers, talking with Ken Venturi about the victory he had just won in the 1960 Masters, when a great roar came sweeping up the hillside and into the room. We knew it was Arnold Palmer's gallery, down on the 17th hole.

From the 14th hole on, Palmer had needed two birdies to beat Venturi, who was already in, and he hadn't gotten one. But then someone came in and told us Palmer had birdied the 17th, which meant he could beat Venturi with a birdie on the 18th, tie him with a par. Venturi said, "Whoops," got out of his chair and walked out, saying, "Well, he has one hole to play. He can beat me, tie me, or lose to me."

Arnie beat him and won the second of his four Masters championships. The two birdies he made when he had to have them contributed greatly to his growing reputation as a fearless charger.

"THE HAWK" SPEAKS

How would you like to interview Ben Hogan?

Pin on a press badge—which will get you access to everything at the Augusta National Golf Course except Ike's cottage and the ladies' room—and shoulder through the herd of some six dozen reporters gathering in the lower locker room.

Hogan, The Hawk, is winging again. He shot a 68 yesterday, which, with his opening 73, left him only one stroke behind leader Arnold Palmer as the Masters tournament headed into the third round today.

Reporters know well where Hogan will sit. He has been using the same bench locker for many years. They save his place for him as they crowd around.

Hogan enters the room, stops, and smiles. It is like old times, having sportswriters bursting the seams of the place to talk with him.

The great man orders a drink, as usual, and starts to make his way through the crowd to his appointed place, then stops.

"Who you fellows waiting to see?" he asks with a smile.

"Nobody," somebody bellows. "We're having a meeting."

"Well," says Hogan, sitting down, "do we have a quorum here?"

There is a moment of silence, and Hogan asks, "Well, what can I do for you?"

"Go over your score for us hole-by-hole," is suggested.

Hogan launches into a detailed report on his round.

"Drive and four iron to the first green, missed a six-foot putt. Five iron five feet from the hole at the eighth, made it. Seven iron 12 feet from the hole at 14, made it.

And then the questions and answers begin in serious.

Q: "Putting has been your trouble for a good while. What do you think caused your putting to go back before the rest of your game?"

A: "I don't know. I guess it was nerves. My putting really drives me crazy. It has for five years now."

Q: "You seem to be taking more time with your putts now than you did when you were putting well."

A: "Hell, that's because I can't get that putter back. I spend less time studying the putt, because I know when I step over that ball it's gonna take me a long time to force the putter back away from the ball and hit that thing. I don't give a damn where the ball goes, all I'm worrying about is breaking that freeze that gets me when I step over the ball and getting that putter moving."

Q: "How do you feel while you're standing over the ball ready to putt?"

A: "I feel like that hole is filled with blood, and the ball can't possibly get in."

Q: "When you were here last year, Ben, you said you were working on building a putter that might help you. Did anything come of that?"

A: "Yeah. It wasn't worth a damn."

Q: "How much golf do you play when you aren't getting ready for a tournament?"

A: "Well, the National Open was played last June. After the Open, I played only three pleasure rounds until I went to Florida a month ago to get ready for the Masters. I don't play golf. I watch football games on TV."

Someone says thank you and the session breaks up.

PALMER—THE CONFIDENT MASTER

The power of Snead, the composure of Hogan, and a confidence as peculiar to himself as to anyone have carried Arnold Palmer to his second Augusta Masters championship in three years.

The solid-oak Pennsylvanian birdied the last two holes yesterday—knowing all the while what he had to do—and edged Ken Venturi by a single shot for the title many say is the greatest of all. Palmer's fantastic finish gave him a 70 for a 72-hole total of 282. Venturi, who appears damned to tragedy in this championship, also shot a 70 but started the day one stroke behind Palmer.

Others who started the day as contenders fell like wheat before a reaper, victims of their own burning passions for victory. Only Venturi and Dow Finsterwald, playing in the same twosome, seriously threatened Palmer. Finsterwald scored 71 for a 284 and third place, bogeying the last hole to lose his classic head-to-head struggle with Venturi. Ben Hogan, Julius Boros, and Bill Casper also started the final round one stroke out of the lead, but Casper's 74 left him fourth, Boros' 75 dropped him to fifth, and Hogan's 76 left him sixth.

Palmer was playing the 14th hole when word reached him that Venturi was in with a 283. He needed at least one birdie to tie and two to win and set about the grim business of getting them, but they were slow in coming.

Venturi was being interviewed as the champion as Palmer walked the 17th fairway. Little chance was held out for Palmer to tie, much less win, and the line of questions and answers in Venturi's interview was one of victory.

But the smile faded from Venturi's face, and the writers fell silent as a great roar rolled up from the valley.

"That's Palmer's gallery," someone said.

Seconds later, a messenger burst into the room and said, "Palmer just holed it from all the way across the green for a birdie at 17!"

"Whoops," said Venturi, and he rose to leave. "Well," he said, "there's one more hole to play. He can beat me, tie me, or lose to me on that hole," and he walked out. Somehow, remembering the many great heartbreaks that have befallen young Venturi in the Masters, the first suspicion that Palmer might win it all at the 18th crept in.

Palmer had holed a 37-foot putt at the 17th, a putt that was 22 feet longer than any other he made during the week.

His drive on No. 18 split the middle. With most of the gallery close to 40,000 making a canyon of the fairway, Palmer studied at great length the uphill stretch that could lead to glory or defeat, then chose a six iron and sailed the ball true to the green.

It came down short and to the right of the hole, bounded forward and then spun left, grazing the hole as it darted by, and stopped five feet away.

Nothing else in the world mattered as Palmer studied his putt, stepped over it and tapped it toward the left corner of the hole. It rolled lazily, turned slowly to the right, and dropped in, and the quiet Augusta countryside exploded with the thunder of the thrilled thousands.

Art Wall, the 1959 defending champion who could not defend this year, watched as Palmer was whisked away from the 18th green to the privacy of the clubhouse by Pinkerton men.

"You have to have a helluva lot of confidence to do something like Palmer just did," he said.

This, probably above all else, was the story of Palmer's great win.

Never once did he back away from the danger. Even at the 12th, a hole that probably cost him the title last year and that has haunted him with bad luck whenever he has played here, was attacked boldly.

A seven iron would have been safe, but he chose the eight, risking a watery fate in the pond fronting the green, for the chance to birdie the hole. He kept hitting the ball hard, almost recklessly, always fearlessly, never trying to guide it with softness.

"I felt I had to give myself a chance to birdie every hole," he said.

When he came to the 17th knowing that he had to birdie one of the last two to tie and both to win, his confidence had not flagged. He confessed he had been disappointed when he failed to birdie either the 13th or the 15th, both par fives which he normally handles under par, but said, "Going to that 17th tee, I knew I still had a chance, and as long as I have the faintest chance, I believe I can do it."

Contrary to what many might have thought as they watched this mighty machine at work yesterday, Palmer is human. He confessed, "I was a little nervous putting that last putt. I felt the tension."

The Masters was Palmer's 19th tournament victory in the five years he has been playing professional golf. Nobody else has won that many during that span. This, plus the fact that two of the 19 were major titles, has placed Palmer a cut above the others as the probable successor to the greatness that is being rapidly relinquished by Hogan and Snead.

It was the fifth tournament victory of the year for the former Wake Forest varsity star who was born in a home beside a golf course, grew up on the fairways, and met his wife on the links. He won $17,500.

NOTES AND OBSERVATIONS

Dow Finsterwald bogeyed the 18th hole from a sand trap and was forgotten. A two-stroke penalty incurred in the opening round for practice putting on the fifth green was the difference between his score and Palmer's, but Finsterwald shook it off.

"I never thought of it today," he said. "I'm just lucky they didn't put me out of the tournament. If I hadn't had that penalty, I might have played differently and still lost."

1961

You will hear varying stories about how the idea of a "modern" Grand Slam came about. Bobby Jones had given us a Grand Slam by winning the U.S. and British Opens and the U.S. and British Amateurs. When Ben Hogan won the Masters, U.S. Open, and British Open in 1953, he didn't even play in the PGA Championship, where he could have completed the modern Grand Slam. He couldn't play in the PGA, because it was the same week as the British Open.

It was around the late 1950s or early 1960s that the modern Grand Slam became a goal, and it may have been Arnold Palmer who popularized it. In 1960, he won the Masters and U.S. Open and missed getting into a playoff for the British Open by a shot. That stretch made a Slam seem to be within his reach.

It was with that in mind that he arrived in Augusta in 1961, but with victory virtually in hand, Arnie double-bogeyed the last hole, and Gary Player, a great player and a worthy champion, slipped into the green jacket. That year, the tournament ended on Monday because rain washed out the Sunday round.

Beginning with Palmer's victory in 1958, he, Player, and Jack Nicklaus ran off a streak in which they won eight of nine Masters between them and had five second places in that span.

NOTES AND OBSERVATIONS

Arnold Palmer, who won over $80,000 last year, had to borrow a dollar from Sam Snead to tip the waiter at lunch yesterday.

Don Cherry, the amateur who is better known for his singing, chirped, "Why don't you ask Sam for his blood? He'd rather part with that than a dollar."

TOMMY SHOOTS A BOLT AT SLAMMER

NOTES AND OBSERVATIONS

Tommy Bolt's terrible temper flared anew yesterday, its flames licking in the direction of Sam Snead.

Snead's drive on the 11th hole narrowly missed Bolt, who was playing in the twosome ahead. The forecaddy stationed there to give the all-clear signal on the blind hole failed to warn Snead that Bolt was not out of the way.

As Snead walked toward the clubhose after the round, Bolt, practicing his putting, shouted, "Hey, Sam, you trying to run everybody else off the golf course? When you get two or three over par, you try to horse around."

Snead replied, but his words were too low to catch.

Bolt added vigorously, "You've already won your money. Now how about giving me a chance to win some?"

Bolt later said he was only kidding Snead, but he wasn't very convincing.

Fourth-place Jack Nicklaus, the young wonder who won the National Amateur in 1959 and was runner-up in the U.S. Open last summer, felt he could "easily have shot 63 or 64" if he had putted well. He missed 12 putts of five feet or less, 11 of them for birdies and one for an eagle, in posting a 70. . .Co-leader Rosburg made a 100-foot putt for a birdie at the 14th hole. . .Doug Ford's neat 71 included two chip-ins—his first of the year. "Breaks like that can get a fellow going again," commented the 1957 Masters king.

Palmer's best shot of the day, by his own measure, was a three-iron that settled six feet from the cup on the wicked par-four 10th hole. He spoiled it by three-putting, missing the second stroke from 18 inches. . .Billy Joe Patton has played the Masters since 1954 and had never put a ball into the water on the par-three 12th, but finally did it yesterday and got a double-bogey. He found water again at the par-five 13th and took a bogey six, winding up with a disheartening 78.

Snead, who, according to legend, buries his money in tin cans, gave Cherry a friendly snarl and forked over.

BANTAM BEN PLEASED WITH PLAY

NOTES AND OBSERVATIONS

There was a time not too many years ago when Ben Hogan wouldn't have grinned at a million dollars if he had double-bogeyed the last hole, as he did here yesterday.

He needed only a par four on the last hole to shoot a one-under-par 71, but his tee shot hit a limb and fell behind a huge pine. He wound up with a six on the hole.

Furious? Not Hogan. He was beaming as he settled into his accustomed place in the locker room and ordered his usual post-round drink.

"Best I've putted in 10 years," he said. "I holed putts from everywhere."

And therein lay the reason for his good cheer. His putting has been poor for about five years, even atrocious at times.

Nothing could spoil it—not even that big pine tree— when, finally, he had another good putting day.

He did say, however, "I'd like to make some wooden clubs out of that big old pine."

Someone asked Gary Player, co-leader with Arnold Palmer after 36 holes, if he had checked the scoreboards as he played, to see what Palmer was doing.

"Yes," he said and, after a long pause, added, "frightening."

Jimmy Demaret played just ahead of Player and couldn't concentrate on his own game for watching the refreshing young South African fire the ball at the hole.

"If Player had putted today," said Demaret, "he would have been 10 under par. That kid's knocking it a mile."

Player hit the ball into the cup on the fly on the par-three 12th hole but, instead of a hole-in-one, he wound up with a par. The ball bounced off the lip of the cup and wound up 15 feet away . . . Australian Peter Thomson, four-time British Open king, shot a 76 for 149 and barked, "I'm putting like a blind man. I shouldn't be allowed on the course."

THEY CHEERED ARNIE'S FALL

Those who have seen Superman Arnold Palmer laugh at pressure in winning two Masters and the U.S. Open felt an urge to turn away, ashamed to watch the great champion as he endured the indignity of this tragic moment.

Slowly, agonizingly, he destroyed himself with six strokes—one too many—while thousands stood by and watched, and millions more peered at him on their television screens. Needing only a par four at the final hole to culminate another of his dramatic comebacks and win the Masters again yesterday, he buckled, and Gary Player, sitting in the clubhouse with a shaky 74 and 72-hole total of 280, became the champion.

It was like watching Dempsey writhing on the canvas. It was like watching Williams strike out with the winning run on base. It was like watching an innocent man being lynched.

And yet, many cheered as Palmer the superman reduced himself to the stature of mere mortal. At another time and another place, this might have been shocking, but it wasn't yesterday, for it demonstrated the grip that Player had taken over the Masters patrons and the grip that he undoubtedly will take over more of the golfing public of this country as he goes about winning additional championships in the future.

Although the 25-year-old South African stands only 5-7 and weighs a mere 150, he belts the ball as long as the muscled Palmer and does so with precision.

Player dies an agonizing death with each putt as it curls toward the cup, and when it drops, he does a little Indian war dance.

He almost always dresses in black trousers, black shirt, and black sweater, because black makes him feel strong. He eats dried fruit and nuts during a round to give him additional strength, and keeps himself in shape by doing fingertip pushups in the morning.

He has a happy, impish face, a fetching smile, and a delightful British accent. By his own admission, he is a showman. He once appeared on the first tee at stuffy St. Andrews wearing trousers that had one white leg and one black leg.

"You should have seen those old fogies training their field glasses on me," he laughed. "I couldn't have caused more of a stir if I had fanned the ball on the first tee."

It is to Player's credit that he is one of those people to whom everything happens.

On the Sunday night prior to the Masters, the house in which he and his family were quartered caught fire. He had carelessly tossed a carpet over a heater, and it had started a blaze. He awoke to find the house filled with smoke and attempted to stamp out the fire with his bare foot, suffering a slight burn.

When questioned about the fire, Player said, "Oh, it wasn't much really. All of us got out safely. We would have been dead in five minutes if I hadn't awakened, though. There was so much smoke, I couldn't see my wife lying in bed next to me."

On Thursday, something strange happened to his car. It went of its own accord, and he didn't have to step on the accelerator as he drove to the course.

"I just had to work like the devil on the brakes to keep the bloomin' thing from running away from me," he said.

As the car pulled up in the parking lot, smoke began to billow from under the hood.

"I still don't know what happened," grinned Player. "I just jumped out of the blasted thing and took off running before it blew up in my face."

Player's tribulations here recalled a classic incident of some two years ago when he drove a friend's car from one tournament to another.

En route, he encountered heavy rain, and the windshield wipers quit working. He had them replaced and set out again, but as he sped along, the hood blew up. He tied it down with his shoelaces.

Under way again, he became entangled in a cloverleaf intersection and couldn't get off. When he finally did find his way out, he forgot what country he was in and was barreling down the left side of the road when he met a car and narrowly managed to swerve to the right before crashing, cursing the stupid driver of the other vehicle as he went.

A short while later, he had a flat tire. He pulled over onto the shoulder and began to jack up the rear end of the car. He pumped feverishly for a long while but nothing happened. The jack had simply buried itself in the soft turf.

As Player sat with chin in hands, in a state of complete surrender, a policeman drove up and barked, "Hey, what do you think you are doing?"

To which Player replied, "Frankly, officer, I have no idea."

This is the kind of fellow Gary Player is. This is why they cheered yesterday when Arnold Palmer let him win.

1962

The most exciting period ever in golf was the early 1960s, when Arnold Palmer was becoming the most popular figure golf has known. He not only had the game and the charisma, he had the benefit of some great competition in Jack Nicklaus and Gary Player.

During a seven-year span in the '60s, Palmer, Player, or Nicklaus won the Masters. In 1962, the world was treated to an 18-hole playoff between the two of them, Palmer and Player, along with Dow Finsterwald.

In the fourth round on Sunday, Palmer was three shots out of the lead, playing the 16th, and hit his tee shot there over the green. He appeared to be finished but holed a 50-foot chip for a birdie and then birdied the 17th to gain his tie.

"He makes Willie Sutton look like Shirley Temple, the way he keeps stealing these tournaments," said Ken Venturi. "He must sandpaper his fingers before he hits his shots on the last few holes."

Venturi hadn't seen Arnie's tee shot on the fourth hole. Palmer popped up a one-iron shot on that par-three hole that traveled roughly 50 yards. It was probably the worst shot he ever hit in Augusta. He made bogey.

Palmer shot 31 on the back nine on Monday to run away with the playoff and his third Masters title and talked about winning the Grand Slam. That day, it seemed possible.

NOTES AND OBSERVATIONS

Former U.S. and British Amateur champion Deane Beman helped himself to a steak in the grill and observed, "If you let Jack Nicklaus hit the drives, Ben Hogan hit all the other shots, and Billy Casper putt, they could shoot 65 on any course in the world. Hogan might drive more accurately than Nicklaus, but Jack would give you that extra 50 yards."

DESPITE FAULTY PUTTER,
PALMER'S MAN TO BEAT

"Iron Man" is Arnold Palmer's caddy and has been for the past seven years. He calls his player "Par."

Consulted for his word on the eve of the first round, "Iron Man," a tall, drawling fellow, replied, "Par hittin' the ball just as good as ever, but he's puttin' worse than I've ever seen him putt in a long time. 'Course, he putted better today, but he ain't as sharp on the greens as he was last year. He ain't too worried, though, and I ain't either. When they ring the bell, he'll be there. He lays one up for a birdie, he'll make it."

PLAYER RATES PALMER'S
MUSCLES OVER MIRACLES

Arnold Palmer, Gary Player, and Dow Finsterwald, the grand triumvirate of this 26th Masters Championship, had tied themselves into a 280-stroke knot on the golf course and had disappeared under a deluge of protective gray Pinkerton uniforms.

They were hiding out from the milling thousands, who had trampled the National Golf Club's green byways into brownness on a Sunday afternoon filled with more drama than should be allowed in the interest of public health.

Palmer, as has become customary in recent years, had risen from his knees, where he had been knocked by the golf course he loves so dearly, and had roared in with spectacular birdies on the 16th and 17th holes to overtake Player, who was his partner, and Finsterwald, who had finished half an hour earlier.

They played off for the title today, teeing off at 1:45.

As they sat in Clifford Roberts' apartment on the east wing of the National Clubhouse yesterday, exchanging congratulations and pondering today's fortunes, Ken Venturi, an also-ran who has loved here a couple of times and lost, sat in the grill wearing a look of astonishment.

"It's unbelievable, truly unbelievable. He just keeps on performing miracles," he said.

The miracles have won two Masters, one U.S. Open, and one British Open title for Palmer in the past five years. They could win another Masters for him today.

Player took a far more realistic view of the playoff, though. With surprising forthrightness, the bouncy little South African looked past Palmer's patented heroics and said, "If either has an advantage in the playoff, it is Arnie, because of his strength.

"He is so much longer than Dow or me. That is a great advantage on this course. He can be fairly certain of reaching some of the par-five holes in two strokes, perhaps all of them, while neither Dow nor I can go for those on the back nine without considerable gamble, if at all."

The par fives on the back—the 13th and 15th—are both fronted by water. Many a title has been won or lost there. Palmer's muscular advantage there proved to be of no avail yesterday. He reached both but three-putted the 13th from 120 feet and hit over the green on the 15th, chipping back and two-putting.

At that stage, Palmer looked like anything but a man destined to tie for the Masters title, much less like the superhuman that his deeds have created in the eyes of the world.

He had blown putts as short as 18 inches, and hit a one-iron so fat it would embarrass any duffer, had repeatedly driven into trees, three-putted greens, and generally butchered the whole thing. With three holes to play, he was par in for a 77 and an ignominy equal to or surpassing what he suffered here last year when he needed only a par on the last hole to win but hacked out a double-bogey.

Even the most unreasonable Palmer idolaters must have doubted his chances of retrieving a piece of first place when he hit his tee shot over the green at the watery, par-three 16th. He trailed Finsterwald by three shots and Player by two at that point, but—only the Good Lord knows how or why—he chipped in from 50 feet for a birdie two.

The roar that went up from that green valley must have been heard in Valdosta.

It was matched decibel for decibel on the next hole when he planted an eight-iron 15 feet short of the pin and rammed it home to catch up with Player and set himself up for a tie.

Palmer started the last round with a two-stroke lead on Finsterwald, a four-shot edge over Player, and a chance to break Ben Hogan's record of 274 for 72 holes by shooting a 68.

The record wasn't even threatened. Palmer shot 75, Finsterwald 73, and Player 71.

"I'm not even sure I deserve to be in the playoff," Palmer said. "I played rinky-dink golf.

"I've been getting off to a slow start all week, but today I pitched my third shot 18 inches from the pin on the second hole, and it looked like I was going to make a birdie. I sort of laughed to myself and said, 'Well, I've got it now.'

"But I missed the putt, and it shook me up. After missing that one, I was very conscious of my putting for the rest of the day, and I didn't make anything except that one on 17. I kind of lost all feeling. It was like playing a practice round.

"I certainly feel fortunate to be in the playoff."

Finsterwald bogeyed the 17th hole to open an avenue for Palmer and Player, hitting over the green, chipping back six feet short, and missing the putt. He said he felt, while playing the hole, that he would need par to win.

Player was six shots behind Palmer after three holes but birdied the fifth, sixth, eighth, ninth, and 11th holes to take a three-shot lead on Arnie and a one-shot edge on Finsterwald. He bogeyed the 12th, then parred in.

Gene Littler, who started the day five strokes behind, birdied the 17th hole to give himself a chance, but couldn't get the tying birdie on 18, scoring a bogey instead to finish fourth at 282.

"IF MR. PALMER DO THAT, LOOK OUT"

Arnold Palmer was in trouble, so deeply in trouble that the 15,000 lining the picturesque 10th fairway of the National Golf Club wondered if he hadn't at last found a challenge too big for even his miraculous powers.

Unable once again to conquer the first nine holes, which had scornfully withstood the great champion's peerless skills throughout the tournament, Palmer stood on the 10th tee yesterday, one stroke over par and three strokes behind Gary

Player in what Dow Finsterwald had reduced to a two-man playoff for the Masters title by shooting himself out of it with a 40.

Palmer jerked at the glove on his left hand and tugged at his trousers as he peered down the green slope that tumbles sharply away from the National Clubhouse.

He drew out his driver, set it down behind the ball, paused, waggled the club a couple of times, then unleashed the mammoth power that is stored in his brown muscles.

The ball screamed off into the Georgia sky, hung there, and then plummeted to the green earth.

Palmer slid the driver back into the bag and walked impatiently while Finsterwald drove. When the disgruntled Dow had hit, Palmer stuck his neck out and began to stride swiftly down the fairway.

He was on his way to Palmer's Paradise, the back nine, and the devil beware.

Those watching this classic duel between the two most exciting golfers in the universe could have saved themselves considerable shortness of breath, beating of heart, and jangling of nerves had they known what Palmer's caddy, Iron Man, knew.

"When Mr. Palmer's gettin' ready to make his move, he jerks at that glove, pulls up his britches and starts walkin' fast," said Iron Man, who has toted for Palmer eight years now. "When he do that, everybody better watch out, he gonna stampede anything that git in his way."

Palmer birdied the 10th hole, running down a breaking 25-foot putt, and the most knowledgeable and polite gallery in American golf suddenly turned into a mob of bleacherites.

"Go get 'em, Arnie, baby!" they bellowed.

"Atta boy, Arnie, get hot, baby."

And when Player missed a six-foot putt for his par, they lost their heads completely and cheered, an unheard-of violation of cow-pasture etiquette.

Palmer passed Player on the 12th hole, a birdie to a bogey, and started pouring it on. The cheers grew with the margin, and The King slugged two more birdies at the 13th and 14th.

He was hunting a 30 for the back nine when he reached the tee on the par-five 15th, a masterpiece of beauty with the water running on three sides of the green.

His drive faded too far to the right, though, hit a spectator's chair, and bounced back some 20 yards behind Palmer's "go" spot—the point where he considers it safe to try to reach the green in two strokes.

"Aren't you lucky," grinned Finsterwald. "Now, you can play safely, gracefully."

Palmer laid up to the water, then pitched eight feet from the cup. He had a good shot at his fifth birdie in six holes and, lying directly in the path of Finsterwald's 12-footer, he could "go to school" on Dow's putt.

There was considerable delay as Palmer twice summoned an official to witness repair work on the green. He later related that there was a worm poking its head out of the earth directly in front of the cup. The unfortunate insect was removed from the best seat in the house to make way for first Finsterwald, then Palmer.

Finsterwald's putt fell sharply off to the right of the cup and long. Palmer noted this and putted his too far to the left.

"Sorry I didn't help you," Finsterwald apologized. "I hit a bad putt. I cut it, and it broke more than it actually should have."

Palmer strode to the 18th hole with a four-stroke lead. It was here that he smote a seven-iron into the sand and made a double-bogey last year when he needed only a par to win or a bogey to tie.

Iron Man pondered the distance up the hillside and advised his man to hit an eight-iron.

"Nope," said Palmer, "I'm going to hit a seven-iron."

He swung softly at the ball, put it on the back of the green, and two-putted for a 68 to beat Player by three strokes and Finsterwald by nine.

"It was really an eight-iron shot," he admitted later, "but I hit the seven purposely. Iron Man thought I was making a mistake, but I wasn't. I just wanted the pleasure of knocking the seven-iron up there. I'm mad at this hole."

1963

As we have noted earlier, the masters of the Masters will bend the rules from time to time. In the 1963 tournament, Japan's Koichi Ono unknowingly violated a rule involving dropping a ball. It called for a disqualification, but tournament officials decided to simply give him a two-shot penalty and let him play on.

Even more generous was the decision to let old-time great Horton Smith ride in an electric cart while he played. He was in poor health, and age was overtaking him. Three decades later, Casey Martin petitioned the PGA Tour for the right to ride in a cart because of a problem with one of his legs and won permission.

Jack Nicklaus won his first Masters in 1963, and newspaper accounts of it mentioned nicknames such as "Ohio Fats" and "Baby Beef" and one that endured, "Golden Bear." He edged "Champagne Tony" Lema, a popular figure who was among the best of his day but would die young when the plane in which he was a passenger crashed into a golf course.

Nicklaus used a yardage book at the Masters. He had been using a book for two years but never at the Masters. To the best of my knowledge, it was the first time anyone had used a yardage book in a big professional tournament.

NOTES AND OBSERVATIONS

Lloyd Mangrum, once one of golf's magic names, is a spectator now after seven heart attacks. "I just came back this year to heckle some of my old buddies. I'm not playing in competition anymore. Twenty-two years ago, I moved some old fellows over and made a place for myself. Now some of the youngsters have moved me over. After 22 years, I think it's time."

HORTON RIDES ELECTRIC CART

The Masters broke a long-standing rule and let aging, gravely ill Horton Smith ride in an electric cart to play. Despite the fact that he can hardly move around anymore, he showed some of his old greatness and determination by shooting a 42 on the first nine holes and a 92 for the round.

THANK GOODNESS FOR JACK

Jack Nicklaus ran a pudgy paw into his hip pocket, fetched out a scorecard, and then passed it around for all to see.

Beside each hole, where the scores go, there were such notations as "First tree on top of the hill," "Last ridge," "Little lone tree," and "Little pine."

They sound like titles for folk songs or the fevered mutterings of a Joyce Kilmer nightmare, but, in truth, they are the book on the Augusta National Golf Course, authored by Nicklaus. The notations are guideposts from which Nicklaus calculates the distance to each green from his tee shots.

Using this handy little ready reckoner, he salvaged some pride for the heralded Big Three in the second round of the Masters championship yesterday.

It was no simple task. Gary Player, "The Black Panther" of the grand triumvirate, scuffed around in 74 strokes to fall six shots off the 139 pace being set by Mike Souchak. Arnold Palmer, "Par" to his caddy, "Corporation" to his agent, fussed and squirmed and scrambled irritably to an unbecoming 73 and stood eight shots behind in his bid for an unprecedented fourth Masters crown.

Nicklaus responded handsomely to the challenge being tossed down at his feet of his rich and famous clan. Consulting his notes faithfully, and measuring each shot to the green from that "little lone tree" or the "last ridge," he figured out a six-under-par 66. This, coupled with an opening-round 74, left him only one stroke behind Souchak, and looming as large as his tent-sized trousers in the title chase here.

Nicklaus has been doing this bit for two years, but strangely never bothered to lay the yardstick down on the Augusta National until this year. Having met with only moderate success here in three previous attempts, he decided it might be wise to pace off the green acres this trip.

Of course, there was more to his 66 than the natural milestones. He miss-hit only two of his 66 shots and hit all the others "as good as I can hit them."

"You can't play much better than I played," he said, and rattled off the six birdies he had made, several other opportunities he had created, and concluded with the information that he had not missed a green until the 18th hole.

Neither of his stablemates could make that claim.

Palmer had worked himself into such a rage by the 12th hole, he told his playing partner, Jay Hebert, "Just let me get the hell off this golf course."

"And he would have gone, too," said Hebert, "if he hadn't holed a putt for his par on 12."

Palmer's beloved National Course tossed him an early flirtation—a missed opportunity for a birdie on the first hole and a fair but wayward shot at an eagle on the second—but turned her back on him there.

The great champion played like a weekend duffer at times, hitting wedge shots far off line, dumping irons into traps, chipping horribly, and leaving his putts shockingly short.

Hair tousled and shirt-tail out, Palmer gritted his teeth and suffered until the pretty lady finally relented and granted him birdies on 13, 15, and 17 that drew him back to even par. But he took the edge off his typically Palmerish burst by scoring a bogey five on the last hole.

"Yeah," he said, "I drove a lot better today, better than I have for most of this year. No, my putting wasn't good. Yeah, my chipping killed me. It was like hitting putty.

"My game was ragged all the way around. I guess I am getting tired."

"All that money you are carrying around is weighing you down," kidded Hebert. Palmer smiled, but it was only a polite smile.

BESIDES ALL ELSE, CARY RAN INTO A SNAKE

NOTES AND OBSERVATIONS

If, after shooting an unbelievable 87 in the first round and an only slightly less credible 81 in the second round, Cary Middlecoff wants to claim he was "snake bit," who can argue with him?

He found his ball, nestled in a coiled snake behind the 12th green yesterday.

"If that little so-and-so hadn't been there, the ball would have rolled back onto the green," snorted Middlecoff. "As it was, I had to lift the ball, move the snake, then place the ball back where it was lying.

"I tried dropping it over my shoulder, according to the rules, but it rolled closer to the hole, so I had to place it there on that steep hillside, leaving myself an awful shot to the pin."

He bogeyed but accepted his fate philosophically, for after all, what is another bogey when you are playing the way he was?

Jay Hebert, the handsome Louisianan who is tied with Jack Nicklaus for second place behind Mike Souchak, took a strange putting lesson before the tournament opened.

It was administered by veteran Horton Smith without benefit of a putter. They struck up a conversation at dinner about putting, carried it outside into the darkness and wound it up sitting in a car outside their hotel.

Hebert thinks the moonlight lesson has helped him into his lofty position.

Ed Furgol's shot to the 15th hole went over the green, struck a woman in the face, and bounded back across the green and into the water. A hospital report said there were no broken bones.

Furgol survived the shaking experience and a bogey to shoot a 71 and tie for fourth place.

"I never have had much luck with women," he said.

THE GREEN JACKET FITS JACK NICKLAUS

Jack Nicklaus, a peach-faced young man with a high-pitched voice, thoughtfully rubbed his pudgy hand across his green jacket, symbol of victory in the Augusta Masters golf tournament.

For a moment, he looked like a kid, and you remembered that despite all of his glory, he is still just 23 years old.

And then he speaks like a man.

"I don't know what size this jacket is," he said, "but I think it's much too large for me."

The jacket fit well. It was just his way of expressing how humble he was at the moment he won the championship he had coveted most of all since winning the U.S. Open last June.

They can't find a jacket too big for Nicklaus. If his success in the past four years is any gauge of what to expect from him in the future, they will have to start tailoring them even larger.

The mighty 205-pound Ohioan has won the Masters, the Open, and two U.S. Amateur championships in four years. Since becoming a professional last year, he has won two of the five major championships in which he has competed.

As the youngest champion in Masters history and one of the youngest ever to win the Open, his future in the game appears unlimited.

Already he has achieved what many thought impossible by establishing himself as the equal to Arnold Palmer, who had things pretty much to himself until Nicklaus came along.

Starting the final round of the Masters yesterday with a one-stroke lead over 45-year-old Ed Furgol after rounds of 74-66-74, Nicklaus shot an even-par 72 for a total of 286. He beat Tony Lema by one stroke, as "Champagne Tony" closed his first Masters with a 25-foot birdie putt on the last hole for a two-under-par 70.

Sam Snead, bidding for his fourth Masters title at the age of 50, made a gallant run down the stretch but faltered when he bogeyed the 18th. He finished tied for third with Julius Boros, the casual Moose from Mid Pines, North Carolina.

Nicklaus, who admitted he "had as many butterflies as anybody on the first tee," lumbered across the damp fairways, making par after par until he ran into trouble on the eighth hole and bogeyed.

He bogeyed again on the 12th—and made a 12-foot putt to do it. Snead, three holes ahead of him, birdied the 14th and 15th to take a two-stroke lead in relation to par at that point.

"I knew I was two shots behind going to the 13th tee," said Nicklaus, "but I also knew I had a couple of birdie holes coming up."

He meant the 13th and 15th. He got his birdie on the par-five 13th but missed one on the par-five 15th. Instead, he ran down a 12-foot putt for a bird on the watery, par-three 16th, then parred in, letting Snead kill himself.

"I wasn't trying to play just for par," insisted Nicklaus. "I attacked. I just missed umpteen million putts for birdies.

"I was just playing along, confident I was going to make some birdies, because I was hitting the ball so close to the hole. I wasn't nervous until I holed that birdie putt on the 16th."

If his nervousness showed at all, it was on the final hole.

His first putt on the 18th rolled three feet past. He had to make it coming back to win. If he had missed, he and Lema would have been tied and would have played off today. The ball rolled into the left side of the cup.

"I honestly thought I had made my first putt," said Nicklaus. "I was so surprised to see it go so far past the hole. I was more surprised when I made the second one.

"I don't know where it went in. All I know is that it went to the bottom of the cup."

1964

You could still buy tickets to the Masters during tournament week in 1964, and some of us raised our eyebrows at the cost, which seemed a little dear—$7.50 for Saturday or Sunday. Later, tickets were sold only to "patrons" whose names were on the list. The waiting list grew so long, the club stopped accepting applications, noting that the applicant would probably have died of old age before making it onto the list proper.

Gary Player had tonsillitis. Ben Hogan was 51 years old but was saying he had conquered, to some degree, the putting yips that had effectively ended his career as a championship threat. Arnold Palmer and Jack Nicklaus were everybody's favorites to win. And a club pro named Davis Love Jr. played well while awaiting at any moment the birth of a son, Davis Love III, who is now one of the top stars in golf.

Arnie won by six shots, claiming his fourth green jacket. Jack finished second and predicted Arnie would win two, three, or four more Masters, but Arnie never won another one. Hogan shot 73-75-67-72-287 to finish tied for ninth. Player had his tonsils taken out in an Augusta hotel on Monday. And a sportswriter named Green played the course the day after the tournament—same tees, same pins—and shot 86, which doesn't sound like much, but Mr. Green was quick to point out that it was only six shots higher than Jerry Barber's Sunday score. He failed to mention that Barber finished last.

NOTES AND OBSERVATIONS

THE HAPPY AGONY OF AUGUSTA

The major league has come to this minor league town this week.

This is Masters Week, when the queen of American golfing classics is played. Tomorrow, by twos, they will whistle their tee shots up the first fairway, the greats out of the past like Hogan, Nelson, and Sarazen; the greats of today like Nicklaus, Palmer, and Snead; the near greats, the amateurs, the foreigners, and a light scattering of relative unknowns.

Everything at Augusta National Golf Club will be as orderly as an operating room. Everything everywhere else in town will be chaos.

For 51 weeks of the year, Augusta lies dozing in the Georgia sun, soft, charming, quiet. And then, like locusts descending on a wheat field, here come the big, shiny cars with license plates from every state in the union.

They whisk into town and deposit thousands of strangers.

Most have learned by now that to come to Augusta without a room reservation is to try to crack Ft. Knox, but some still gamble that they will find a place to rest their heads when day is done.

Some manage ("I'm living in a house vacated by Jeter Lester," said one sports writer.). Some don't, and drive as far away as Columbia, S.C., a distance of 60 miles, to find a bed for the night.

To possess a room is no guarantee against perishing in the streets at midnight. People move from dining room to restaurant to waffle shop, seeking sustenance. Every seat is filled from dusk to the wee hours.

The city's most popular restaurant, a downtown steak house, has people filling its many tables, its bar, its anteroom and spilling outside far down the street every night.

These inconveniences are viewed tolerantly by the invaders, for this is the week of the Masters, and no price is too high to pay (not even the $7.50 for a Saturday or Sunday ticket).

Although no figures are ever released on the attendance, veteran observers believe the Masters attracts the largest galleries in golf. The event has grown so popular in recent years that officials have ruled that once the acres of parking space are filled, no more tickets will be sold.

What is the great attraction of the Masters?

The course itself is a great part of it. From the fat, shiny magnolias lining the driveway into the course, past the old colonial-style clubhouse, down the gently tumbling hillside that is much of the golf course, to the farthest reaches of the layout, there is nothing but magnificent beauty.

Plush green fairways, softly rolling hills, towering pines, flowering shrubs, blue ponds, serpentine creeks, and glistening white sand present a breathtaking scene, but one that is deceiving—for on these tranquil premises, a man can die a thousand deaths with a golf club in his hand.

The field is carefully selected, and it, too, is a great lure. You might see Arnold Palmer paired with Ben Hogan, Jack Nicklaus paired with Byron Nelson, or Billy Joe Patton playing in the company of Gene Sarazen.

Bobby Jones, founder of the tournament, is always there riding around in a golf cart to lend glory and dignity to the event that no one else can impart.

The battle is always fierce, the finish always dramatic, the prize always rich in prestige and money.

This is the Masters. The inconveniences are unimportant.

SOME BIG NAMES FALL BY WAYSIDE

NOTES AND OBSERVATIONS

Sam Snead, Julius Boros, Art Wall, Cary Middlecoff, and a raft of other sparkling names in professional golf were gone from the Augusta National Court today, victims of the 36-hole cutoff that reduces the field to the lowest-scoring 44 players. But Davis Love Jr., home pro at Charlotte Country Club, was still here and, even better, still there among the leaders.

Love, the slender, scholarly 29-year-old who shocked the country by shooting an opening-round 69 on Thursday and tying for the lead, came back yesterday with a three-over-par 75, and there were only eight players ahead of him as the third round opened today.

"I enjoyed myself even more today," said Love, who readily recognizes the measure of incredulity attached to his performance. "I didn't putt as well as Thursday. That was the difference. Naturally, I was a little disappointed at not playing better, but being up there in the thick of the fight made it more enjoyable to play."

Love said he didn't have the putting touch and thus was unsure of himself on the greens. He missed some short putts on the first nine that got him into the uncomfortable position of being three over par at the turn.

"As I started down the back nine," he said, "I told myself that if I could par the next three holes, three of the toughest on the course, I would be okay."

He didn't make it, but as things turned out, he was willing to settle for what did happen. He three-putted the 10th for a bogey, birdied the watery 11th with a 25-foot putt, bogeyed the 12th, then birdied the 13th and 14th.

Love came to the 18th needing only a par-four to stand one under par for the two days, but hit into a bunker, exploded out eight feet from the cup, and missed the putt.

"I get as nervous as anybody," he said. "But I'm not losing any sleep over this thing, and I'm eating well. I'm getting a lot of messages from back home in Charlotte, but so far, none from the stork."

His wife, Penta, is expecting a baby any day now.

A HOT DOG AND THE KING

You have to see and hear Juan (Chi Chi) Rodriquez to believe that he exists and is not merely the creation of some late-working journalist who has just staggered out of the Bull Bat Lounge, one of downtown Augusta's more fashionable watering troughs.

This may account for the puzzled but amused interest devoted to him by his playing partner, Arnold Palmer, during the second round of the Masters championship yesterday.

Chi Chi is as thin as a strip of bacon. "I whay whan hondered twenny pounds," he says with some pride. He has features as sharp as the blade of a nine-iron, and they are forever decorated with a pair of dark glasses and a dangling cigarette and shaded from the Georgia sun by a snappy straw hat.

He gives off the air of a cool cat, which one suspects is the idea.

How the gods of the Masters arrived at this pairing is open for wide speculation, but promptly at 11:30, Arnold Palmer and Chi Chi Rodriquez swapped blows on the first tee and set off up the hillside with several thousand $5 customers at their heels.

Now you are no doubt familiar with Arnie's Army. This is the multitude that gathers about him on any golf course in any town. Nowhere are his forces out in greater numbers or in better voice than here at the Masters. They cheer him here if he so much as scratches his nose or shoos a fly.

There were among the legions on this day, though, a smattering of Chi Chi Rodriquez disciples. Lest they go unnoticed among Arnie's Army, some of them displayed signs reading, "Chi Chi's Bandidos."

Palmer's force's retaliated by air. A plane flew over, towing a sign that read, "Go, Arnie, Go."

Arnie went, but so did Chi Chi.

Palmer would whack one of his mighty drives up the fairway, and Chi Chi would step up, leap off the ground and knock it past him. You see, Chi Chi has a secret for getting distance, or rather had one, until he published it recently in a book that was thinner even than he. They say if you lifted the preface and the summary from it, nothing would remain but the covers, but Chi Chi explains, "You can't give the peeble too much at wall time. They will get confused."

The slugging match came out about even, but the scores didn't (Palmer shot 68, Rodriquez 73) and neither did Palmer's temper.

Chi Chi likes to clown around on the course.

Many times when Palmer walked onto a green, the crowd would applaud him lustily as they traditionally do the established greats of this classic.

Palmer would acknowledge the applause ever so lightly by touching the visor of his cap. Rodriquez would acknowledge it— apparently presuming it to be for him as well—by waving his hat violently, bowing to the customers, and generally taking on like a vaudeville comic making curtain calls.

In addition, he offered conversation with the galleries, anguished or joyous contortions of his lean frame, and assorted other routines that Palmer found a trifle distracting as he went about the business of playing one of the finest rounds from tee to green that he has ever played in the Masters.

In baseball, Rodriquez would be called a hot dog—in show business, a ham. Palmer was spared further discombobulation by a ruling last year in which Masters officials requested that Chi Chi no longer do the twist after hauling out a putt.

Chi Chi's performance may have delighted the crowds, but it burned Palmer up.

Asked how he liked playing golf with Chi Chi, Palmer replied, "I have a very definite opinion to offer on that.

"I like Chi Chi very much, and nobody likes to clown around or joke more than I do on the course, but there is a time and place for it. In a tournament that has the dignity of the Masters, it should at least be spread out."

Upon hearing of Palmer's comments, Chi Chi was one crushed fellow.

"Whell," he said, "that's the way it goes.

"In Puerto Rico, it is considered proper to tip your hat to the gallery. It is a Spanish courtesy.

"My father always tole me, 'Son, when they cheer for you, you tip your hat.'"

It was not clearly established by nightfall how many casualties Palmer's 68 and Rodriquez' 73 had inflicted on "Chi Chi's Bandidos," and Chi Chi didn't hang around to find out. He was throwing a cocktail party in honor of his book.

CRITICS ARE SILENCED AFTER BLITZ BY KING

For the fourth time in seven years, Arnold Palmer yesterday slipped into the green jacket that is delivered, alterations free, to the Masters golf champion.

Then, in a tone that sounded strangely wistful for a vital, wealthy, and remarkably successful young man of 34, he said, "It's kinda like a new life for me. I feel like going out now and playing golf."

He had not exactly been playing hopscotch for the past four days. In wrenching scores of 69-68-69-70-276 out of the exacting Augusta National Golf Club, Palmer played what equaled, if not bettered, any golf he has ever played in winning seven major championships.

He called it the most exciting victory of them all.

"There were so many things depending on this tournament for me," he explained. "First, I didn't win a major championship last year, and so I started this year a little unhappy about that. I had one thing definitely in mind, and that was to try to win at least one major title this year. I didn't say anything about it, because it would have sounded silly in January for me to say I was aiming at winning the Masters in April, but I did set my sights on it.

"If I hadn't won the Masters, then I would have aimed toward, and worked for, the U.S. Open.

"Then there was the matter of my quitting smoking. It was a mental block for me. I felt like I had the jitters, and my game seemed to indicate that I did. I know now I've got that licked."

He came then to the pièce de résistance, the essence of his satisfaction with his smashing victory here.

His failure to win this year had raised the question in many minds of whether The King was at last slipping.

"When anyone questions your ability," said Palmer, "you always like to prove them wrong. I don't object to some of the criticism when I don't win, but I'm human."

When he finally did silence the critics, he didn't want to do it politely. He hit them right in the mouth with four rounds of golf that defending champion Jack Nicklaus said, "put the rest of us in another class."

The scoreboard indicated as much. There was Palmer up there at 276, just two shots off Ben Hogan's Masters record, and nobody was closer to him than six strokes. Nicklaus finally found his touch on the greens to close with a five-under-par 67 and tie little tiger Dave Marr for second place at 282.

A WRITER PLAYS AUGUSTA

When Henry Longhurst, England's most gifted golfing author, was invited to play that portion of the Augusta National course that Arnold Palmer had left unscorched on the day after the Masters, he declined.

With typical British regard for royalty, he said, "No, thank you. To inflict my golf game upon this great course would be a travesty."

The American writers have an equally high regard for the tossing hills and tall pines of this verdant golfing cathedral, but when dawn broke yesterday morning, they were out by the dozens to play the course, a travesty in every bag.

This rare privilege is a gesture of appreciation on the part of the Augusta National officials for the unparalleled coverage given the Masters each year by the news media. It is a high price to pay.

For the golf writers of this nation—or any other—to play golf on the same ground that just a day earlier has been trod by such as Palmer, Jack Nicklaus, Tony Lema, Ben Hogan, and other giants of the game, is like following filet mignon with hominy grits.

With the writers' first shot, the door is slammed shut on all of the charm and dignity of the previous week, and the hallowed course weeps tears of shame.

It is like walking up to a queen and kicking her in the tail.

No one committed more dastardly deeds at the Augusta National than my foursome, and I must confess to many of the crimes, sad to say.

Ah, what a pity. And I was so well prepared.

Fearful of being overtrained for this long-awaited challenge, I scheduled my preparations very carefully. I played only nine holes during the 10 weeks prior to setting my first peg into the lush green turf. I trained on five to six hours of sleep a night during the Masters, ate press-room hot dogs for lunch at noon, and exercised strenuously each evening by wrestling old ladies and young children for a table in the dining room at 11 p.m.

I felt ready—sleepy and tired, but ready—when at last I came to battle the giant that had known combat with such names as Hagen, Sarazen, Hogan, Snead, Palmer, and Nicklaus.

The tee markers were still back there where they were on Sunday for the final round of the Masters. The pins were still stuck behind the traps or off in the corners where they had dashed the hopes of all but the mighty Palmer.

That's just the way we wanted it. We asked no quarter.

Somewhere along the line, I obviously made an error in my preparations.

My tee shots lacked the carry of Nicklaus' and the accuracy of Snead's. My irons, carefully chosen and aimed, strayed far more than Hogan's ever did. And my putting was hardly as deft as Billy Casper's.

It could be that the gallery upset me. Everywhere we turned, there were people. Oh, sure, we had a gallery.

There were dozens of fellows walking around in the woods, picking up empty beer cups. There were truck drivers rolling their mounts across the fairways, hauling away the litter of Sunday's throngs. There were workmen rolling up the ropes that had restrained the milling thousands.

I tell you, for a man not accustomed to playing in front of a crowd, it was a little disconcerting.

I played the course boldly, the way Arnie does, which may account for several of my lost strokes. Like on No. 4, I tried to play for position on the green and wound up in a jungle of cane, and that cost me a triple-bogey six. Or take 13. I tried to cut the corner of the dogleg, hoping to go for the green in two, but caught the trees, and it took me a few more than two to get to that green.

I hit it 86 times, I think it was, but you must remember, it was my first time around the course as a player, and what with the galleries and all, well....

1965

It was in 1965 that Bobby Jones uttered the famous words about Jack Nicklaus: "He plays a different game, a game with which I am not even familiar."

Nicklaus had just torched Augusta National with scores of 67-71-64-69-271, breaking Ben Hogan's tournament record by three shots and winning by nine. Jones called it "the greatest tournament achievement in golfing history."

Nicklaus' power was awesome for that period of time, and he used it to great advantage on a course that played uncommonly fast, but it wasn't just muscle. He played the par threes in seven twos, seven threes, and two fours.

It was about this time that the fans began to accept Nicklaus, the man who had come along to challenge their favorite, Arnold Palmer. Nicklaus had endured a lot of indifference and outright hostility, but the realization that they were seeing greatness eventually silenced the critics and won him the acclaim and acceptance he deserved. Nobody, not even the great Jones, ever conducted a life and a career at such a high level with more dignity.

Nicklaus would go on to win a total of six Masters championships, his last at age 46.

NOTES AND OBSERVATIONS

"ROWDY" SETTLES DOWN

Except for the fact that he looks good around the clubhouse and signs pretty scorecards, there is little about Doug Sanders to suggest that he is one of professional golf's star performers.

He has one of the most unstylish swings on the tour, and by his own proud admission, some of the poorest training habits.

But that is Doug Sanders, take it or leave it, and whatever your opinion about his style on or off the golf course, he can play the game.

He has been demonstrating this ever since he majored in golf for a couple of years at the University of Florida, beating the pros to win the Canadian Open while he was still an amateur, and he was still demonstrating it in the opening round of the Masters Tournament yesterday.

Looking quite snappy in light blue trousers, navy blue shirt and socks, and navy-and-white shoes, he pegged his ball up on a matching light blue tee and shot a three-under-par 69.

This was the occasion for delving into the fabled habits of the handsome son of Cedartown. Word has been around for weeks now, since he won the Doral and Pensacola Opens back-to-back to become the leading money winner on the tour this year, that dashing Doug has subjected his nightlife to some reformation.

Doug Sanders, pro golf's leading advocate of la dolce vita, reformed?

"Let's get this straight," said Sanders with an impish grin, "I've given up drinking, and I started getting some sleep. Those are the only sacrifices I've made.

"I haven't had so much as a beer in four months, except a couple of times. That's no world's record, but it's pretty good for old Doug.

"I celebrated after I won the Doral and Pensacola. After Doral, I jumped out of the Mr. Clean bottle into the champagne jug. The next morning, I felt like I had been hit in the head with a stick.

"Say, I wonder how far Cutty Sark stock has dropped since I quit drinking."

Someone asked Sanders if he had given up smoking.

"Me?" he said. "Man, I already make a mill town nervous. If I quit smoking, you couldn't hold me in a 10-acre field. I don't know how many I smoke a day, but I use four books of matches, if that's any hint."

Sanders has been married twice, but at present is playing unattached.

Sanders makes no apologies for his rakish habits. "It's the way I've always lived," he said. "It's what I wanted.

"I've tried to do better recently, though, and I feel a lot better, and my golf game is better."

He got his basic training early. His astonishingly short back-swing evolved from the early days when he used to sneak out on the course as a kid and play a hole that had water on one side and honeysuckle on the other. He couldn't afford to lose a ball, so he shortened his swing to keep it in play.

He learned some other shortcuts along about that time.

"I used to pick cotton for about $2 a hundred pounds," he remembered. "I might still be back there in Cedartown working in a cotton mill if it hadn't been for golf. No, I think I had too much ambition to stay in a cotton mill. I believe I would have at least have gotten myself a pool cue and started hustling. I was a pretty good pool player. That's how I paid my expenses in college."

Some, pondering his success on the fairways and recalling incidents in his life, think Sanders leads a charmed life. They fetch up the story about the time he and Al Besselink, fellow boulevardier, were broke, but won $20,000 betting on bowl games on New Year's Day when they didn't have a nickel to pay off if they lost.

"We'd have had to leave the planet if we had lost."

But it hasn't been all dollars, dolls, and dollops for Sanders. They could write a medical book on the injuries and illnesses that have plagued him since he became a golf pro. Many of them have knocked him out of action for several weeks at a time.

He keeps coming back as bouncy and brassy as ever. And this time, perhaps better than ever.

BEN HOGAN PONDERING ABOUT FORM

NOTES AND OBSERVATIONS

When golfers speak of perfection in golf swings, they invariably mention the name of Ben Hogan, but the Texas Hawk says maybe he has had the wrong idea all along.

"A lot of these fellows look good swinging at the ball," said the golfing immortal, "but watch them in slow-motion films, and you see all sorts of jerks and hitches.

"Maybe that's the thing to do. They are winning. Maybe I've been working the wrong side of the street."

Asked to name some players who have good swings, he passed over a lot of men who are regarded as sweet swingers and named Bruce Devlin of Australia and Chi Chi Rodriquez of Puerto Rico.

"Devlin has a helluva swing," he said. "Chi Chi doesn't look so good, but watch him in slow motion. His swing is real good. He has a wonderful pattern."

The Masters was a sellout again yesterday, with the gates closing behind an estimated 35,000 people. No tickets are available for today or tomorrow.

Arnold Palmer says he has used a different putter every day for two weeks. After shooting a 68 yesterday, he was asked if he planned on another change for today.

"Oh, chances are about 50-50," he said.

Palmer's wife, Winnie, says the caddies here try to set a Masters record of their own. They try to top the payoff the caddy for the previous year's winner received. The record is $1,800, held by "Iron Man"—Palmer's caddy—here for 11 years.

BIG JACK RELAXED, ARNIE EDGY, GARY HUNGRY AT START

Jack Nicklaus had curtailed the Masters Championship by 24 hours on Saturday when he waddled around the Augusta National Golf Course in 64 strokes, trampling fallen bodies and records with a big grin on his fresh, round face, but he and the other guys showed up yesterday anyway to play out the farce.

Gary Player had a trace of a chance of catching up from five shots behind Nicklaus' 54-hole record 202 and people who believe in miracles thought Arnold Palmer, who has practiced magic here before, might pull out the greatest trick of all and come back from eight behind. The rest though, came just to get their slice of the $140,075 wages.

One by one, they drifted in and out of the heat to lounge in the locker room and await their turns on the tee.

Dan Sikes—tied with Palmer eight shots off Nicklaus' pace—sat down with Mason Rudolph, Bernard Hunt, and Gene Littler and had a glass of iced tea. He had been paired with Nicklaus on Saturday, when the awesome Golden Bear had tied Lloyd Mangrum's 25-year-old record of 64.

"I shot 71," said Sikes, "and he made me feel like I was about five over par. That man plays a different game from the rest of us.

"He's got it six under par, and he drives it behind those trees in the fairway at 15. He's got to play it safe and lay up short of the water. Anybody would. Not him. He bends a five-iron around the trees and makes another birdie.

"I tell you, he's different from the rest of us."

At 11:20, Palmer came in. He nodded to a couple of acquaintances, then pulled some telegrams out of his locker and rifled through them. A commercial photographer asked him about posing for some publicity pictures someone had commissioned him to shoot.

Palmer is a remarkably patient man, but that cracked him. "What the hell do they think this is, a publicity show or a golf tournament?" he snapped. "No pictures." And he walked out and went to the practice range.

At 11:40, Player arrived, carrying a golf glove, some mail, a Bible, and a banana. He put the Bible, which he had taken to church with him, in his locker, sat down on a couch, read his mail and ate the banana.

Cary Middlecoff walked up behind him and said, "Hey, Gary, you're playing pretty good to be five shots behind. Man, you shoot 69, and Jack runs off and leaves you."

"Yeh," said Player, "what do you do, Doc? You're a doctor, you tell me. Do I need pills?"

Doug Sanders, the bon vivant of the fairways, was over in the corner, stripping down and changing into brilliant yellow slacks, shirt, and shoes. "I heard we're on color TV today," he chirped.

At noon, Tony Lema strolled through and went to his locker. Someone remarked they had heard his name mentioned in church.

"They introduced some of us golfers at church today," he said. "Can you imagine that? It's ridiculous. First thing you know, we'll be getting appearance money to go to church."

At 12:05, the man arrived—Jack Nicklaus. Neither he nor Player nor Palmer nor Sikes was ready to admit it, but they knew that, barring miracles, it was his tournament. All he had to do was play it out.

He smiled and said hello to the people in the room as he moved through. He looked relaxed, fresh, confident, and so very young to be in such complete command of one of the world's premier golf tournaments. He had slept10 hours and had put away a hearty breakfast of melon, bacon, eggs, and toast.

He sat down with Deane Beman, the amateur, sipped a glass of water, and exchanged conversation with Ben Hogan, who was at an adjoining table.

"That 12th hole really shakes me up," he told Hogan. It's a par three guarded by water, sand, and assorted other devilish problems.

"I knocked it eight feet from the hole there yesterday, and I was so shook up about hitting the green, I didn't even come close on the putt."

Hogan smiled and nodded, "That hole shakes everybody up," he said.

Nicklaus went to his locker and changed shoes. Writers clustered around and kidded him about one thing and another, and he laughed heartily.

"Well," he said, getting up to go, "off to the war."

He won it by nine shots, broke Hogan's 72-hole record by three, and won $20,000. And somebody said war was hell.

NICKLAUS' 271 "GREATEST EVER"

Bobby Jones, in whose lifetime the most illustrious golfing accomplishments of all time have transpired, viewed the ruin of his beloved and formidable Augusta National Golf Club yesterday afternoon and declared that young Jack Nicklaus' second Masters victory was "the greatest tournament achievement in golfing history."

Nicklaus, still 10 years short of the acknowledged prime age for golfers, sent Ben Hogan's lofty record of 274 for 72 holes crashing to the lush green turf with a 271 total that beat the field by nine shots. Nobody had ever won by more than seven.

On a day that could have been anticlimactic after he had virtually clinched his second Masters title in three years with a Saturday 64, Nicklaus thrilled the milling thousands with his relentless play.

With a five-stroke lead starting the day, Nicklaus faced a situation that dictated a careful 72 or 73, but the great youngster from Ohio, relaxed and confident, gave the National another lusty thrashing with a three-under-par 69, the best round of the day.

Looking back across Nicklaus' 67-71-64-69, the immortal Jones said, "I would never have believed anyone would shoot a score like Jack shot here, no matter what the conditions."

It is a game few can approach or ever have approached. He drove the ball so far that he reduced the par-five holes to par fours and played the par fours with his wedge so often that a British writer asked him in jest if it ever caught fire from excessive use.

Proving that it was not his power alone that destroyed the myth of the dogwood-scented acres and left his competitors struggling far behind, he handled the par-three holes in seven twos, seven threes, and two fours.

Four-time Champion Arnold Palmer and one-time winner Gary Player, who tied for second at 280, lost 10and nine strokes, respectively, to Nicklaus on the short holes.

Palmer labeled the smashing triumph, "probably one of the outstanding performances the golf world has ever seen." Player said simply, "It was fantastic."

Nicklaus didn't know exactly what to say.

"It will take a while for this to sink in," apologized the husky, golden blond who, in addition to two Masters, has won the U.S. Open and PGA Championship since turning professional in 1961.

"The first time I won here, I wasn't sure I should have been up there. I had the lowest score, but several players faltered to let me win.

"This time, I felt I had control of it all the way. I drove the ball as consistently long as I've ever driven it, and I hit only one bad drive all week. It was as good a putting tournament as I've ever had.

"I've never played a more enjoyable round of golf in my life than this last one today. I felt confident all day that I could hit the shots."

He said he thought about Hogan's record throughout the round, but made no conscious "charge" for it until after he had gotten safely past the troublesome 13th hole.

He might have sliced another shot off the revered record had he not gone too boldly for a putt on the 15th green and come up with his only three-putt of the tournament.

Nicklaus, already one of the leading money winners of all time, was awarded $20,000, a gold medal and a green jacket, symbolic of victory in the Masters.

"I wouldn't care if I hadn't won any money in this tournament," he said. "That gold medal and that green jacket were enough."

Palmer, seeking his fifth Masters and his second in a row, never holed a putt longer than 10 feet throughout the tournament, and yet he and Player shot scores that would have won 22 previous Masters tournaments. He had hoped either he or Player could make an early move yesterday and put some pressure on Nicklaus.

"If we could have started pushing him," said Palmer, "we might have done something, but we couldn't get close enough for him to know we were even in the field. It was no contest."

Palmer closed with a 70, Player with a 72. Each collected $10,200 from the $140,075 pot.

Total attendance figures were not available, but it was believed that more people saw this tournament than have attended any other four-day golfing event.

1966

In 1966, Jack Nicklaus won the Masters for the third time in four years. He finished second the one time he failed to win in that span. The resentment that galleries had felt when this beefy young blond intruded on Arnold Palmer's kingdom should have been gone and forgotten by then, but it still lingered.

He was still the rich, overweight kid they liked to call "Baby Beef" and "Ohio Fats." He was overweight, and his wardrobe had not yet been laid out for him by a special designer. It had seemed in 1965, when he set the scoring record at Augusta, that he had won over the crowd, but in 1966, some actually urged his ball away from the cup, loudly. It has often been said that the galleries at the Masters are among the most knowledgeable, but their treatment of Nicklaus brought that into question.

In time, he would lose weight, have his own popular line of clothing, and win the crowds over with his unbending class and his unparalleled golf. Nicklaus would grow to be one of our most beloved golfers. He never betrayed his game or his name. Nobody, including the great Bobby Jones, ever conducted a career in golf with more dignity.

NOTES AND OBSERVATIONS

TREACHERY IS HER NAME

One of the most beautiful spots and unquestionably the most cursed at the Augusta National Golf Club is that plot of bottom land that serves as the 12th hole of the golf course where the Masters Tournament is played each spring.

It's a pleasant little nook, the kind of place you'd choose for a picnic, except that the language there at this time of year is not fit for children's ears.

The 12th is the shortest hole on the course, measuring only 155 yards, and to the spectator's eye, it is no more menacing than a glass of warm milk. There's a nice little creek ambling along in front of the green, a couple of glistening white sand traps at the front and rear of the long, thin green, and some shrubbery and heavy grass on the hillside to the left and rear of it all. Lovely spot.

But the world's greatest golfers cower on its tee. The creek looks like the Atlantic to them, and the sand traps are twin Saharas. The wind, driving down the neighboring fairways, pauses to swirl there and baffles them when they start to choose a club.

Every hole on the course is named for a flower or shrub. They call this one "Golden Bell." Doug Sanders, Sam Snead, Arnold Palmer, and some of the others who are handy with words call it other names.

Gary Player, who has traveled much of the world playing golf, calls it probably the greatest par-three hole built anywhere, any time, but then he made a birdie on it yesterday, and he was prejudiced.

Another golfer walked away from "Golden Bell" yesterday after making a triple-bogey six on it and said, "Playing that hole is what I imagined it was like going to hell."

"Golden Bell" respects no man. Palmer is the king of golf and a four-time winner here, but his highness triple-bogeyed this hole on the final round in 1959 when he appeared to have the title wrapped up, and Art Wall won. The pretty little wench got Arnie again yesterday.

The wind quit blowing when he hit his tee shot and the ball buried in the back bunker. He didn't get his first blast out and made a double-bogey five and finished the round two over par.

Sanders is the hottest man in golf at the moment, coming here on the heels of back-to-back victories, but "Golden Bell" fixed him. It took one of the orange shoes right off the fairway fashion plate. Sanders hit his tee shot right into the mud at the edge of the creek, and in order to hit out of it, he removed his right shoe and stood with his foot in the cold water. The crowd cheered. It was like a striptease show.

Four times, he almost tumbled into the water as he struggled to figure out a way to hit the ball. Each time the crowd would gasp. He tried kneeling on one knee on the bank, and that didn't work, but he must have said a prayer while he was down there, because he finally figured out something, swung away, and the ball plopped on the green about 15 feet from the cup.

Sure, he missed the putt.

Billy Joe Patton is a member of the Augusta National Golf Club, but it didn't mean a thing yesterday. He was going pretty good up until the 12th hole, but "Golden Bell" ignored his credentials, hid his ball under some shrubs, and made him work like the dickens to hack it out for a double bogey.

Master putter Billy Casper, who can get down in two from the deck of a burning ship, three-putted it. He wasn't too unhappy about it, though. He made an eight there last year.

All told, 28 of the world's premier golfers bogeyed the hole, 21 double-bogeyed it, and three took sixes on it. Only three courted birdies out of "Golden Bell"—Player, Ray Floyd, and Tony Lema.

Player got his with a miracle. He buried his tee shot behind the rear trap and hit six inches behind the ball just trying to dig it out and move it a foot or two so it would tumble into the trap so he could make a bogey or double bogey from there.

Instead, it shot out across the trap, landed on the green, and rolled into the cup.

"If I may be a bit immodest," said the little South African star, "that not only was the greatest shot I ever hit, it was the greatest I've ever seen. If I stood there and hit that shot the rest of my life, I couldn't get it within 10 feet of the cup, much less in the hole."

Well, there's a bit of ham in "Golden Bell," too.

LAUGHS BEFORE THE WAR

It was Easter morning, the day that was supposed to be the last of the Masters Tournament for this year until Jack Nicklaus, Gay Brewer, and Tommy Jacobs got themselves knotted up and were invited outside to settle it today. The clubhouse was crawling with contenders, nervous men trying to appear relaxed.

On one side of the room, Arnold Palmer sat amid a clutch of writers. Ray Floyd, the youngster from Fayetteville, walked in, noticed the new blue cap sitting on Palmer's receding hairline and said, "You look funny in a cap."

Palmer acted offended and said, "I'm glad I have to wear a cap to look funny."

"Another couple of years," said Floyd, "and you are going to need all kinds of caps. You are going to need a transplant of hair from me."

Palmer looked at Floyd's thick, wavy locks, and shot back, "Well, at least I don't have to put mine up in curlers."

Jay Hebert said something about how fresh these young kids are nowadays and fretted over whether he would be warm enough in one sweater.

"Just three-putt the first green, Pierre, and you'll be hot enough," cracked Palmer.

Across the room, another group of writers chatted with Ben Hogan, who was in prime position to win despite his 53 years.

"You know," he said, "I listen to these other fellows telling about their rounds and they're saying, 'I hit a wedge to No. 7 and a wedge to No. 9 and a wedge on this hole and that hole!' They don't need a whole set of clubs. They just need a set of wedges."

Jacobs was worrying aloud about getting a plane out last night. He's anxious to get home and see his new son, born last Thursday.

"Just win this tournament, and you won't need a plane," Palmer told him. "You can just spread your arms and fly."

Jack Nicklaus came in carrying a red sweater, sat down at his locker, and looked awesome.

Somebody told him that his caddy was being interviewed outside by several writers.

"Yeah," said Nicklaus. "Willie's telling them how 'we' birdied those holes yesterday, and how 'I' bogeyed them."

And then, one by one, they moved out to fight their lonely battles in front of tens of thousands on a sunny Sunday afternoon.

"IT HURTS, BUT WE SMILE BIG"

Jack Nicklaus is going to Las Vegas this week to play in a golf tournament, but he's planning to have some fun out there while he's at it, just like any ordinary businessman on a convention.

After that, he'll take his family to Florida for a week's vacation, and then he and some pals are going fishing in British Honduras.

All of which proves that the man who yesterday won the Masters golf championship for the third time in three years—in a playoff with Tommy Jacobs and Gay Brewer— is a human being, a fact that many have questioned.

Watching Nicklaus play golf is like watching a bulldozer move dirt. Gary Player, his partner in the Big Three of golf, is emotional, showy, expansive. Arnold Palmer, the other member of the Grand Triumvirate, is animated, a slam-bang gambler who has a mystic communication with his worshipping galleries.

Nicklaus is none of these things. He is a nice guy, but he can't seem to get that point across, because he can play golf better than anybody on the planet, and a lot of people seem to resent his particular brand of excellence.

Perhaps because he has won so much so soon, and perhaps because he fetches up visions of a big kid beating up on little ones, the big bear is not the most popular champion ever to win here.

While he was hammering out a two-under-par 70 to Jacobs' 72 and Brewer's 78 in the flaming brilliance of the Augusta National Golf Club yesterday, many among the estimated 18,000 who tramped around trying to see a shot here or there not only pulled for Jacobs, and to a lesser degree for Brewer, they pulled against Nicklaus.

They didn't do it silently and discreetly, as is expected of a well-mannered golf gallery. They loudly urged his ball away from the cup at times, which put Nicklaus back where he was before he won with a record score here last year. There were indications in 1965 that the big, peach-faced 26-year-old with the cornsilk hair and the blacksmith arms had finally been accepted as a good guy, but he was back playing the villain again yesterday.

It's a bad rap. It's like pulling against Sandy Koufax simply because he's the best pitcher in baseball.

Nicklaus shrugs when you ask him about it.

"You're going to find that anywhere," he said. "The crowd always pulls for the man who's behind. They want him to catch up and make it a game."

Which didn't explain why, with Nicklaus tied with Jacobs, the crowd waved its arms and shouted at Jack's ball to keep going when it started to roll back off the ninth green yesterday. This is strange behavior for people who watch golf.

"I came out here to see Nicklaus get beat," said a guy in the gallery. "He's a good 'un, but I hope he gets beat. I'd like to see Jacobs win."

Nicklaus' caddy, Willie Peterson, who has been toting the Golden Bear's bag since 1960 and has seen his man become the only one ever to win two Masters back-to-back, says it breaks his heart to hear the people applaud Jack's misfortunes, but added, "We got a deal. When that happens, we both just smile big. We hurt inside, but we smile."

Because of his build, Nicklaus looks awesome, but he's as friendly as a preacher.

When he speaks, it is in a high-pitched voice that fits his boyish appearance. He likes to kid around, and he laughs a giggly laugh at his own jokes.

On the course he doesn't transmit his feelings to the crowds, because it is not his nature. He will raise a casual hand or touch his hat in response to applause, and when he holes a long putt, he might kick his left leg and punch the air with a right fist that looks like it could fell a water buffalo. But he doesn't come across.

He plays with more controlled power and precision than any active player today. He suffers out there like the rest when things aren't going well, and he is just as happy to win as anybody, but his emotions can't escape from that massive frame.

1967

Not all Masters are won by true masters. Some are won by golf's working class, men who have won a few Pensacola Opens but never a major championship, men who have not and will not capture the public's imagination the way a Nicklaus or Palmer or Player could.

Such a winner was Gay Brewer in 1967. There was atonement in his victory, though, that made it feel good. The year before, he had three-putted the 72nd green to fall into a tie with Jack Nicklaus and Tommy Jacobs, then had shot 78 in the playoff, shanking one of those 78.

The true highlight of this tournament was the 30 on the back nine, 66 total, that Ben Hogan shot in the third round, when he birdied 10, 11, 12, and 13. While Brewer, who had once caddied for Ben Hogan and who had once worked at Augusta National, parking cars during the Masters, was making his way into a green jacket, Nicklaus, going for his third straight Masters title, shot 79 in the second round and missed the cut.

It's not meant to be, but sometimes it is a funny game.

NOTES AND OBSERVATIONS

NICKLAUS DOES HAVE A HEART

As he talked, Jack Nicklaus kept touching his left eye. It was twitching from time to time. "Must be my nerves," he said, smiling.

While her husband was playing the par-three tournament that has become a Wednesday tradition here, pretty Barbara Nicklaus said, "It's nerves."

"The eye just started doing that since he got here. It did the same thing down here two years ago.

"I think Jack's a little more excited this year than he has been in past years but he controls it well. He has such a wonderful temperament for his profession.

"He is quite emotional, even though he may not show it. He can be at a very high pitch for a round of golf.

"At home, though, he and our oldest son, Jackie, will sit down to watch TV, and the house could burn down and they wouldn't know it. I call Jack "Stonewall," because he never hears what I'm saying when he's concentrating on television. It's like talking to a stone wall."

SUNDAY MORNING COMING DOWN

It was Sunday morning at the Masters. Outside, the day laughed a spring laugh, and the people, a brilliant montage of color, filed into Augusta National Golf Course by the dozens, then hundreds, then thousands to watch one of sport's greatest dramas unfold.

In the locker room, which doesn't even look like a locker room because the lockers are disguised as walls and benches, one of the early arrivals was Gardner Dickinson, who emulates Ben Hogan in dress, manner, and to a lesser degree, swing.

"That Hogan," he said, his cigarette dangling in Hogan-like fashion from between his teeth, "imagine him playing 10, 11, 12, and 13 in straight birdies yesterday. I didn't even think they could be played in pars."

Hogan had shot the back nine in 30 strokes for a 66, to move into the thick of the fight on this fine, sunny day.

Ken Venturi, the former U.S. Open champion and several times a contender here, came in with that jerky walk of his and chirped, "Ah, the working press! You guys better be ready to stay over tonight. There's going to be a playoff tomorrow."

Then, unprovoked, he resumed the bleating that had been heard from him all week. Bitter because he had been virtually ignored by the couple of hundred writers on hand, Venturi said, "You guys are losing the knack for spelling my name. My press this week hasn't been exactly overwhelming."

A writer dryly replied, "Look for your name in the summaries."

That's where Venturi's scores—76-73-71-73—were listed.

Sam Snead came in whistling. He wasn't going to win anything but money. Gene Littler walked by carrying one of the popular new Ping putters. Snead took it and swung it a couple of times.

"Oh, geez," said Littler, "don't put that awful stroke on my putter. It may stick."

The next arrival was George Archer, winner of the Greater Greensboro Open the week before and very much in contention on this day.

"Hey, George," Lionel Hebert shouted, "you get all the featured pairings."

Archer was matched with Ben Hogan.

"Yeah," he said, "I wish it was a best-ball tournament."

And then came Hogan. He looked like a million dollars, fresh, hard, his steely eyes bright. He sat down at his accustomed place, the same place he has sat throughout history, lit up a smoke, and had a few laughs about the old days, about Clayton Heafner, and Jug McSpaden, and Johnny Bulla.

Gay Brewer, the man who would win, passed, paused to shake Hogan's hand and said, "Beautiful round, Ben. A little 30. Hmmm." And then Brewer changed his shoes and asked Hogan if he remembered playing an exhibition match in Lexington, Kentucky, back in the '40s when Gay caddied for him. Ben couldn't remember.

By now, you could hear an occasional thunderclap of cheering from far down the valley as the Art Walls and Bruce Cramptons and Don Allens, the non-contenders, moved around the course.

Gary Player, winner of the four major titles of the world, arrived wearing his traditional black outfit and carrying a golf glove and a banana. He sat down on a couch and was granted solitude. He played well here, but for some reason, never really appeared to be a contender this time.

Arnold Palmer's presence caught the notice of everyone in the room, but few spoke to him. The great god of the fairways is friendly, communicative, but on Sunday morning at the Masters, he's often moody. He rifled through a dozen telegrams, chatted softly with U.S. Golf Association official Joe Dey, leafed through a golf magazine, then got up, hitched up his trousers and went out to practice.

A reporter tried to get Julius Boros, one of the leaders, to talk about his easygoing nature and his syrupy swing. Well, what he really wanted to know was whether there was a heart and soul, liver and lights inside this quiet man.

"Look," said Boros, bothered by the question, "you're skinny, and I'm fat. There's not much either of us can do about the way we are, right?" And with that, he went off to work on his iron shots.

Bobby Nichols attacked a steak sandwich in the adjoining grillroom. His striking blue eyes were big and happy. Tied for the lead with just one round to go, he looked as if he might burst out laughing. He was turned on.

Bert Yancey, the third man in the tie, was just the opposite. He seemed to be in a daze, didn't hear much of what was said to him and answered those he did hear in brief sentences. He seemed tense.

One by one, they drifted back out of the clubhouse to do their day's work. The working conditions were ideal, and the pay was good, but the only one who was happy when he came back in late in the day was Brewer. He had won.

MASTERS KING ONCE PARKED CARS THERE

Gay Brewer once caddied for Ben Hogan, parked cars at the Augusta National Golf Club, and went to the University of Kentucky on a football scholarship to play golf.

He has a pug-nosed face that looks like Babe Ruth's, and there is some distance between his looping golf swing and purity, but yesterday Brewer, a tough 36-year-old Kentuckian, added the Masters golf championship to his identifying features and credentials. With it, he added a check for $20,000 plus ancillary rights.

Where just a year earlier he had three-putted the final green to let victory slip out of his calloused grasp and had then staggered through an embarrassing 78 in the playoff won by Jack Nicklaus, Brewer this time shot a five-under-par 67 that the great Ben Hogan described as "fantastic" and one that left no doubt.

Some, like Hogan and Julius Boros, stumbled in the final round of this 31st classic, not a day perfect for golf, and an Augusta National course that had its cups cut to test severely the nerves and skills of the competitors as the pressure grew with each moment. Others, like Bobby Nichols, Bert Yancey, and Arnold Palmer, hung on grimly.

Nichols, Brewer's tall and handsome pal from Kentucky and his playing partner yesterday, turned out to be his closest competitor. Nichols led much of the way through the pressurized final round but finished with a two-under-par 70 and a 281 total for the 72 holes, one stroke too many, as Brewer nailed his 67 onto earlier rounds of 73, 68, and 72.

There was no handling Brewer this time, though. He bowed those sloping shoulders of his, set that weak chin, and methodically cut the course apart with fighting, if not especially stylish, golf.

Before he teed off, Brewer, who just two weeks ago shot a 61 and a 64 in winning at Pensacola, sat in the locker room and reminded the aged Hogan of the time their paths crossed many years ago.

"It was, oh, I don't remember, somewhere in the late '40s," said Brewer. "You were playing an exhibition match in Lexington, Kentucky. I caddied for you.

"You made me mad, too. On one hole, you asked me what club to hit and I said, 'All you've got,' and you said, 'How do you know how much I've got?'

"You remember that?"

Hogan said he didn't.

Hogan will not forget yesterday's round, though. He had shot a brilliant back-nine 30 for a 66 on Saturday to move into contention, but his nerves frayed early yesterday, and he went down.

He complained that he had never seen the pin placements as consistently difficult as they were for this round, and he felt, therefore, that Brewer's round had been "fantastic."

Brewer, a consistent money winner but a most inconsistent tournament winner during his 11 years on the tour, can recall the year he parked cars at the Masters.

He was stationed at nearby Ft. Gordon. He took the job simply so he could see some of the tournament, in which Sam Snead beat Ben Hogan in a playoff.

Brewer may be the poorest football player ever recruited by Bear Bryant. He spent two years taking fishes and loaves from Bryant at Kentucky under the pretense of being a specialist in the art of holding a football for placekickers.

It was Bryant's way of helping Brewer through school without jeopardizing his amateur standing. Brewer held footballs in practice, but never on Saturday, and prayed constantly that a kicker wouldn't miss and mess up his golf grip.

Gay, at six-foot, 168 pounds, said he remembers the 1966 Masters, that fateful three-putt on the 72nd hole that cost him the title and then that blushing 78 the following day that wasn't even close to winner Jack Nicklaus, but he remembers it only when someone mentions it.

He still uses the same putter that did the foul deed last year.

Yesterday, he and Nichols shook off the rest of the competitors by shooting birdies on the 13th, 14th, and 15th holes. Brewer broke Nichols' heart with a 10-foot putt on the 15th that produced a one-stroke lead. "I knew then I had to birdie something else from there in to catch him," said Bobby.

Brewer wasn't so certain of that. Someone handed him a cup of water as he walked off the 16th green, and he was shaking so hard, he spilled it.

"I had a pep talk with myself walking down the 17th fairway," he said. "I can't tell you what I said, but I settled down."

1968

I always felt that Bob Goalby was the real victim in 1968 when Roberto De Vicenzo signed an erroneous scorecard and was dropped from a tie with Goalby into second place, leaving Goalby to pull on the green jacket rather than face a playoff the next day.

De Vicenzo was, of course, a pitiful figure. He was a beloved 45-year-old international campaigner who was not likely to challenge again. He had shot a wonderful 65 in the final round to tie Goalby, who had shot 66, but Tommy Aaron, keeping De Vicenzo's score, put down a four on the 17th hole instead of the three Roberto had made, and once De Vicenzo had signed the card, he had to accept the higher number.

This caused a storm of protest around the country, and probably around the world. Almost lost in the noise was Goalby. He had won not just by a ruling but by his golf clubs, as well, but there was a resentment that lingered through the years, an asterisk beside his finest moment.

Goalby dealt with it well enough. His pleasant nature and strong mind carried him on into a successful career on the PGA Senior Tour, which he helped to form and lead into widespread popularity.

THE MONKEY AND THE DUCK

NOTES AND OBSERVATIONS

The happy Argentine, Roberto De Vicenzo, describing his round of 73, said in broken English, "I knock the ball into the trees on No. 6, and I play like a monkey." And later, "I knock the ball into the water on No. 16 and I play like a duck."

It was a day of dramatic developments, the most dramatic being Arnold Palmer's failure to qualify for the final 36 holes largely because he shot an eight on a par-five hole the way you or I might do it—by knocking two shots into the water.

Almost as dramatic, though, was an eight on the par-four 11th by Australian Bruce Devlin. He had caught fire on the front nine and was pulling away from the field but bogeyed the 10th hole, then butchered the watery 11th.

Devlin, who was a master plumber before turning pro, couldn't do anything about that water, but he played steady golf from there in to finish with no worse than a 73, which left him only three shots out of the lead.

"Wouldn't it be something," he mused, "if I could win the tournament after making that eight?

"I'm pleased to be as close to the lead as I am, but had I not made one bad shot and had I made any putts (he holed only one putt of any size), I might have run away from the field."

THE MASTERS JACKET WAS UNCOMFORTABLE

In his finest hour, Bob Goalby was a villain.

He won the Masters golf championship yesterday in a scrambling, fighting style that has typified his 12-year career, but in the end, he won it because of some poor arithmetic by the popular Argentine, Roberto De Vicenzo.

The 45-year-old De Vicenzo, dazed by the pressure of the chase and a bogey five on the final hole that had snatched almost certain victory from his grasp, signed a scorecard that showed a four for him on the 17th hole when, in fact, he had made a birdie three.

This error, which made his total 66 instead of the proper 65, cost him a tie with Goalby. Once he had signed it and turned it in to the officials at the scorer's table, it had to stand. Goalby, shooting a closing 66 highlighted by an eagle three on the 15th hole, thus collected first prize of $20,000 with his 72-hole score of 277, 11 under par, for four days of ideal golfing conditions.

The mistake, which three-time champion Jack Nicklaus estimated will cost De Vicenzo a million dollars, was De Vicenzo's, as he readily admitted, and the victory was Goalby's, no strings attached.

By rights, all of the glory that normally comes to the winners of the Masters—one of the four major tournaments of the world—should have swirled around the handsome, 37-year-old Goalby, but his victory was darkened— no, blackened—by this most stunning finish in all of major golf.

In the too stiff-necked championship presentation, Masters officials acted as if they had a corpse on their hands and wished aloud that they could crown two champions. Most of the thousands of spectators who had walked the course on this dramatic, overcast day left without realizing what had happened. Those who lingered for the presentation ceremonies heard the news. Many cursed the ruling, and the crowd lining the ceremonies applauded louder and longer for the runner-up than they did for the champion.

The dream Goalby said he had dared not dream, victory in the Masters, had come true, but he couldn't fully enjoy it. He wasn't treated exactly like a villain, but he wasn't treated exactly like a Masters champion, either.

"I'm happy I won," said Goalby. "I'd be a liar if I told you any different. The Masters has always been something special to me. I've played more golf tournaments that anybody on the tour in the past 12 years, mainly because I like to play golf, and I've played the Masters nine times, but this is the first time I've ever played well here.

"I don't think this is the way to win a golf tournament. I would prefer to have won in a playoff. But I think the rule is correct. It is just unfortunate the way that it happened to Roberto."

De Vicenzo, the reigning British Open champion and a popular figure because of his happy-go-lucky approach to life, said in his struggling English, "I play maybe 30 years, maybe all over the world. I sign so many scorecards, and I never be wrong. What a stupid I am to be wrong here. Nothing be better for me than to win the Masters.

"I feel sorry for me. I feel very close to winning this tournament today. Now, I feel too far away from it. I think I am too old to have another chance like this."

De Vicenzo played virtually flawless golf to make Goalby's task extremely difficult. The big-chested, balding Latin holed a 135-yard nine-iron shot on the first hole, then birdied the second and third with putts of less than two feet to leap from the pack into the lead. He never faltered but kept slicing away at par until he hit his only poor shot of the day on the 18th, a hooked four-iron, and took a bogey five.

Goalby, aware of what was going on in front of him, put handsome figures up on the scoreboard, too, making his only bogey at the 17th when he three-putted, but his round was marked by six missed greens. Not once did he fail to get down in two, though, and twice he putted in from the fringe of the green.

The six-foot, 180-pound former University of Illinois substitute quarterback, winner of nine tour tournaments but almost unheard from this year, altered his game slightly and credited that with his victory.

Bothered throughout his career by a devilish hook off the tee, he found a way this week to control his drives. The rest of his game has always been good.

On a perfect day for scoring, first one, then another player made threatening gestures toward the title. As it turned out, there was Goalby with 66 for a 277 total, then De Vicenzo with his 65-turned-66, worth $15,000; Bert Yancey with a 65 and a total of 279 for $10,000, closing with four birdies on the last six holes; Bruce Devlin, fourth with a 69-280 for $7,500 after he opened with three successive birdies but couldn't make any more; and Jack Nicklaus, a three-time champion here, trying to rise above the masses with a 67 but finishing at 281, tied for fifth with Frank Beard.

Many others scorched the course to the delight of the milling thousands. It was a great tournament, but it had the wrong kind of ending.

1969

In 1969, we took it upon ourselves to anoint a tall young man named Tom Weiskopf the next superstar of golf. That's always risky business, and Weiskopf eventually showed why. He won a British Open and some other tournaments—five of them in eight weeks in 1973—but he never reached superstardom. He had classic form and great power, but there was something lacking inside him. He was runner-up four times in the Masters, including the 1969 tournament, but never won it, and was runner-up once in the U.S. Open.

Some financial facts, ordinarily guarded by Augusta National members, came out in 1969. Clifford Roberts, director of the Masters, revealed that television rights to the tournament had been sold for $750,000. Today, it's in the millions.

Ticket sales were estimated to bring in $1 million.

The Masters was said to bring in more money than any other tournament, and yet first prize remained at $20,000 for several years. That's what George Archer got for winning in 1969. Several other events on the PGA Tour paid more.

As the years went by, prize money went up. In 1999, José Maria Olazabal won $576,000 for finishing first. Series badges, though, remained priced at $100. Concession prices were among the lowest at major sports events. Parking and pairings sheets were free.

It is not only one of the greatest events in sports, it is the best bargain anywhere.

IT'S A NEW YEAR AT THE MASTERS

Roberto De Vicenzo, the barrel-chested Argentine who last year signed an erroneous scorecard that cost him a tie with Bob Goalby for the title, laughs heartily and in his broken English, says, "Now, I even read carefully the letters from my wife. Har, har, har. Last year, after I make the mistake, Jerry Barber asks me at Wilmington how I can do such a thing, why I am not more careful. Then he plays nine holes in the Azalea Tournament with one club too many and gets penalty on every hole. Har, har, har."

NOTES AND OBSERVATIONS

Amateur Bruce Fleisher, playing here for the first time, said, "I try to make myself think of this as just another junior college tournament, but it's hard to do." . . . Of his playing partner, Arnold Palmer, Fleisher, the U.S. Amateur champion, said, "The people love that man. It's a tremendous psychological lift for him to have them with him."

Bert Yancey, a perennial threat here, almost aced the par three 16th hole en route to a 69. His seven-iron shot rang the cup. When he tapped in his 18-inch putt there for a birdie, it marked his fifth straight deuce on that watery hole. He had four of them here last year . . . Yancey was heading for a mediocre round until he rammed in a 35-foot putt on the testing 11th hole for a birdie to go one under par. That set him afire for a good finish . . . watch him in this one. It may be his year.

Billy Casper, the tournament leader with a 66, will probably avoid sausages and peaches for the remainder of the week. He opened up as the leader last year but complained that his sausage-and-peaches breakfast the second day made him too ill for a couple of days to remain a contender, and he finished far down the line...

Mason Rudolph posted a three-under-par 69 despite a second shot into the menacing pond on the 11th hole that cost him a double bogey . . . Former U.S. Open champion Ken Venturi, who used to be a threat here year after year, shot an awful 83. When a fellow Californian, a sportswriter, attempted to commiserate with him, Venturi blew up at him and invited him to take off in no uncertain terms . . .

MAN CALLED CASPER

Friday was a hot day, and the Masters crowd arrived as white as the dogwoods and went home as red as the azaleas. Honest sweat made dark circles on the belly of Jack Nicklaus' shirt. Thoughts of skinny-dipping in Rae's Creek while Arnold Palmer putted on a nearby green played whimsically through the mind of at least one sportswriter.

Spectators shucked what they could and still be decent, and a couple of those short-frocked ladies who dominate the scenery at the Masters may even have exceeded those bounds, but nobody seemed to mind.

There in the blazing Georgia sun, though, trudging up the green slopes in a heavy alpaca sweater, was Billy Casper, who just can't help being different from everybody else. He never removed the sweater, just kept on perspiring and making pars and birdies until he had shot a one-under-par 71 that gave him a two-day total of 137, tying him with Australian Bruce Devlin for the halfway lead.

"I like to stay warm," he explained. "I like to sweat and stay supple. Sometimes, when you have to wait long between shots and there's a breeze, you stiffen up."

If Casper showed up nude in a snowstorm and broke 70, it wouldn't surprise the tour regulars. Casper is golf's greatest flake. He is also its finest player at the moment. Arnold Palmer may still have the charm, Jack Nicklaus the potential, and Gary Player the guts, but Billy Casper has turned the Big Three into the Big One.

"He's been the best player in this country for the last three years," said Devlin.

"If you took a poll of all the players on tour," said Dan Sikes, "they'd tell you Casper is the last guy they'd want to meet in a playoff, he's so steady. Some people say he does it all with his putting. That's a bunch of baloney. He can play."

Casper has been a player of major importance for more than 10 years, winning over 40 tournaments, including two U.S. Opens—and over a million dollars—but he seems to be getting better by the years, and he's already 37.

"I feel I'm still on my way up," Casper said, which should make his banker rub his hands in glee. Billy won over $200,000 last year.

"I'm still learning; I feel I have six or seven more extremely good years of golf left. I plan to play until I'm about 50." That should make his competitors cry.

There's no reason he can't do it. He has a perfect temperament for the game. He doesn't get overwrought about anything. He plays too fast to get upset, waiting just long enough for the ball to stop rolling before hitting it again. He has supreme confidence, figuring every putt is going to drop, and every hole is a potential birdie.

His game requires little work. He has never completely gotten away from the days when he was a fat kid too lazy to practice. Last year, he spent seven weeks in the Orient entertaining troops, came home, blew the dust off his clubs, and promptly won the Greensboro Open.

He hadn't touched a club for eight days when he came here.

The reason he hadn't played before coming here is part of the strange side of Billy Casper. He played in Miami a couple of weeks ago and had an allergic reaction to the pesticide used to spray the course. He got all splotchy and swollen and had to go home to California. His fingers are still a little numb, and his feet hurt the other day when he wore a pair of shoes "contaminated" in Miami, so he got rid of them.

He used to be known as "Crazy Fatso, The Putting Fool" or just plain "Jelly Belly." He was also known as a man with all the charm of a rattlesnake. He was only 33, but he felt 53, and he was a grouch.

A Chicago doctor put him on a diet of exotic food, things like hippopotamus, whale, and buffalo, and he began to shed weight and feel better. He straightened out his mental problems by turning to the Mormon religion.

Now, he moves lightly and contentedly through life, making birdies and friends and veering only to avoid things to which he is allergic.

ARCHER'S PUTTER MASTER(S)

One of the reasons the Augusta Masters golf tournament is placed up there among the great sports events is its unfailing knack for producing the dramatic.

Gene Sarazen made a double eagle and won. Billy Joe Patton hit the water and lost by a shot. Jack Nicklaus, winning by a mile, posted an incredible round of 64. Ben Hogan, in the twilight of his career, birdied the toughest stretch of holes here. Arnold Palmer has won it and lost it spectacularly.

They waited a long time to salvage the 1969 Masters. For the first three days, it was one of the less exciting chapters in the history of this classic.

Palmer, Nicklaus, and Gary Player, the guys who have made it bristle with excitement for the past decade, were shooting themselves into obscurity, and the man up front was Billy Casper. He doesn't have all the color in the world, anyway, and this year he was ho-humming it around, playing ultraconservative golf, refusing both birdies and bogeys.

By gambling and/or knocking down some dandy putts, George Archer, George Knudson, Tom Weiskopf, Miller Barber, Charles Coody, and Lionel Hebert, not exactly the golf hall of fame, had managed to stay close, but the whole thing had a serious case of the blahs until yesterday afternoon.

Archer, a very tall Californian with a twangy voice that seems to come out of his prominent nose, finally won it, scrambling to a closing round of par 72 for a 72-hole total of 281; one shot better than Weiskopf, Casper, and Knudson. Archer collected $20,000, while Weiskopf's 71, Casper's 74 and Knudson's 70 earned them $12,333 apiece.

Charles Coody shot a stumbling 72 to tie fast-closing Don January (66) for fifth spot and $6,750.

Casper had bogeyed only two holes in three days when he set out on the final round yesterday under cloudy skies that put a little chill into the light breeze. He and Archer got into an early struggle, and it appeared it would settle into a two-man race, but Casper's game went to pieces. He hit only two of the first 10 greens, and by the time they had finished nine holes apiece, Archer had a four-stroke lead on Casper and a three-shot lead on the field.

He wasn't home free, though. Coody, who has all the glitter of, say, Spiro Agnew, holed a birdie putt at No. 11 and a long eagle three at 13, and found himself a stranger in paradise, tied with Archer for the lead. Two holes later, when he birdied the par-five 13th, the lead was his alone.

Charlie Coodys don't win the Masters, though, and like a faithful puppy, he faded with bogeys on the last three holes.

Casper rallied sharply with three birdies on the back nine but couldn't make it reach. Weiskopf was tied for the lead with two holes to play but hit a TV camera cart, then a sand trap, and bogeyed the 17th to fall behind. Knudson made a late bid but had too far to go. January came from nowhere and was never really a threat.

The rest faded into the backdrop of towering pines and blossoming dogwood.

By Palmer standards, Archer is a relatively colorless character, but he has been known for several years to have one of the soundest games on tour. He's one of the best putters, and it was his ability to make the key putts that won for him yesterday.

Those who are a little careless with their words call him a cowboy, but he admits, "what I did on the ranch back home in Gilroy was clean out the stalls and water troughs and paint fences. Certain fellows used to ride horses on the ranch, but I never got to be as high class as a cowboy."

He started playing golf after he was kicked off the junior high basketball team for missing practice. He used to caddy for Harvie Ward, once a University of North Carolina golfing great, and has always held him as an idol. After high school, he tried to make a living hustling, but went broke in six months and went to work in a furniture store.

The man who owns the ranch, Eugene Selvidge, sponsored him on the tour in 1963, and Archer's been doing nothing but making money since.

1970

There was a rumor that Arnold Palmer had suffered a heart attack out on the course. There was a true story that Jack Nicklaus had taken an eight on the eighth hole. And there was a gripping conclusion to the 1970 Masters. Billy Casper, who had earned a reputation as a flake because of his habits and his diet, defeated fellow Californian Gene Littler, a beautiful swinger and pleasantly mannered man, but who was no more colorful than water.

Casper was probably the most underrated player the game has seen. He is a Hall of Famer, of course, but he was much more than that. He won two U.S. Opens, a Masters, and 48 other PGA Tour events, played on eight Ryder Cup teams, and won the Vardon Trophy for scoring five times. He then became a top-level performer on the PGA Senior Tour. He was acknowledged as a master with the putter, but you don't win all those tournaments with the putter alone.

THE TENSION IS TOUGH FOR GARY

Wednesday was the kind of day the good Lord saves for the Masters, blue and sunny with a light breeze nudging the dogwoods and pines, but the threat of trouble lurked about.

Out on the first fairway in a glistening white outfit, Gary Player walked shoulder-to-shoulder with Tony Jacklin and Tom Weiskopf as they began their final practice round before the start of the great tournament today.

They chatted and seemed relaxed, but whenever Player plays now, there is apprehension. There have been veiled threats against the little South African, winner of all four of the world's major titles, because of his country's apartheid policies. His caddy for nine years here, Ernest Nipper, has suddenly changed to another golfer, and a fellow caddy says Nipper was warned by militant activists not to work for Player. Nipper isn't talking.

Back among the pines, as Player and his companions made their way up the first fairway, a voice shouted, "Someone throw a firecracker." Nobody laughed.

The scene within the restraining ropes was no different from that which has taken place here thousands of times, but outside the ropes, jostling through the crowd at a fast pace with their eyes darting from Player to the spectators and back again, were several uniformed Pinkerton men.

There were three other men rushing ahead of Player. They wore business suits and hats and carried notebooks, and when they found a point on the course where Player would cross paths with the spectators, they stopped and discussed the situation among themselves and with the men in uniform.

A Pinkerton, puffing along the edge of the fairway, paused long enough to say, "I don't know what to expect. They didn't tell us. It's just a damn job. They just told us to see that nothing happened to him."

The situation has existed since Player's return to the United States five weeks ago, but it is believed if trouble comes, either in the form of a physical attack or something less violent, it will happen either Saturday or Sunday, when the tournament is on television.

Player refused to discuss the matter, saying he made his statement when he arrived in the United States. At that time, he said he would not criticize his own country while he was out of it and pointed out that he had no ill feelings against any man, regardless of his color.

"I'm an athlete," he said, "and politics have no place in athletics."

There is no escaping it, though, except in the clubhouse, where he relaxes with the other golfers and the writers, tells jokes, and seems to be in good spirits.

On the course, if anyone approaches him—and it is usually an autograph seeker nailing him at the tee—the Pinkertons swoop in and stare at the intruder, their chests pushed protectively against Player's back.

Despite the threats, Player continues to play the best golf on the tour. Leaving his ranch in South Africa to play in 16 tournaments here last year, the boyish, crew-cut little muscle man finished in the top five 10 times, winning once, finishing second three times and third three times, making $123,897 for his relatively short visit. Nobody matched that record on a pre-tournament basis.

This year, he has continued to shoot well, cresting last weekend with a victory in the Greater Greensboro Open, and his play in practice rounds here has ranged from good to superb.

Despite the gloom hanging over him, he appears to be the best bet to win the Masters this week. He looks ready. He made seven birdies in his final tune-up yesterday. He was driving as far or farther than the big-hitting Weiskopf and putting extremely well.

One of his fellow golfers looked at Player, whose round eyes give him the appearance of constant surprise, and said, "Of all the people in the world, he's one of the last anyone should ever hurt. When he won the U.S. Open, he gave the $25,000 back to the U.S. Golf Association to benefit the game. He's religious, friendly, incredibly dedicated, all the good things I can say about him.

"He doesn't deserve this kind of treatment."

It is relatively inconsequential now, but among other things, this kind of treatment could cost him his second Masters title.

CALM CLOUDS THE STORM OF AUGUSTA

NOTES AND OBSERVATIONS

Arnold Palmer hadn't planned to play yesterday, but finally came out for nine holes, which gave him a total of only one and a half rounds of practice here.

The four-time champion, who, on occasion, has come here a week in advance to practice, remembered, "I played only one and one half rounds here in 1958. I lost a playoff to Howie Johnson for the Azalea Open title in Wilmington on Monday, then came down here and, on Tuesday, played with Ben Hogan and shot an 80. Hogan didn't say anything, he just looked at me kinda funny.

"The next day I played nine holes, and then I won the tournament."

MASTERS COURSE TURNS MONSTER

Chi Chi Rodriguez, who says he's so skinny, they used him as a ramrod for a 102 Howitzer in the Army, arrived back early, laughing. He shot a 70.

"That green coat (symbol of Masters victory) makes you choke," said the leathery little Puerto Rican. "I missed putts on 11, 12, and 13 I would have made in any other tournament. But today when I got over those putts, I looked down at my knees, and they looked like castanets. My caddy helped me a lot. See, I read the greens in Spanish and putt in English, and that's not so good."

Tommy Aaron, the leader with a 68, played beautifully, his long, flowing swing producing neat, consistent golf. He was interviewed at length, and people shuffled their feet and hemmed and hawed before finally getting around to the thing they had on their mind—the four he put down on Roberto De Vicenzo's scorecard here two years ago when the Argentine had made a three. It cost Roberto the tie for the title.

"It was a terrible thing and, of course, I felt badly about it," said the scholarly, bespectacled Georgian, "but if you play by the rules, well, it's not my fault. He's responsible for his scorecard.

"I knew, though, that people would make me the heavy, people who are uninformed about the rules.

"Heck, it happens all the time. I corrected a mistake on my card at Greensboro last week. The fellow keeping my score wanted to give me a four when I really made a five."

Who was it?

"Arnold Palmer."

A KING AND HIS NERVES

At about 2 o'clock yesterday afternoon, a rumor ripped through the Masters press room: "Arnold Palmer's had a heart attack on the 13th hole."

A communications man put through a call to central control, reported the rumor, and asked for a check. The reply came back, "Palmer in the 14th fairway, three over par for the tournament. And standing up."

Nobody ever figured out how the ridiculous rumor got started. Palmer looked as healthy as a glass of milk. The only thing he was suffering from was a fractured confidence and a swollen score.

IT WAS BLOOPER TIME AT MASTERS

Friday at the Masters was one of those delightful days when Jack Nicklaus stepped on a banana peel, Bob Goalby got hit in the face with a cream pie, and Gary Player had the chair pulled out from under him.

That is to say, the computers hit some clinkers just like us duffers, proving they are human and can look just as foolish as the standard Saturday morning hacker at times.

Nicklaus' goof was perhaps the most heralded of the day, he being the giant of the game that he is, and the consequences of his blunder being what they were.

It had been assumed up until now that Big Jack could knock a golf ball right through a tree, but we learned yesterday when, on the par-five eighth hole, he whacked his second shot (which he had tagged for the green) into the woods on the left. It hit a tree and bounded deeper into the forest and was never seen again.

A couple of hundred people searched for it, but it was gone. Nicklaus said he thought it must have dropped into one of the several holes in the vicinity, which are believed to be Billy Joe Patton's old divot marks.

Nicklaus had to return to the point from which he hit the shot and hit another, which he did—into a bunker. He blasted out 15 feet past the cup, putted up 15 inches away and missed, taking a big, fat, sloppy triple-bogey eight—just like us guys.

MASTERS: AND THEN THERE WERE TWO

After four days of bitter struggle, thousands of shots, and a blazing four-man battle down the stretch, the Masters golf championship came down to the best putter in the universe hunched over a slippery downhill 10-footer to win it all.

If you had to select a man to putt a 10-footer for your life, you would choose Billy Casper, but even he couldn't coax the ball into the cup on the final green yesterday when one of the world's four major championships was at stake. It dipped into the edge of the hole but pulled back out and eased away.

The huge crowd, frozen for hours by the intensity of the drama unfolding on this gray Sunday down the wicked back nine of the Augusta National Golf Course, gasped.

They had watched Casper, Gene Littler, Gary Player, and Bert Yancey battle all afternoon, with first one, then the other winning, and then it had all come down to the half inch or less it would have taken for Casper's putt to fall into the cup.

The wayward stroke left Casper tied with Littler, a fellow Californian with whom he has played golf since they were in knee britches. Both shot 279, nine under par for the four rounds, and met today at 2:15 in an 18-hole playoff for the Masters title.

Player almost made it a three-way playoff but miss-clubbed on the final hole, hit into a sand trap with a six-iron, blasted out seven feet beyond the cup, and then missed the putt.

GROWTH OF A GOLF NUT

Professional golf is one big fruitcake, full of nuts.

Friends call Bert Yancey "Fog" because he often gives the impression he's in one. Arnold Palmer changes his putters more often than he changes clothes. Half the guys on tour are walking around wearing copper bracelets that are supposed to cure what ails you. Gary Player trains on bananas and raisins and does push-ups in the bathtub.

You could run your finger down the list of players competing in the Masters here this week, and you'd get a blister before you found one who doesn't have something flaky about him. It's an occupational hazard. They are all a bunch of left-handed baseball pitchers who wound up in the wrong sport.

One of the grade-A flakes is Billy Casper, who was playing off today with his boyhood buddy Gene Littler for the Masters title after they tied at 279 strokes yesterday in a heart-stopping finish to a week of real golf.

For example, he has a certain routine he follows before, during, and after each shot, a certain way he takes the club out of the bag, a certain way he waggles and swings, a certain way he drops the club so that it falls, grip up, against the bag.

If anything occurs to upset his pre-stroke routine, he stops and starts over.

You know, of course, about his diet. It is less exotic than before, now that he has trimmed about half a ton of blubber off his middle, but he still likes such things as broiled shrimp, avocado, and pompano for breakfast and Lord knows what for dinner.

He still has this thing about allergies, and he doesn't play golf in Florida because of it. A couple of years ago, he discovered he was allergic to certain pesticides used on golf courses, and he now skips all of the Florida tournaments because the chemicals are prevalent there.

That meant a five-week layoff for him prior to the Greensboro Open two weeks ago. During the layoff, he played only five rounds of golf, but he came back, playing well, and he has been super-sharp here.

Most guys train like slaves, beating golf balls until their hands are bloody. Casper rarely hits a practice ball and can lay off indefinitely and come back winning.

Most of the pros find real or imagined flaws in their clubs more often than teenagers find pimples, and they throw them aside and grab a new set. Casper is just the opposite, lending strength to his image, as well, as an odd sort.

He played golf with the same woods from 1957 until this year and with the same irons from 1960 until this year.

He had them re-gripped, of course, and broke three of them and had them re-shafted. But he won a million dollars with them and simply wouldn't give up the battered old weapons.

He estimates he tried out two dozen new sets in that time, but never played more than one round with them. And then, during that recent layoff, he tried another new set, and as soon as he took them out of the box, he thought he was going to like them.

He did. He loves them, and he believes they are partly responsible for his drive to at least tie for the Masters title. They are Wilson clubs with a new extra-light steel shaft. He says they have given him 20 to 30 yards more distance off the tee, and he has demonstrated it by hitting some enormous drives. One of particular note was a 336-yarder on the 10th hole in the second round.

Casper is not a picture swinger, but his ability to keep the ball in play and his absolute genius at the short game have made him one of three million-dollar winners on the tour. He misses a lot of shots, but he makes "good misses."

That he has been at all successful on the tour has been a surprise to some who watched him in his formative years. Paul Runyan, a former PGA champion and a noted authority on the golf swing, played a round with Casper in 1955 and told his friends Billy would never make it as a touring pro.

Casper made it, big. He has won two U.S. Open titles and today had the chance to add the Masters. The playoff complicated matters a bit for him, though. You see, he finished up all of his pompano yesterday morning.

1971

From time to time over the years, I've walked 18 holes with
Winnie Palmer, Arnie's wife, or Barbara Nicklaus, Jack's wife. For
several years, I made a point of talking with them before the Masters
started to see how their husbands were feeling, what they were
thinking. Wives offer an insight that others can't.

In 1971, I walked around with Winnie, a celebrity in her own
right who was constantly shaking hands and exchanging pleasant-
ries with people who approached her. I listened as she commented on
Arnie's play, which that day was not championship stuff.

I found Winnie and Barbara to be comfortable in their roles
as wives of legendary figures, as likely to leave the course early to do
some grocery shopping for the family dinner that night as to sit
under the umbrellas on the clubhouse lawn and chat with the rich
and famous.

There's a line in a song that says, "It must have been cold there
in my shadow," but I never sensed that either of those two felt that
she was in the shadows of her husband. They were as admirable in
what they did as Arnie and Jack were in what they did.

The PGA Championship is played in August nowadays, but in
1971 it was played in February. Nicklaus won it and came to
Augusta in April with a Grand Slam on his mind. He had been
listed as a 5,000-to-1 shot to win the PGA, Masters, U.S. Open, and
British Open all within a calendar year, but after he won the PGA
in Palm Beach Gardens, Florida, his odds dropped to 100-1.

Nicklaus just couldn't quite win the second stage, though. He
shot 70-71-68-72 and tied Johnny Miller for second, but Charles
Coody, who had bogeyed the last three holes to lose the Masters in
1969, played the last three in one under on Sunday to win.

When he had putted out, Coody walked over to Nicklaus and
said he was proud to be the Masters champion, but he was sorry
about the Grand Slam.

The gallery was sorry, too. Nicklaus had become, as one maga-
zine put it, beautiful and loved, a trimmed down, modishly dressed,
long-maned figure whose following lifted some of the loudest roars
heard at Augusta over the years.

A ROUND WITH WINNIE

Several thousand spectators chased Arnold Palmer around
the Augusta National Golf Course Thursday, his wonders to
behold. I chased his wife, Winnie.

We hiked together through the dogwoods, pines, and
milling crowds to watch Arnie, the great god of golf, open his
bid for a fifth Masters championship. He responded by playing
what he later accurately described as his poorest round of the
year—a one-over-par 73 that looked more like a dog-eared 78
while he was putting it together.

Winnie, blue-eyed, freckled, cute, and at 5-3, about two
feet too short to watch golf tournaments, kissed three women
friends and four new friends, shook hands with four dozen more
people, and smiled at a couple hundred like a campaigning
politician as she made her way around the course. She instinc-
tively turned to watch every shot.

She has a remarkable knack for spectating, knows just where
to stand, knows the shortcuts, can judge the worth of a shot by
the crowd reaction, is conscious of things like pin placements and
wind direction. And yet she gives the appearance of just another
gabby galleryite while she takes care of the niceties expected of
her.

As we started up the first fairway at noon in brilliant sunshine, Winnie pondered the hooked drive that had left Arnie
behind some trees and said, "The first hole is very important to
him. If he birdies it or bogey it, it can affect his entire round. I'm
always concerned about the first hole."

Palmer scrambled a par four, holing a four-footer, and as
she headed for the second tee, Mrs. Palmer remarked, "A good
putt to make, a bad one to miss."

She seemed a little put out with him when he drove into a
fairway bunker on the second hole.

"Would you believe Arnold's in that trap?" she said, in the same way she might say: "Would you believe he still hasn't fixed that lawn mower?" Sort of a hands-on-hips exasperation.

Arnie hit another shady drive on the third hole, and she seemed to sense this wasn't going to be his day. "Those are the three worst drives I've seen him hit in a long time," she said. "I guess here you get a little overanxious in the opening round."

She doesn't. She said she quit being nervous a long time ago. So she doesn't show much emotion when things go so poorly or when they go well. When Arnie holed a par putt after coming out of a trap on No. 4, seemingly a key putt at the time, the crowd erupted, but Winnie remarked very calmly, "That was a good one to get."

She ordinarily tries to cross paths with her husband once or twice in a round, in case he needs a soft drink.

Her rendezvous spot here is between the fifth green and sixth tee, but as she moved toward Arnie, she found herself jostled by big, hurrying men, and she missed contact.

No matter, Arnie birdied the sixth. "Remember the ice cream on a stick?" Winnie suddenly recalled with a girlish giggle as she walked with a woman friend. "One year here, we ate one of those ice creams on a stick every time Arnie made a birdie. We almost got sick."

Palmer birdied the seventh from beneath some pines, but tried to get home with his second shot on the par-five eighth and hooked into trees. "He's done that before," she said. "He's trying to make a three."

As she walked along the restraining ropes up the hill, Arnie passed her and saw her for the only time during the round. "This is hard work," he said, never breaking stride as he went by.

He bogeyed the hole, and in describing it later for a friend, Winnie said he "hit a couple of indifferent shots there." As she stood along the ropes on the 10th hole, Arnie's drive sailed straight and true. A man who didn't know her said, "Well, that is the first one he's hit straight all day."

She turned away without a word to him. "Sometimes," she whispered, "I'm tempted, but I never say anything when they criticize him. I'd rather they not even know who I am. Tommy Bolt's first wife, Shirley, used to get into some fierce arguments with the spectators. She had a temper like Tommy's. But I just ignore them."

The 10th ruined Arnie's day. He trapped his second shot and three-putted for a double-bogey six, missing an 18-inch putt.

"Oh, Arnold," said Winnie with exasperation in her voice. "He just won't learn to be more careful with those little putts. Well, we'll just have to make an eagle or two."

The eagle didn't happen—not much of anything good happened—and Palmer finished the first round seven strokes behind leader Charles Coody. I wondered, as we walked up the 18th fairway, what emotions were running through Winnie's mind.

"I try never to get emotional one way or the other," she said. "It wouldn't help. It wouldn't change his score. I know Arnie's upset. He'll probably practice his driving when he's finished, as he should. That's what it's all about—hard work."

She tried to speak to Arnie as he was whisked away from the 18th in a golf cart to the interview room, but too many people were in her way. She sat down on the lawn in front of the club-house and waited.

THE NEW "FAT JACK"

Exactly what it has to do with golf has never been satisfactorily explained, but Arnold Palmer introduced it into the game, and if chewing gum, shampoo, and cigars can have sex appeal, why not golf?

It has been widely suggested in recent months that even Jack Nicklaus had acquired it and was flaunting it from coast to coast. A golfing magazine that usually gives its attention to things like how to get a downhill chip shot up and how to get an uphill chip shot down carried a cover story entitled, "How Fat Jack Became Beautiful and Loved."

As men go, Nicklaus is beautiful and loved. If he should win the Masters championship for the fourth time tomorrow afternoon, it would be an extremely popular victory, which is something that couldn't be said for his first three.

The galleries no longer follow Jack Nicklaus simply to wonder at his incredible power and his exquisite skill and to root against him secretly and hope Arnie wins. They still hope Arnie wins, but if Jack beats him, they won't hate him for doing it the way they once did.

They like him now. He's no longer a fat, rich kid in ill-fitting khaki-colored trousers and a yellow golf shirt. He's built like a fullback now, 188 pounds of muscle with eight inches of tail starved off.

He is modishly dressed in blue-and-white striped trousers with a wide, white leather belt, a navy blue shirt, and white shoes and with his long, blond locks blowing rakishly in the breeze.

Young girls and middle-aged women trail after him the way they do after Arnie. Guys who used to bellow things like "Let 'er go, Fat Guts" now applaud reverently when Nicklaus approaches a green, and sometimes they are moved to shout an irreverent, "Go get 'em, Jack." The insults that used to hurt and baffle him no longer ring in his ears.

Along with his new image, Nicklaus is held in awe because of his ability. He can walk through a locker room full of famous players, and every eye will turn toward him, every ear listen for his comments. He can go to the practice tee and draw hundreds of spectators with him. There has never been a player quite like him—as powerful and as skillful. Bobby Jones won 13 major championships. Nicklaus, at 31, has won 11 and has made it clear he intends to win more than Jones did.

The excitement surrounding Nicklaus this week is almost insufferable for his fans. He has already won the PGA title this year and is aiming for the greatest achievement the game has ever known, a slam of the PGA, Masters, U.S. Open, and British Open in a single year.

His efforts to win here have been frustrating through the first two rounds, though. He has all that enormous power, but the par-five holes have troubled him, and he knocked two balls into the water on them. He is acknowledged as one of the game's deftest putters, but he has gotten down only two putts of any length in 36 holes.

"Gosh," he said yesterday afternoon when he had hammered out a 71 to go with his opening 70. "It's really been frustrating so far. I've played a lot of good shots, but I've hit too many fliers (iron shots that travel farther than normal because of the thick grass in the fairways) and missed so many putts, I'm kind of disappointed."

Someone asked if he thought he might shoot in the 60s today. He smiled and said, "Damn, I hope so. I sure feel like I'm playing well. I'm just gonna have to knock in a couple of putts. I'm sure getting impatient. This tournament is half over, and I've only had six birdies.

"I had a chance to really bust it wide open today and missed some putts and hit some shots that were absolutely ridiculous."

At 141, Nicklaus is, relatively speaking, in as good a position as leader Don January at 138 or any of the others who are ahead of him or tied with him.

His game goes with major championships. He is still the man to beat.

His mind goes with major titles, too. He thinks in terms as precise as any golfer. He says things like, "I had a 110-yard wedge on the 17th, but I hit a flier and it went 130 yards, and there's just no way I can hit a wedge 130 yards, and then on 18, I had a 140-yard shot to the flag but the wind was at my back, so that made it a 125-yard shot."

And he is genuinely interested only in winning the major titles. He said if he wins here, he may not play more than one or two tournaments before the U.S. Open in June.

And his image now goes with major championships. He has sex appeal. He's beautiful and loved. And that—going from villain to hero in a year—may be his biggest victory of all.

COODY CHARMS THE MASTER

Billy Charles Coody ate sweet potato biscuits, wore some old green trousers, marked his ball with an English half-penny his daughter gave him, and sure enough, they all worked.

The drawling son of Abilene, Texas, whose most famous feat until yesterday was blowing the 1969 Masters in a blinding flurry of late bogeys, slipped into the green jacket that is traditionally fitted onto the Masters champion late yesterday afternoon, while down in the valley, the dust settled over the corpse of Jack Nicklaus' bid for a golfing Grand Slam.

Coody, 33, tall, dark, and good-looking in a country boy sort of way, shot a closing 70, bearing up better than the steely

Nicklaus under the late pressure, and finished with a 279 total, two strokes better than Nicklaus and late-surging, young Johnny Miller.

Nicklaus, surprisingly edgy and having difficulty swinging with his accustomed fluidity, shot a bland 72, the sort of round one might expect of a Coody. Miller, a lean, mod 23-year-old, holed miles of putts and led after 15 holes, but bogeyed two of the last three holes, as the unwritten rules dictated that he must.

When the last putt had been struck, Coody walked out to the edge of the 18th green, shook hands with Nicklaus, and said he was mighty proud to win the Masters, but he sure was sorry about that Grand Slam.

It was, in one way, poetic justice that the lovable Texan should redeem himself after walking off the 69th green two years ago leading the tournament and winding up three holes later in fifth place. What made it double sweet for him was a birdie on the 16th hole yesterday, where all his trouble started two years ago.

After a birdie on the watery, par-five 15th, Coody's caddy, "Cricket," told him if he made three pars going in, he would win it. Coody replied, "How about a birdie?" and whipped a six-iron in 15 feet behind the hole and made the putt.

Sweet justice, no doubt about it.

And yet there was something strangely ludicrous about Coody's victory. Here was a superstitious, meticulous, workman-like, and unglamorous plugger shooting holes in the great Nicklaus' Grand Slam aspirations.

Nicklaus had already won the PGA championship and planned to win the Masters, U.S. Open, and British Open, golf's greatest feat. Yesterday he was sidetracked by the Texan.

He has been eating sweet potato biscuits all week and playing well, so he had some more yesterday morning, for the sake of superstition.

He wore a pair of light green trousers yesterday, not because they would go well with the Masters jacket.

"I wore 'em on April 11, 1969," he said, "and I had the low round of the day here, a 69. I wore 'em on April 11, 1970, and I had the low round of the day again, a 68. I wore 'em again today. I didn't have the low round, but I did have the low total, didn't I?"

He told about the coin his eight-year-old daughter gave him to use as a ball marker on the green and admitted he had some other superstitions, but said, "Aw, y'all don't want to hear about all of 'em."

Coody is known for his penny-pinching. His close friend, Frank Beard, says Charlie (they didn't call him Billy, because he had so many cousins named Billy Bob and Billy Joe, etc.) frets if he can't account for every penny he and his wife spend.

"The only guy on the tour who's tighter than Charlie is me," said Beard.

Coody also keeps a chart of every shot he hits in competition and has a file on it going back several years. He uses it to study the trends in his game and determine where he needs work.

Oddly, Coody appeared relaxed before and during the round, while Nicklaus, with whom he was tied starting the day, seemed uneasy.

And when the firing had died, Nicklaus insisted he might have been too relaxed, too confident, while the winner, ol' Billy Charles, said, "Anybody who says you don't feel pressure on those last few holes is trying to fool you or fool himself. That's true in any tournament, but especially in one like the Masters.

"I felt nervous, keyed up all day, and I think that made me concentrate more.

"When we got to those last three holes this time, it was different. In 1969, I had the lead, and everybody was trying to catch me. This time, I was a shot behind Miller. I was trying to catch up."

Coody shot rounds of 66-73-70-70. The two critical moments of the tournament for him came in the second round, when he butchered the first 12 holes with four-over-par golf but then got himself together, and then on the closing three holes yesterday, when he murdered the ghosts with his birdie on 16 and scrambling pars on 17 and 18.

Nicklaus had a strange tournament in which he hit a ball into the water every day and could not overwhelm the par-five holes with his great power. When he needed birdies desperately yesterday, he couldn't hammer a birdie out of either the 13th or the 15th, both par fives he can easily reach in two strokes. He three-putted both.

Miller stormed into the game with six birdies on the first 14 holes but was bunkered on the par-three 16th and bogeyed when his putt lipped out, then took another bogey on the finishing hole when he hit his only poor tee shot of the day and came up short of the green.

"I'm disappointed I didn't win," he said, "but I'm not a great player like Nicklaus. I know he doesn't feel this way, but to me, finishing second in this tournament is just great."

Coody won $25,000. Miller and Nicklaus earned $17,500 apiece.

1972

Not every Masters is a glorious walk through the azaleas. In 1972, Lee Trevino had a problem with Masters officials that was never clearly explained. A black activist showed up with plans to ask Trevino to sign some sort of statement about the Masters and minorities, but Trevino brushed him aside, saying what had happened was just a misunderstanding.

The golf course was not up to its usual standards and neither was the play. Jack Nicklaus shot 74 in the final round and won by three shots.

Even though I had seen Nicklaus win his fourth Masters jacket, I left Augusta feeling unfulfilled.

SUPER-MEX STILL LAUGHING

If Lee Trevino wins the Augusta Masters this week— which he thinks is a remote possibility—it will be yet another tribute to the patience of the gum-popping, fast-talking, wise-cracking Super Mex.

He's the hottest item in town this week, including Miss Flame, who does her number in a topless joint down on Main Street. On Monday they tried to remove his automobile driver (don't call him chauffeur—Mexicans don't have chauffeurs) from the luxurious premises of the Augusta National Golf Club because he didn't have the right ticket. Trevino threatened to leave, too, but the matter was quickly resolved and dismissed as nothing more than a minor misunderstanding.

Yesterday, he had to deal with the issue again, this time quelling an attempt to twist it into a racial incident.

From the 18th green to the parking lot, where Trevino's red Dodge was waiting with a bumper sticker reading "This is Trevino country—El Paso, Texas," is no more than a long-iron shot, if you carry over the plantation-style clubhouse. It took Super Mex about 20 minutes to cover the distance and get away yesterday after completing a practice round.

Here's the way it went:

A television crew—portable camera, microphone, and interviewer—worked on Trevino as he walked. The interviewer asked a typically inane question, something like "What do you think of Arnold Palmer?"

Trevino shrugged. "Well," he said, "any man who's won four Masters on a golf course like that has got to be great. We call him The King."

The cameraman broke in to point out to his fellow crewmen that dammit, he was having to walk backwards, and if somebody didn't steer him, he was going to fall on his duff. One of the others took him by the belt and led him along, and the announcer said, "Now, would you mind stating that over again?"

Trevino didn't stop in the clubhouse. He went through the caddy lot and was finally brought to a halt in the parking lot by a couple dozen newsmen.

A man with a tape recorder asked Trevino to relate what had happened Monday. The man who won the U.S. and British Opens last year to climb onto a plateau of prominence with Arnold Palmer and Jack Nicklaus tried to dismiss it as "just a misunderstanding" and explained it again in detail.

A black man with a tape recorder broke in to say something about "racial harassment," and Trevino's brow furrowed.

"They don't care what color you are here," he snarled. "If you qualify to play here, you can play here. If you don't qualify, you can't play, no matter what color you are."

Another black man identified himself as a representative of the NAACP and said, "I have a statement here I thought you might like us to make, but in view of what you just said, I don't think we should release it to the press."

Trevino read the first few sentences, handed it back to the man and said, "No, there's no need for that. No sir."

Someone shouted at Trevino from the grandstands between the parking lot and practice range. Trevino looked up. It was Chi Chi Rodriguez.

"Hey," said Rodriguez, "they don't allow Mexicans in here." Trevino laughed and said, "Okay, I'm leaving."

A writer stopped him as he started to get into the car.

"You said after the 1969 tournament you wouldn't play here again because you couldn't handle the course. Why have you come back?"

"Jack Nicklaus told me I was crazy for not playing here," he said. "He told me there wasn't a golf course in the world I couldn't play, and if Jack Nicklaus tells you an ant can put up a bale of hay, you better hitch him up."

Trevino remains unconvinced, though.

"I still don't think I can play this golf course," he said. "I don't hit it high enough. I've shot some good rounds here in the past when I got some lucky bounces, but when I got some bad bounces, I shot a 79 and an 80. I'm hitting the ball higher, but I don't know."

He slapped his caddy on the shoulder and said, "Now Robert, you stay out of jail tonight," climbed into his car, put his cap on sideways, and somehow exited laughing.

BIG JACK OPENED DOOR TO "SLAM"

Jack Nicklaus' attempts to discourage talk of his winning the Grand Slam of golf received a severe setback Sunday when he won his fourth Augusta Masters championship.

Even he had to admit that his relative easy triumph in the first leg of the slam, which also includes the U.S. and British Opens and the PGA championship, would fuel the flames.

"I guess the odds against not winning the Grand Slam have dropped from about 100,000 to 1,000," he joked.

Whatever the odds, Nicklaus' victory here, his 12th in a major, leaving him only one short of the late Bobby Jones' record total—has lent great excitement to the game. By his own admission, this is his best year to win the slam if he's going to do it, because all four of the events are being played on courses he likes and plays well.

He played well here, all things considered, but this will probably go down as the Masters that the 32-year-old Ohio belter won by default. He shook off a poor start in the first round, played six holes in six under par on the back nine, finished with a 68, and was in command the remainder of the tournament.

He began yesterday's play with only a one-shot lead over pudgy Jim Jamieson and a three-stroke edge, but both fell back early and nobody else moved up to challenge him.

Left with only his own thoughts and an uncommonly testy Augusta National Golf Club course to contend with, Nicklaus played cautious golf on the final nine holes and frittered away part of his lead, but there was never any serious doubt throughout the chilly, sunny day that he would win.

He finished with a two-over-par 74, which, grouped with his earlier 68-71-73, gave him a 282 total, the highest winning score here since 1966. He won $25,000.

Tied for second place were Weiskopf, who shot a closing 74; Australian Bruce Crampton, who finished with a 73; and Bobby Mitchell, who also posted a 72.

Of the top nine players chasing Nicklaus, only Crampton broke par on the final nine holes.

This could be attributed in part to Nicklaus' smothering omnipotence and in part to the condition of the golf course.

The greens were firm, fast, and bumpy, because they had been invaded by patches of poa annua.

Nicklaus said he kept looking over his shoulder yesterday for someone to move up on him, but the challenge never came, and as a result he played a cautious brand of golf that he rarely employs.

"After I got the ball over the water on No. 12 (a scary par three), I was playing safely on every shot," he admitted.

"I figured I had the tournament won then if I didn't make any dumb mistakes. If someone had started to move up on me, I think I could have turned it on a little, because I was hitting the ball better than I had all week. If I had been pressed, I would have taken different tactics and probably wouldn't have made as many bogeys.

"When you're playing conservatively, that's the time you have to concentrate the hardest.

"During the week, I had several opportunities to blow the tournament open, move ahead by seven or eight shots but I didn't. Today I was just playing to win the tournament."

Nicklaus, employing his awesome power, birdied the second hole—a downhill 555 yarder—with a drive, a four-iron and two putts from 15 feet and the uphill, par-five eighth with a nine-foot putt. When he made the turn in 35, he had a five-stroke lead on the field. Jamieson played a ragged round and went out of contention early before rallying to shoot 74 and finish tied for fifth. Weiskopf's bogeys on the first, third, and fourth holes put him out of the picture until very late.

Nicklaus took bogeys on the 11th, 14th, and 15th holes, three-putting two of them after cautious approaches.

Now the unchallenged ruler of the game says he will turn his thoughts to the second leg of the Grand Slam, the U.S. Open at Pebble Beach in June. He has won two Crosby tournaments and the U.S. Amateur there.

While Nicklaus set his sights on that lofty goal of a Grand Slam, some other of the game's most notable players were taking aim simply on getting themselves back together again. Arnold Palmer, a four-time winner here, shot a closing 81 for an even 300. Player tied for 10th but was never a serious contender. Billy Casper shot 74-294, and Lee Trevino, playing here for the first time in three years, shot a final round of 72 for an even 300.

1973

You won't find a column about the final round of the 1973 Masters here. I had fallen ill midway through the tournament and gone home. Before I left, though, I had written about the eventual champion, Tommy Aaron, who until then, was noted for three things—a beautiful swing, a penchant for finishing second ,and some bad arithmetic. He was the fellow who put down a four for Roberto De Vicenzo on the 17th hole when De Vicenzo had made a three.

It was a special week, because Ben Hogan flew in for a ceremony hosted by the Golf Writers Association of America. With no golf to play, Hogan relaxed and talked, and the result was a rare look inside the mind of the great man.

I left the party and went back to my hotel room and wrote the interview, anxious to beat my rival newspaper. I did. It was precious stuff. I still consider it to be.

HOGAN REMEMBERS

Ben Hogan is 60 years old and has made only rare appearances in tournaments for the past several years. He has played a full 18 holes of golf only once since last summer and has played only nine in the past five months.

But the Texas Hawk, regarded by many as the greatest player of all time, revealed here last night that he would like to play in the major championships again if his injured left knee heals enough.

Here to receive the Richardson award from the Golf Writers Association of America, presented annually to a person who has made major contributions to golf, Hogan specifically mentioned the Masters and PGA as tournaments in which he would like to compete again.

"My knee would have to get much better, though, before I could do it," he said. "There's torn cartilage in it, the result of that bus accident many years ago. The doctors say they can take it out, but none of them will assure I'll be better, and none of them want to fool with it, because I also have a circulatory problem in my legs as a result of the accident, and they're not sure I'd heal properly."

Hogan flew in yesterday and out today without even visiting Augusta National Golf Course, where he was once the ruler of the game, winning the Masters three times and finishing second four times. In his last four appearances there, in 1967, he shot a 36-31-67, scoring birdies on the dreaded first holes of the back nine.

At the reception last night at a downtown hotel, he wore a black suit with narrow lapels, a white shirt with a short collar, and a narrow necktie. His face has changed little in recent years, though his hairline has receded a bit more.

"I don't know what I've done to deserve this award," he said. "But there are some things I've avoided doing in order to uphold the dignity of golf on a pedestal, and I want it to stay there."

Hogan, who has won four U.S. Opens and is one of only four players ever to win the U.S. and British Opens, the Masters, and the PGA, looked back over his career and concluded that the reason he didn't win a pro tournament until he was 27 years old is that he got to play so little amateur golf ("The last amateur tournament I played in, I had to sell my watch to pay my caddy"), he didn't play as much as youngsters play today, and most important, "had to figure everything out for myself."

"Boys today can start out where a lot of us left off, because we spent 25 years perfecting our games."

He said that he watches a lot of golf tournaments on television and complained that he rarely gets to see many shots hit, with most of the emphasis being placed on the putting.

"You know," he said, "nowadays when these fellows miss 30-footers, they jump up and say, 'Oh,' like they'd been shot in the back with an arrow. I was never a super putter myself. I was a good putter, but not super.

"When he was winning, Arnold Palmer was probably the greatest putter who ever lived."

Hogan said his most satisfying victory was in the British Open at Carnoustie, because it was the first time he had played in Great Britain and the only time he had played in wind, cold, and rain for three days.

Hogan said the greatest disappointment of his career came in 1960, when he failed to win the U.S. Open at Denver—the one Palmer won by shooting a 65 in the last round.

"I had played just about as good as I ever played and putted atrociously, but going to 17, I was tied for the lead," he said. "The pin was very close to the edge of the green, near the water. I knew I had to wedge within two feet of the cup to make the putt, and I needed a birdie there because there was no way to birdie the 18th because of where the pin was cut.

"I gambled and lost. The ball fell short and went into the water. I don't mind taking gambles, but I've thought many nights about that one. I'll never forget it.

"And you know, I've never figured up whether I might have tied or won if I had played safely onto the green and made my par. And I don't intend to ever figure it up."

BEN CRENSHAW NICKS NICKLAUS, POUNDS PALMER

NOTES AND OBSERVATIONS

Ben Crenshaw, the University of Texas student who had the tournament lead for a long while yesterday before finishing tied for 15th, was paired with Arnold Palmer and Jack Nicklaus in the first two rounds and has beaten both. "Yeah," he said, "but both had off days. It was a tremendous experience for me, though, playing in a great tournament like this with the two greatest players in the world." Crenshaw and Nicklaus took turns outdriving each other, with neither ever getting more than a 10-yard edge.

If Gay Brewer wins the Masters—and he was tied for the lead after two rounds—look for a heavy run on the new clubs with carbon graphite shafts. He hits the ball 20 to 30 yards farther with the new shaft in his driver, he says, and pros who have been paired with him agree. The clubs are expensive, though, about $90 apiece.

Former British and U.S. Open champion Tony Jacklin's game was in a shambles for a round and a half, but when it appeared he would fail to qualify for the final 36 holes, he rallied sharply to finish birdie-birdie-par-birdie-birdie-par-par. His charge fell one shot short of the mark. Another Briton, Brian Barnes, a Ryder Cup star, blew himself right out of the tournament and said there was no way he could compete here by playing only one week in this country. "If they invite me back next year," he said, "I'll decline." . . . His fellow countryman, British Amateur champion Trevor Homer, had a horrendous 88, due in great part to a 10 on the 13th hole, when he had to take three penalty drops in the woods, but he said he'd be back if they asked him.

HE ALSO RAN

If Tommy Aaron was the only entrant in a golf tournament, he would finish second. He's won over half a million dollars on the pro tour, but he's more famous for arithmetic than for his birdies and pars. His golf swing is so pretty, he can't win with it.

Such is the ill-starred life of the tall, closely shorn, bespectacled Georgian who was leading the heck out of the Masters early in the third round yesterday but stood four strokes back of Briton Peter Oosterhuis going into the final round today.

By nightfall, he could be wearing the green jacket symbolic of victory in the Masters. He is capable of stringing together some remarkable golf. It would be a surprise, though. Aaron seems destined to live out his life as a decorative piece.

He is perhaps the most gifted also-ran in golf. Since he graduated from the University of Florida in 1960 and hung out his shingle on the PGA tour in '61, he has won $650,000, which places him 16th on the all-time list.

But in all those years, he has won only one official PGA co-sponsored tournament, the Atlanta Classic. He had beaten Sam Snead in an 18-hole playoff to win the Canadian Open the year before, but it wasn't official because it was in conflict with another tour event at that time.

TOUCHY SUBJECT

Until he won in Canada, Aaron had been runner-up nine times—four times in 1963. He was also second four times last year. His record in official playoffs is 0-4.

Mention it to him, and the syrupy-voiced, mild-mannered Aaron bristles as best he can and says, "That runner-up business has been played very much out of proportion. It's an erroneous label. Look at the records.

"I checked recently and found Jack Nicklaus has finished second more times."

Nicklaus also finished first more times, a lot more.

"Lou Graham has been second twice and third once in his last three tournaments," said Aaron, talking as he devoured a steak sandwich and ice cream in the Augusta National clubhouse. "He led all three tournaments. Everybody says he's playing super. If I'd done that, I'd have been getting a lot of heat about it."

Aaron thinks he acquired the reputation as "runner-up champion" in 1963 when he lost a sudden-death playoff to Tony Lema in the Memphis Open and dropped an 18-hole playoff to Arnold Palmer at Cleveland.

Adding to the irony of Aaron's situation is the fact that he wrote the wrong number on Roberto De Vicenzo's scorecard in the final round of the 1968 Masters.

Aaron shrugs now and says, "I'd give anything if it hadn't happened. But I don't let it bother me anymore."

1974

Gary Player has always talked in superlatives, to the extent that some news media people imitate him at times. He likes to call places or things or moments the "greatest" or the "finest" or the "best," things like that, and he no doubt means it at the time. He has great enthusiasm, and it shows in everything he does.

When he had won his second Masters in 1974, he said he practiced as hard as any man who ever lived, traveled more than any athlete ever had, and exercised as hard as any man. That was not the idle talk of a man enthralled by the moment. What he said was the absolute truth.

Player was the second-most remarkable golfer I've ever seen, from a physical standpoint. Sam Snead was No. 1, ageless, richly gifted in natural ability and suppleness, and ever young in his mind and heart. If he ever worked out, I didn't hear about it. He just walked golf courses day after day, winning tournaments or bets off of people who considered it an honor to lose money to the Slammer.

Player did everything he could to stay at the peak of fitness, and that, along with a strong mind, enabled him to travel the globe, playing in tournaments and maintaining his strength and concentration.

He is a remarkable man, small in stature but a giant in mind and heart.

NICKLAUS APPEARS READY TO EXPLODE

NOTES AND OBSERVATIONS

Jack Nicklaus, who has played a game that the late Bobby Jones once said was "unfamiliar to me," was spectacularly un-spectacular again Friday, tacking a one-under-par 71 onto his opening-round 69 to stand three strokes off Dave Stockton's pace at the halfway mark. Five players had better scores, and four more were tied with him as he stalked into today's third round, but the Golden Bear remained a solid favorite to win his fifth Masters come tomorrow afternoon.

He looks and talks like a man who is ready to explode.

"The course looks awfully good this year," he said. "It's just sitting there waiting for somebody to shoot an awfully low score—and somebody's going to do it before it's over."

Out in front of the clubhouse, Nicklaus' caddy, Willie Peterson, was talking with Jack's wife, Barbara, and two of their sons.

"We've got a 66 in the bag," he said, patting Jack's sticks, "and it's gonna come out tomorrow or Sunday."

Nicklaus made an eagle three on the dogleg 475-yard 13th hole with a three-wood off the tee, a six-iron approach, and a 20-foot putt. "I thought, 'Now, I'm going to get something going,'" he said, but he knocked his second shot into the water on the 15th and bogeyed where he expected to make a birdie, and that took the fire out of his round . . . His playing partner, Dan Sikes, matched Nicklaus' 71 and his 140 total. "He's a great guy, and I love to play with him," said Sikes, "but the crowds following him are so huge, they become a factor. He's used to playing in front of 15,000 people every day, but I'm not. I didn't try to play his game. I just played the course."

The most spectacular exit of the day was made by George Archer. He was assessed a two-stroke penalty on the second hole for moving a branch of a small tree "other than in the course of fairly taking his stance," as the rulebook says. He turned in a 38 and asked his playing partner, Bruce Crampton, if he would mind playing alone. Crampton said okay, but Archer decided to stick it out to the bitter end. He promptly made a triple bogey on the 10th. Capping it all off, Archer signed an erroneous scorecard when Crampton gave him a five on the 13th when he had actually scored a six. This disqualified him, but it didn't matter because he had missed the cut, anyway.

Trevor Homer, the Englishman who had been made a 5,000-to-1 shot to win by a London bookmaker, closed with a blazing 33 for a 72 but missed the cut with a 149 total. The bookie had also offered 3-to-1 odds that Homer wouldn't break 80 in both of the first two rounds, but he showed 'em . . . . Arnold Palmer shot the back nine in 34 for a 71 and 147 total that got him into the last 36 holes by a single stroke . . . Lanny Wadkins, one of the favorites here, missed the cut for the third week in a row when he shot 80 with a triple-bogey eight on the eighth hole and a double-bogey seven on the 13th. Instead of taking next week off, as he had planned, he's going to stay with the tour and try to learn what's wrong with his game. He admits right now he has no idea.

Tony Jacklin, former U.S. and British Open champion who had 81 on opening day, shot 11 straight fours to start his second round and posted a 71 but also departed . . . Phil Rodgers fired a 69, which matched the score of his playing partner, Tom Weiskopf, but he said, "I felt like a 99 handicap playing with Tom. His 69 was the best round I've ever seen" . . . Weiskopf bogeyed only one hole, the long, par-three fourth, and was resting at 140, looking like a very serious threat to win his first Masters . . . Among the missing today was Tommy Aaron, who never got it going and shot 77-73-150.

PLAYER WINS MASTERS

Gary Player, who faded from glory last year when he won only one tournament after two serious operations, returned to the preeminence he shared with Jack Nicklaus and Arnold Palmer in bygone years when he won his second Masters and seventh major championship here yesterday.

The South African pixie, who stands only 5-6 and weighs 150 pounds, got home with a finishing 70 for a 72-hole total of 278 just ahead of a rainstorm that struck Augusta National and was symbolic of the thunder and lightning hurled at him by some of the game's best players in the last four hours of this classic.

As he walked off the 18th green, the candid Player told his playing partner, Dave Stockton, "I deserved to win. I played the best I've ever played from tee to green."

Later, when 1973 champion Tommy Aaron had held the

champion's green jacket for him to pull on for the second time in 13 years, Player said, "I've sacrificed, I've been dedicated, I've practiced, I've exercised.

"I practice as hard as any man who ever lived. I travel more than any other athlete ever has. I've exercised as hard as any man. Because of that, I think I get more satisfaction out of winning a major championship than a lot of people.

"And yet, when you win, you've got to be very, very grateful."

Though the battle raged furiously across the hills and through the valley of this leafy playground that Bobby Jones built on what was once a nursery, Player said he never lost faith that he would win.

"When I teed up on the first hole in the first round, I was never so confident as I was then. I just had so much confidence in the way I was hitting the ball. I'd swing, and the ball would just shoot right toward the flag," he said.

His certainty that he would win the title he first won in 1961 was not shared by his competitors. He overtook third-round leader Stockton on the sixth hole with a birdie two and passed him when he birdied the ninth as Stockton bogeyed.

But he was far from home free. Tom Weiskopf made a determined run at him on the back nine, and as late as the 15th hole, was tied with him for the lead, but Weiskopf knocked his tee shot on the watery par-three 16th hole into the placid blue pond fronting the green and bogeyed, finishing with a 70 to tie Stockton, who shot a 73, for second place at 280. Hale Irwin and the terrifying Jack Nicklaus also had shots at him in the late going, but faltered and finished tied for fourth with Jim Colbert, who hauled out an eight-iron for an eagle two on the final hole for a 281 total.

Player carried a card in his hip pocket on which he had written two thoughts that he said helped him to victory. One was something Billy Graham told him: "I can do anything through Jesus Christ who strengthens me." He declined to say what the other was.

Player didn't putt well in the final round, but his shots were so accurate, he didn't have to. He admitted he became frustrated, though, after missing a flock of short ones.

Frustrated, but never lacking in confidence.

He came to the 17th hole leading Weiskopf, Stockton, and Irwin by two strokes. He told his caddy, Eddie McCoy, "Before this year, I don't think I've hit this green more than six times in all the years I've played here. But it won for me in 1961 and it's going to win for me again. I hit my approach eight inches from the cup.

"I didn't even follow the flight of the ball. I knew it was good. I said to Eddie, "You think we'll have to putt this one?"

Weiskopf was distraught at his failure in the stretch.

"That shot that went into the water on 16 put me out of it," he said. "I tried as hard as I could on 17 and 18 (he lipped out a birdie putt on the final green), but Gary proved to be the best player.

"It's the most empty feeling I've ever had."

Stockton went into the final round oozing confidence, but he had the heart cut right out of him when he hit the first nine greens in regulation and had eight two-putts and a three-putt. He hung in until the 17th, hole when Player put him and the field away with his eight-inch birdie.

Player two-putted for par from seven, eight, 25, 12, and two feet before he dropped a 12-footer for a birdie on the sixth. He missed a three-footer for a birdie on the long eighth, then nailed another bird from six feet.

He bogeyed the 10th from a trap, one-putted the 11th from six feet for a par, missed the 12th green and bogeyed, made a six-foot bird putt on 13, two-putted from 8 feet for par on 14, parred 15 out of a trap, missed from 14 feet, and parred 16. And then came the fateful 17th.

It was the 17th victory on the American tour for the 38-year-old and earned him $35,000. It left him one U.S. Open short of a double grand slam. He has won two Masters, two British Opens, two PGAs, and one U.S. Open.

He is the only foreigner ever to win the Masters.

Along with the blazing battle for the championship, two other developments had a massive crowd roaring on this sticky, overcast day. Four-time champion Arnold Palmer shot a 67 to vault into 11th place, a round that would have put him squarely in the thick of the battle had he not opened with a 76. And the Britisher Maurice Bembridge tied the course record with an eight-under-par 64, shooting 30 on the back nine after playing the dreaded Amen Corner—10 through 13—in birdies.

1975

The 1975 Masters was the best of them all. I didn't write that at the time, I'm sorry to say, but today I have no doubt of it. It was the best because of the golf that was played and the people who played it.

Jack Nicklaus won. He holed an uphill, curling 40-foot putt on the 16th hole for a birdie two that set the stage for his victory, and when it went in, he ran around the green in celebration, leaving what Tom Weiskopf would later call "Bear tracks." Weiskopf and Miller were watching from the 16th tee.

It was all great theater. Miller, who could put together astonishing streaks of golf, had fallen 11 shots behind Nicklaus in the first two rounds, but had strung together six straight birdies on the front nine and shot 65 on Saturday to get into the thick of it. Weiskopf, never to be a winner but four times a runner-up, felt certain he would win, and he was defiant even after it was over, saying he was as good as either of the other two.

In the years since, we've savored that tournament, relived it, compared it, wished for another like it. So far, there has been none.

BATTLE FOR SUPREMACY

The idea that a battle for supremacy of tournament golf has evolved in the past two years between Jack Nicklaus, the ruler, and Johnny Miller, the challenger, may have been created and nurtured by the press. But as the 39th Masters got under-way today, the rivalry of these two blond sensations had even the other players in this select field talking.

This has been billed as something of a showdown for them, although Nicklaus has finished higher than Miller in three of the four tournaments in which both have played this year and tied him in the other. In their last 19 meetings, Nicklaus has beaten Miller 14 times.

Nicklaus and Miller try to shrug it off, but they talk about it, like the others.

Miller Barber says, "All Miller's done is wake up a sleeping bear."

Sam Snead, who used to have a similar rivalry going with Ben Hogan, feels, "You can't take one tournament and say this is for the championship between them. One guy could happen to be playing bad. They'd need to play maybe five tournaments head-to-head."

Dave Hill, sitting across the table from Snead in the Augusta National grill, said, "If it were a head-to-head thing over, say, 30 rounds, I'd like to put Tom Weiskopf in against both of them, and I'd take him."

Billy Casper, who was also sitting there, shook his head from side to side.

"Well," hedged Hill, "the only problem with Weiskopf is his head."

"That's right," said Casper. "He doesn't think as well as those two."

The fourth party at the table, Australian Bruce Devlin, put in, "Jack's the brightest I've ever seen."

"Yeah," said Snead. "He can play gawdawful and still come in with a 69. And I've never seen him get mad. I've seen him color up, get red in the neck, but never get mad."

"I played with him the year he was defending champion and missed the cut here because he shot 77 in the second round," said Devlin. "I'll tell you what, he ground it out until the last hole, and he stood over that last putt as long as he stood over any of the others."

Miller says, "This Nicklaus-Miller thing doesn't mean that much. There's no doubt Jack's the guy to beat. He's always tough in the majors.

"If he's playing his worst, his worst is better than my worst. My best is as good as his best at times. I think he's a lot better performer, more consistent. I may play terrible and finish 35th, which really isn't too bad, but if he plays bad, he finishes in the top 10."

Nicklaus admits that Miller's stunning burst of success early this year—winning three of the first four tournaments and shooting a pair of 61s—may have made him work a little harder, but he insists the thing that made him whip his game into perhaps its best shape ever (he had won two in a row coming here) was the unsatisfying way he played last year when he didn't win a major title.

"Sure," he said, "you see when someone's playing well, and I suppose it gives you a little push, but I can't worry about one guy.

"It doesn't make any difference whether it's Johnny Miller or Sam Snead or anyone else. It was my own lousy game that made me work so hard to get ready this year."

"My inspiration was the fact that I wasn't paying well—not Johnny Miller.

"Miller and Weiskopf have more ability than anybody out there. Miller is going to win a lot of majors. What he has done over the past year and a half is fantastic, something that hasn't been done in a long time, but greatness and a challenge to a position are built over a long period. Gary Player won two majors last year, and I think he had a better year than Miller (who won eight titles and over $300,000, but no majors).

"I don't think Miller's or Weiskopf's record approaches Player's or Lee Trevino's. Gary won eight majors, and Lee's won five."

Nicklaus says his game and his confidence are at a peak. Miller is less enthralled with his but not unhappy.

Real or imagined, their first big showdown of the year is on, and nothing they may say can change that. When it's all over, what will be remembered is their score.

JUST LIKE THE OLD DAYS

In the end, it paled beside the dead-solid perfection of Jack Nicklaus, but for a long time yesterday, the second round of the Masters belonged to a faded hero named Arnold Palmer. Just like it used to be. Words and music by Bill Haley and the Comets. Cokes a nickel apiece.

It was ironic that it was Nicklaus, the man who had de-throned Palmer as king of golf, who turned Arnie's best start here since 1965 into an exercise in futility by making a shambles of the last 12 holes at Augusta National Golf Club. When night fell on the halfway mark of this classic, Jack had shot 68-67-135 and had made only one bogey with some of the most flawless golf these storied fairways have ever seen. He did it like a machine. Palmer, with 69-71-140, was tied for second place but a distant five shots behind. He did it like Palmer, thrilling 'em all the way.

Before the late-starting Nicklaus had begun to unload his barrage, Palmer was out there raising thunderclaps of noise from his huge gallery—just like the old days. Shirttail out, hair tousled, shots whistling off his clubs.

Arnie owned this place back then. He won here in 1958, 1960, 1962, and 1964, and when he didn't, he had them looking over their shoulders for him. He was the hero of the aristocrat and the common man alike, and he made the game what it is with his hell-bound drive for the prize, scoffing at peril, winning or losing spectacularly.

But he hasn't won here since '64. He was second in 1965, fell to fourth in 1966, was fourth again in 1967, and hasn't been a factor since.

Not until now.

Suddenly, there he is again, lurking in position to challenge if Nicklaus makes a false move. He has played better this year after going winless on the tour for two years. Some of his old swashbuckling confidence has welled up again. He no longer complains about his short game that brought on his fall from glory. He is playing and thinking like a man who could possibly win again.

At one time yesterday during the mid-day gloom and rain, he was leading the tournament, bringing people galloping from all over the course when they heard. His game wasn't as sharp as it had been the day before, when he shot 69, but when he made a mistake, he pulled his white visor lower, tugged at his trousers in that old familiar way and went off after it like a man getting ready to whip some tail.

He one-putted eight times, four of them for birdies and four to save pars. One of the saves was vintage Palmer. It came on the par-five 13th hole, which doglegs left and is fronted by a creek and dares you to go for the green in two.

Arnie had just blown his lead, three-putting the 11th hole and bogeying from a trap on the tricky par-three 12th. His drive on the 13th was too close to the trees to the left. He could see the green only through the branches. He fiddled around a long time before pulling out a four-wood, but later said, "I had no hesitation about going for the green in two. All I was doing was deciding which club to hit."

His hooked, four-wood shot plopped into the creek. But he fetched it out, dropped it, pitched a little wedge shot over the water to within three feet of the cup, got his par, and didn't mess up again.

The crowd loved it. Palmer loved it. "In the last seven or eight years, chipping and putting have been my major problem," he said. "After those bogeys on 11 and 12, I got a little concerned, and after I knocked it in the ditch on 13, I got damned concerned. But I am getting the ball up and down better now."

His playing partner, young Tom Watson, a three-year veteran of the tour who still looks like Tom Sawyer, also loved it.

"You know, I've played with Arnie a lot in the past three years," he said, "but this was the first time I've played with him here. I found myself thinking, 'Here I am, playing with Arnold Palmer in the Masters.' I used to think about that when I would watch him on TV. I guess everybody has.

"They cheer louder for him here than anywhere else. I've never heard cheers like that. Ten million decibels.

"I can understand why. He's the man who made our game what it is."

Arnie still has a solid, if not lean, look about him, though he has to wear glasses now, and his hairline has receded some. He still walks with a purposeful stride, like a man who can't wait to hammer that ball again.

But what of his nerves? When he was winning here, he birdied whichever holes he had to birdie to win. Suppose he goes down that awful back nine tomorrow with a shot at the championship. What of the nerves then?

"I don't know," he said. "I haven't led going into the last nine holes in a long time."

FRUSTRATED WEISKOPF
NEVER DOUBTED WIN

They had come at Jack Nicklaus, the king of the pride, from different directions.

Tom Weiskopf had arrived at the Masters fresh off a victory in the Greater Greensboro Open with his game so keen, he said he never doubted from the first shot to the last that he would win. He had fallen five strokes behind in the first two rounds but had overtaken Nicklaus and passed him by a shot with a 66 on Saturday.

Miller had come here with his game shaky and had fallen 11 strokes behind Nicklaus in the first two rounds with scores of 75 and 71. He was fretful, uncertain about his putting, stung by the manner in which the man whose reign he had challenged over the past two years had embarrassed him. Then he had shot 65 on Saturday, stringing together six straight birdies on the front nine, but he still stood three behind Nicklaus, four behind Weiskopf. Catching one of them in the heat of the searing pressure in yesterday's final round seemed remotely possible. Catching both seemed virtually impossible.

But Weiskopf swapped the lead with Nicklaus all the way around, and Miller, hitting enormous drives and dazzling irons and deadly putts, moved up on them. And it came down to two putts. Either could have tied Nicklaus on the last hole, but Miller's long, sensational comeback with scores of 65-66 fell short by inches, and Weiskopf's bid to atone for a punishing bogey on the 16th slid agonizingly by.

Nicklaus was champion for the fifth time, while Weiskopf was runner-up here for the third time, and Miller for the second.

"I don't know how to tell you how I felt when I missed that last putt," said Weiskopf, who has a rather brusque nature and seems uncomfortable talking about emotions. "Let me say this, nobody has a better swing in golf than I do. I listen to Miller talk about how great he is, and I know how great Jack is, but I can play as good as any of them.

"I never doubted all week that I would win. You know, somebody once said you can't explain pain. So I can't explain to you how I felt. Unless you could stand in my shoes out there and experience it, you can't know how it felt.

"But I'm not going to let it get me down. Winning is everything. Nobody remembers who finished second, and I'm going to forget it, too. But someday, I'm going to win here."

The watery par-three 16th hole was Weiskopf's undoing, as it had been last year when he was threatening to win until he knocked his tee shot into the pond. This time, he hit his five-iron fat and left it 85 feet from the cup and took three more strokes to get it in. He had just stood on the tee and watched Nicklaus make a 40-footer there for a birdie. Weiskopf had gone from leader to second place on that pretty little hole.

"It wasn't just that one," he insisted. "You can't say it was one hole. It was one of many over the period of four days. I sure didn't stand there and say, 'Gee whiz, here's 16 again, where I knocked it in the water last year.'"

Weiskopf, who had been paired with Miller, had heard the chesty young blond tell the writers how he had outdriven Weiskopf on every hole but one.

When questioned about that, Weiskopf said, "The 18th hole was the only time I really tried to hit the ball hard all day. I was only 46 steps past him on that one. He can hit it a long way, but when I want to, he can't even come close to me."

Miller's reaction to his near miss was considerably different.

"I really wasn't that upset," he said. "After shooting 75 on the opening day, I really didn't think my chances were too red hot. Today, I was just fighting my guts out trying to catch those two guys and hoping something happened.

"You know, 131 in the last two rounds is not too shabby. I think people will believe now that I can play golf, too. I just can't play golf any better than that. (He birdied 15 of his last 36 holes.) It was just that bad start."

1976

The day before the 1976 Masters began, Clifford Roberts, then 82, announced that he was retiring as chairman of the Masters, a position he had held since the tournament's inception in 1933. He was succeeded by William Lane, a Houston businessman.

Roberts was in ill health and would later take his own life with a pistol on the par-three course that lies just a short distance from the clubhouse.

There would be no obvious changes as a result of Roberts' resignation for several years. He had ruled Augusta National and the Masters with a king-like power, and much of what the club and the tournament are today can be attributed to him. He insisted on the dignity that is as much a part of the event as the fairways and greens, and Bobby Jones was his model.

The Masters is more relaxed now. That's not to say it hasn't retained the qualities that made it great. It is still about golf and beauty and tradition and the fellowship of people who love a game. But now it smiles. I don't recall that I ever saw Roberts do that, although I'm sure he did.

Raymond Floyd, on the other hand, was all smiles after this Masters. He won by eight strokes.

FLOYD BLOWS CHALLENGERS OFF THE COURSE

As has become one of the little traditions among the big at Augusta National Golf Club during Masters week, Chet Baker, the chunky, balding little keeper of the pressroom scoreboard, put up his "Thought For the Day" yesterday. There, just below the figures showing Ray Floyd holding an eight-stroke lead with only the day's 18 holes to play, Baker had penned, "Jesus said, 'All things are possible, to him that believeth.'"

Jack Nicklaus tried to believe. He had five green jackets symbolic of Masters supremacy and had dressed appropriately for a sixth, wearing white trousers and a green shirt.

When Sunday came up windy, tossing the treetops around, Nicklaus, whose scores had gone from 67 to 69 to 73 to leave him eight behind Floyd's Masters record 201 total for 54 holes, was heartened. "If it weren't for the wind, we'd have to shoot something like 63 to catch him," he said.

Larry Ziegler, starting in third place, nine back, tried to believe. "This wind is just what Jack and I need," he said, chatting away in the locker room before teeing off. "If we can shoot a low score in this stuff, we might catch him. It would be tough to catch him on a perfect day, though."

Tom Weiskopf, who had played a major role in the great drama of the day in 1975 when he and Johnny Miller dogged Nicklaus down to the last putt, sat nearby, listening, out of the chase himself, 13 shots back.

"Ray will be out there just trying to make numbers," he said. "The others will be out there trying to make miracles."

Floyd strode into the locker room to change shoes and get ready for the kill. He carried a handful of telegrams from well-wishers, and he read them as he talked to reporters hovering around him. ("Nobody else got any sleep at my house last night, but I did. They're too nervous. I think the wind will help me. The harder the conditions, the less likely anybody's going to shoot a low score on me".)

He said later he knew he had the tournament won before teeing off yesterday. But his hands were shaking slightly as he held the telegrams, and a trace of perspiration appeared on his upper lip.

He went to his locker to get some golf balls. He set his Coke down on the floor of the locker and reached up on a shelf for the balls. He accidentally knocked a box of balls off the shelf. It landed on the Coke, crushing the top of the cup, but the drink didn't turn over.

"I drop a dozen balls on my Coke and don't even spill a drop," said Floyd, his eyes glistening. "See how good I'm doing this week?"

He was going too good.

The challengers went out and tried to make miracles, as Weiskopf said, but after the first few holes, they were playing for second place and admitted it. Floyd wasn't cracking, and they weren't heating up. Of the other nine players in the top 10 along with Floyd heading into the final round, only Ben Crenshaw made any kind of threatening gesture. The others either just held or lost ground.

Crenshaw eagled the 13th hole and birdied the 14th to pull within six shots of Floyd, but the cheers from his birdie had hardly died before Floyd answered it with a birdie of his own on the testy par-three 12th. Just in case the kid had any ideas.

Floyd finished leading by the same margin with which he started, shooting a 70 for a 271 to tie the tournament record.

Crenshaw shot a 67 to finish second, giving the huge crowds most of their excitement for an afternoon that was in reality a dreadfully dull one compared to the drama ordinarily associated with Masters Sundays. The noise was the polite noise of appreciation for excellence, rather than the spontaneous thunderclaps that rumble up the hillsides when the chase is hot.

Floyd played some of the most impeccable golf ever played for 72 holes here, but without a Miller or a Nicklaus or a Weiskopf matching him shot for shot down that dreadful back nine, it wasn't the same.

All things are possible, to him that believeth. But some things are highly improbable, and beating Ray Floyd yesterday was one of them. If anybody else had dropped a dozen balls on his Coke, it would have splashed all over him.

1977

Over the years, many a man has done something awful on the last hole of the Masters to lose his chance at the title. Tom Watson drove into the trees on the right and double bogeyed. Arnold Palmer, needing only a par to win and a bogey to tie, hit his second shot into a bunker and made double bogey, leaving the championship for Gary Player. Greg Norman hit his second shot so poorly, it was to the right of the bunker from which Palmer double bogeyed. And so it has gone, as the pressure—descends on the shoulders of the men about to win a Masters—like a pair of anvils.

Who would have expected it of Jack Nicklaus, though? If you could have picked one man to hit a shot for your life, it would have been Nicklaus back then, but when he heard the roar from Tom Watson's birdie on the 17th hole as he stood waiting to hit to the 18th green, it disrupted his thinking, and he hit his approach fat, into a bunker, and Watson won.

JACK SAYS FIRST MASTERS WAS FLOP

The Bruce Lietzkes, Mark Hayeses, and Danny Edwardses say they aren't awed by the Masters golf course, even though this is their first crack at the championship. Jack Nicklaus knows the feeling.

"I first started giving a lot of attention to the Masters when Billy Joe Patton almost won it (1954)," he recalled yesterday. "Then Ken Venturi almost won (in 1956), and I started thinking seriously about being the first amateur to win it.

"I played here for the first time in 1959. Before the tournament started, I was shooting these low rounds and thinking this course was not so tough. Then the tournament started. I three-putted eight times in 36 holes, shot 150, and was on my way home."

TOM TOOK JACK'S BEST

After you've been around the Masters for a while, you learn to read the roar of the crowds. There are different ones for spectacular shots, for eagle putts, for birdie putts, for good saving putts for par.

Jack Nicklaus was standing on the 18th fairway yesterday afternoon, pondering his second shot up the hill to the green, when an unmistakable roar came thundering up from the 17th green. He knew that Tom Watson, whom he had overtaken with a flawless round to that point to tie for the lead, had run in a birdie and retaken the lead.

Later, after Watson had polished off a 67 for a 276 total that won the title by two shots, Nicklaus, a five-time winner here and a man accustomed to unsettling his opponents but not being unsettled himself, said, "When I heard Tom make that birdie on 17, my strategy was shot. I was going to put the ball on the back of the green, not take any chances with the bunker in front.

"If I made the putt, I would win. If I didn't, I would at least not lose the tournament. I was thinking playoff. But when he birdied, it changed around my mind. I had a six-iron in my hand. It was too much to get the ball close to the hole, so I tried to soft it in, and I hit it fat, into the bunker.

"That was something I hadn't planned on—somebody else making a birdie. My mind wasn't ready for that."

It was a stunning twist of fate, Watson making the birdie instead of the great Nicklaus. And Nicklaus hitting the poor shot instead of Watson. One of Nicklaus' great rounds here—and he has had so many—meant nothing except second place, in which he is not interested.

Nicklaus, his blond mane tousled by the gentle breeze that had wafted across the sun-splashed fairways on this gorgeous Easter Sunday, looked back over the day and said, "It was one of those days when no matter how much I hit it right, somebody else hit it better."

Nicklaus thought he probably helped Watson, who had begun the day three strokes ahead of him and in a tie for the lead with Ben Crenshaw, but that he had hurt Crenshaw badly.

"Tom's not afraid of anybody," he said. "There's no reason for anybody to be afraid. But winning breeds winning, and when you come down the stretch and you're used to seeing a fellow always in contention up there with you, it affects your play.

"Tom probably felt I was not going to give the game away, felt he couldn't lay up, play safe, and that kept him bearing down. It's like when I first came up. I knew Arnold (Palmer) wasn't going to take a dive someplace; I had to beat him."

But it was different, he said, with Crenshaw, his playing partner.

"I felt sorry for Ben," he said. "He was really playing poorly. (He shot a sloppy 76 and dropped from first to a tie for eighth at 285, nine shots off the winning score.) I think he probably expected to be paired with Jim Colbert because of the way the scores were after the third round, but they don't do it that way here. In no other tournament in the world would I have been paired with Ben.

"It was good for me. If I'm three shots behind, as I was at the start, I've got to beat somebody to win, and I like being paired with the leader.

"I think it might be harder for a young kid to win his first major playing with me. I don't think he would've done what he did today if he hadn't been playing with me and I started making birdies."

Nicklaus stroked in a 20-footer for a birdie on the first hole and two-putted for a birdie on the second. Crenshaw parred the first and bogeyed the second, and from then on, the young blond's game went hither and yon, off into places he said nobody had ever been.

1978

*Once he stopped playing in the Masters, after 1967, Ben
Hogan, who didn't like flying, came back to Augusta only twice,
once to accept an award from the Golf Writers Association of
America (after which he left town without ever going to Augusta
National) and in 1978 for the traditional Champions Dinner.*

*It was there, in 1978, that he told his famous story about a
dream he had had in which he made 17 straight birdies and then
parred the last hole and woke up mad.*

*Gary Player won for a third time in 1978 and afterward took
a swipe at the media, who had questioned whether he was over the
hill. He answered that rather dramatically with a closing 64 that
featured nine birdies.*

AUGUSTA DRAMA—PLAYER PROVES HE'S NOT FINISHED ON U.S. TOUR

For the genuine challengers, those with anything close to a
reasonable chance of winning the Masters, the final round began
yesterday on a light note and ended with some of the greatest
drama this 42-year-old golf tournament has ever known.

Shortly before 1 p.m., Jack Nicklaus and Tom Weiskopf
appeared on the first tee wearing—by coincidence—identical
shirts and trousers. Weiskopf said he wasn't going through the
afternoon looking like a bowling team with people asking,
"What's going on here?" He sent someone to get him another
shirt and changed there on the first tee while the crowd cheered.

That was the last bit of levity on this hot, humid Sunday, as
Gary Player shot his way through a thicket of players, who
themselves were producing heroics seemingly every second, to
win his third Masters championship.

Starting seven shots behind third-round leader Hubert
Green, Player nailed together a course-record-tying, eight-under-

par 64, two shots lower than the best finishing round ever by a Masters champion. At age 42, the 5-6, 150-pound South African is the oldest man ever to win this coveted title that he first won in 1961 and claimed again in 1964.

His 277 total edged defending champion Tom Watson, Rod Funseth and Green by a single shot. Victory wasn't assured until the last twosome came to the last green and Funseth left a downhill 22-foot putt hanging on the lip of the cup, and Green, noted as a deadly putter, saw his tying, three-foot putt roll along the edge of the hole, dip as if it might drop, then go on past.

Player, watching Funseth and Green on TV, said, "I was choking."

For Player, it was a return to the glory that he feels has been unfairly denied him in this country. Because he hadn't won on the U.S. tour since 1974, when he won the Masters and the Memphis Open, he has come to be generally regarded as a has-been.

With a dash of anger in his voice, Player told newsmen, "I read last week in a Greensboro newspaper that I was a fading star. Wherever I go in this country, writers come up to me and ask why I'm not winning anymore. Hell, I'm winning all over the world. I won the last three tournaments I played in last year.

"I'd like to see Jack Nicklaus travel round-trip from South Africa five times in a year, play in only about 15 tournaments a year here and still play as well as he does. I mention Jack only because he's your greatest player. He's one of my best friends. But I wonder how many tournaments he would win here with my schedule. My children flew here from South Africa Wednesday and it took them 33 hours."

Player said he had an incentive other than his crumbling status, though. He said he wanted this one to go with his three British Opens, two PGA Championships, one U.S. Open, and two other Masters to tie him with the legendary Ben Hogan in number of majors won.

"I knew I was in the hunt before I teed off," said Player, and he recalled several instances when players have come from seven or more strokes back to win.

"Actually," he said, "I played not one stroke better today than I had the last two rounds, but I made the putts today. I changed my putting stroke last week. I decided to get away from the jab I had used for 24 years and begin stroking the ball.

"My wife has been after me for a long time to make this change. I finally tried it last week in Greensboro and didn't do badly. I finished fifth. I couldn't get it to work in the first three rounds here, but my caddy, Eddie McCoy, kept encouraging me, telling me that I was playing well and not to give up on the stroke."

Player's most vital putts in a round that featured nine birdies and just one bogey under intense pressure came at the 16th, where he holed a 15-footer for a birdie to catch the front-runners, and at the 18th, where he cruised in a downhill 15-footer for another birdie that eventually proved to be the winning margin.

Watson came to the 18th with a chance to tie with a par, win with a birdie, but he hit his tee shot into trees and had to play a fade that didn't turn enough. His ball rolled down a steep hill beside the green. He hit it eight feet from the hole and missed his par putt.

Then Funseth, needing a birdie to tie, missed. And finally Green, also needing a birdie, missed.

Player earned $45,000. Watson, who shot a closing 69, Funseth, 69, and Green, 72, won $21,667 apiece.

1979

Not since the first Masters in 1934 had anyone won the title in his first try, but Fuzzy Zoeller, a wisecracking, easygoing Indianan, did it in 1979. He had to go two extra holes to do it, beating Tom Watson and Ed Sneed in a playoff with a birdie on the 11th hole.

Sneed came into the final round with a five-shot lead and was ahead by three with three to play, but two three-putts and a bogey on the last dropped him into the playoff.

"Maybe next time," he said, but there would be no next time for him as a serious challenger.

IT'S THE "AMEN CORNER"

If you could buy a homesite on Augusta National Golf Club, you'd want one somewhere around the 11th, 12th, and 13th holes.

But you'd want to send the kids to Grandma's during Masters week. For four days there, the language turns the air purple.

It's a lovely spot with tall pines, flowering shrubs and trees, a little pond, and a gurgling brook.

It's a little bit of heaven until you walk down it with a golf club in your hand. Then it's a whole bunch of hell.

In mixed company, they call it Amen Corner, because the golfers say "amen" when they've finished those three holes.

They were cursing the back nine again Thursday as the 43rd Masters began in ideal playing conditions that produced 22 sub-par rounds and 10 more at even 72.

The most prominent and stunning victim was Lanny Wadkins, former PGA champion who is the only two-time winner on the tour this year. He came to the 10th hole four under par and, a half hour and several expletives later, he left over par.

On No. 10, which is named "Camellia," he put his second shot into a bunker, blasted out, and three-putted.

He barely missed the green on No. 11—"White Dogwood"—and just as he took his backswing on his chip shot, the gallery cheered something someone had done on No. 12. Wadkins dumped his chip 10 feet short and missed.

On No. 12, a lovely but treacherous 155-yard par three with the disarming name of "Golden Bell" and with winds that swirl capriciously, he dumped a seven-iron shot into the creek, dropped out, pitched over the creek, and made double bogey.

Everything he had built on the front nine with four birdies and five pars was blown apart.

As he and playing partner Hale Irwin walked down the 13th fairway, Irwin said, "C'mon, Lanny, let's start going the other way for a while. This is not much fun."

"Amen," said Wadkins, or something to that effect. Wadkins was baffled by his self-destruction, which turned a front-nine 32 into a back-nine 41. "I shot six under in practice yesterday," he said. "I had a good practice session before I teed off today. I'm hitting the ball really well. I wasn't surprised when I went four under. I was thinking about shooting something like 66."

Then, the 10th hole and Amen Corner had other ideas.

Before we continue with the gore, let's pause here to look at how kindly the early back nine holes treated Tom Watson en route to his 68. He played them in birdie-par-birdie, which beat Wadkins and fellow victims Masashi Ozaki's 6-6-4 and Gay Brewer's 5-5-6 by seven shots.

"When I knocked my ball onto the green on 12," said Watson, "I told my caddy, Leon, 'I sure am glad to have those holes behind me.' I'd seen on the scoreboard what happened to Wadkins.

"When you play those three holes in par, you're stealing, and I got through them two under. Amen."

Former Masters champion Tommy Aaron turned the front nine in even par and then played 10, 11, and 12 in 5-5-5. Another former winner, Bob Goalby, also made it there even par but left with a 4-6-5.

David Graham was even through 11 and made a seven on "Golden Bell." Tom Weiskopf arrived at 12 in the same shape and made a six. Fuzzy Zoeller was three under until he double-bogeyed the 12th. Ozaki was even par until his twin doubles on 10 and 11.

"The tournament usually seems to be won or lost on those holes," said Watson.

"You've got to hit really, really good shots on them or be lucky," said Joe Inman.

The 12th hole is so scary, even the great Jack Nicklaus takes no liberties with it.

"When the pin's on the right side of the green, as it was today," he said, "I just aim for the middle of the green. That way, if I come up short, I'll land in the bunker in front of the green. If you're short and land in the grass, you roll back into the water."

And on the 11th, he said, "If the pin's on the left and you hit to the right, you're afraid to putt the ball firmly because the grain of the grass runs that way, and the green slopes away from you, and if you putt three or four feet past, the ball might just roll right on into the pond."

It's probably no consolation to Thursday's victims, but it could've been worse. Dow Finsterwald once made an 11 on No. 12.

What he said is not recorded, but it sure wasn't "amen."

NOTES AND OBSERVATIONS

Leader Bruce Lietzke, an automotive buff, drove a truck—one of his collection—to the tournament. "It's kinda hard to be nostalgic driving down Magnolia Lane (the club entrance) in a truck," he said.

Last year, he didn't even qualify for the Masters, and instead of watching it on TV Saturday and Sunday, he worked on one of his cars.

LOSING CAN BE HARD TO SWALLOW
WHEN YOU CHOKE ON A 5-STROKE LEAD

At least Ed Sneed went down fighting.

He can carry that with him and perhaps it will be of some consolation to him as he sits—as he must—and ponders the Masters championship that he lost on Easter Sunday.

That's what will haunt him—he lost it.

The record book will show that Fuzzy Zoeller, playing in his first Masters, won when he made up four shots on Sneed in the last three holes and then beat Sneed and Tom Watson on the second hole of a sudden-death playoff.

But Sneed—unlike the flamboyant Zoeller— is a grim, cautious workman out there on the fairways and greens, and started the day five strokes ahead of the field.

It could've been a nice walk through the springtime for him.

Instead, it became a dismal, grinding battle.

In the galleries, there were mixed emotions. The crowd wanted to see some drama, not a runaway, but as the sturdy, erect, handsome 34-year-old Sneed began to let his lead slip away, there were whispers of sympathy.

It's only a game, but it's a big game, with stakes far greater than the $50,000 first prize, and it's painful to watch a man stripped of his dignity out there.

Reduced to its harshest form, it's called choking.

Sneed bogeyed two holes on the first nine, and his lead was down to two. He bogeyed the 10th, and it was down to one.

He fought back with birdies on the 13th and 15th holes and was ahead again by three, but then he three-putted the 16th and 17th holes and bogeyed the 18th. He could've won it at the 18th. He had a six-foot putt to take it, but left it hanging on the lip.

He played the first extra hole well (the playoff began on the 10th) but on the next, his second shot went into a bunker behind the green. Watson had a birdie putt sitting there. Zoeller had a better one.

Sneed blasted from a devilish downhill lie, and the ball settled into a roll. It looked as if it might go in. But it missed by an inch.

Zoeller birdied, and it was over.

Earlier in the week, after Sneed had added a 67 to his opening 68, one of Sneed's best friends, Tom Weiskopf, had said, "Ed plays a lot better than a lot of guys out there, but there are two parts of his game that are lacking.

"One, he doesn't believe in himself. He doesn't have enough confidence. That's because he's never gone down to the wire and beaten a Nicklaus or a Watson or a Trevino.

"He needs to beat somebody that good to tell him he's that good.

"And the other thing is that he's not an outstanding putter. If he could putt as well as Nicklaus or Crenshaw or Watson, this guy would never be off the leader board."

Weiskopf's remarks were prophetic. You could see them unfolding out there Sunday.

Sneed insisted, though, that he didn't fold under the pressure.

When it was over, he said things like, "I felt in control of the tournament. I didn't feel tight. After a kinda shaky start, I felt good; my swing felt good."

He ticked off the reasons he missed those putts on the last three holes—"maybe I misread it," or "I thought it broke right, and my caddy thought it broke right, but it didn't."

Even after he had bogeyed the 17th, he said, "I still felt good. I still felt I was gonna do it.

"It just didn't happen."

Watson, who lost the PGA Championship in a playoff last year after blowing a five-shot lead, said, "Ed deserved to win. He played well all week.

"I've been there before. I know what it feels like to lose with a lead. But you can't play 'ifs'. The past is past."

Sneed, his face a mask of utter dejection, said, "It'll be tough to forget this, but I'll have to put it out of my life.

"I played awfully well this week.

"Maybe next time."

1980

In 1980, Jack Nicklaus' record of major championships stood at 17. After 23-year-old Seve Ballesteros won the Masters that year, Jack said that of all those playing the game at the time, the young Spaniard had the best chance of winning more majors than he had.

Some players have the ability to excite you, something beyond their golf shots, something that makes you realize you're watching something special. Arnold Palmer had it. Tiger Woods has it. Ballesteros had it. He was powerful, but could play shots around the greens so well, the other golfers marveled. He had nerve, a sense of humor, good looks, and a sense of the dramatic. You could never be bored following him around a golf course. Of all the players I've ever watched, he is one of three or four whom I enjoyed watching most.

Unfortunately, Ballesteros played only a few tournaments in this country each year, choosing to play a heavy schedule on the European Tour. As time went by, Ballesteros demonstrated, through his words, a resentment toward the United States media and PGA tour commissioner Deane Beman, who refused to bend the rules to let Ballesteros play here when he chose if he didn't play the required 15 U.S. events.

The fans never stopped following him and cheering for him, except for one instance I can recall. That was in 1986, when he was threatening to win the Masters again and was battling the 46-year-old Jack Nicklaus around the back nine. While Nicklaus was playing No. 16, Seve was in the fairway on No. 15, needing only a four-iron to clear the water in front of the green on the par-five hole. He made a poor swing and hooked the ball into the pond, and the crowd, so anxious for Nicklaus to win, cheered.

MEET TOM WEISKOPF, NOW HERO
TO THE COMMON MAN

In 15 minutes Thursday, Tom Weiskopf erased—at least for a while—the image it took him 15 years on the pro golf tour to build.

From Tall Tom, the Towering Inferno, the angry and often arrogant villain with one of the game's grandest swings, he became a man America's hackers could love.

He made a 13 on a par-three hole and shot 85 in the opening round of the Masters tournament.

Ordinarily, Weiskopf and his fellow professionals hit shots and make scores the Saturday morning sufferers at Hog Wallow Golf and Grill can't truly comprehend.

But today Weiskopf is a hero of the common man.

Is there one among us who hasn't hacked out a 13 or worse, all logic fleeing from our addled minds, leaving us staring dumbly at the terrifying possibility that we might never finish the hole?

While we feel sympathy for Weiskopf, always a threat to win this great championship, we also feel a certain exultation that it can happen to the best as well as to us.

It happened to Weiskopf on the 12th, a 155-yard hole sitting in a picturesque hollow known as Amen Corner. It looks harmless and is known as Golden Bell for the flora behind it.

But it's actually the most dreaded hole on the course, because the wind swirls down there, and it's always a guess as to which club to use to hit to the skinny green.

Too much club, and you're up on a steep hillside. Too little and you're in Rae's Creek, which flows gently in front of the green. Weiskopf chose the creek for his disaster.

He hit a seven-iron off the tee. The ball cleared the creek but hit short of the green and trickled back into the water. "It was a pretty good shot," said Weiskopf, dressed appropriately in gloomy greys and blacks but remarkably serene in the clubhouse.

He walked down near the water's edge, from where he could've thrown the ball over the water underhanded if it were allowed. He dropped a ball, pitched over, and watched in dismay as it, too, fell short of the green and rolled back into the brook.

He dropped three more balls and knocked all three into the water, never clearing the hazard with either. Finally, he put one on the green and two-putted for his 13.

And his Masters was, for all intents and purposes, dead, drowned in Rae's Creek.

"There was no grass, I mean no grass, in that designated drop zone," said Weiskopf by way of explanation.

Asked why he didn't exercise his option to drop as far back as he chose, someplace where there was more grass, he said—and we can understand this—"When you screw up that bad, you're gonna stand there until you do it right.

"I saw Hogan do the same thing one time at the Champions Tournament. He knocked three balls in the water, two of them from a drop area. When somebody asked why he didn't drop farther back, he said he was going to do it until he got it right.

"That's how I felt."

It wasn't the first 13 ever made here, but it broke Dow Finsterwald's record 11 on the 12th and tied the record for highest on any hole set by Tsuneyuki Nakajima of Japan on the par-five 13th. It was Weiskopf's first double figure ever on the tour.

The worst he can recall having made was an eight on the 18th at Pebble Beach in 1972.

"It was extremely embarrassing to make 13, but more than that, it was very disappointing," Weiskopf said. "There must have been some English people or people of English heritage in the crowd, because when I finished, I got light applause. In England, that's called sympathy applause."

TALK OF THE TOWN

CONSENSUS AT CONCLUSION OF THE MASTERS:
SEVE BALLESTEROS IS ALREADY SOMETHING SPECIAL

The battle had ended, and the smoke was settling late Sunday afternoon over Augusta National golf course, and Severaiano Ballesteros had won the 44th Masters.

As the golfing world contemplated the enormity of the young Spaniard's conquest, one of those who had fought him hardest brought it into focus.

David Graham, finishing six strokes behind Ballesteros' 275 total for 72 holes, despite some of his finest golf, said, "At the age of 23, you just don't tee it up at Augusta National and go out there and win the golf tournament unless you're something special, and I think we all agree, Seve's something special."

More special, perhaps, than most of us can yet comprehend because of the breadth of his talent and charm.

He is younger—three months younger than Jack Nicklaus was when he won the first of his five Masters titles. He is very long, but has a surgeon's touch. He is handsome, so much so that young women have been constantly calling or dropping by the home where he stayed here. He has a keen sense of humor. He has nerve. He has dedication.

He has it all.

Nicklaus says that of all those playing the game today, Ballesteros has the best chance of breaking his record of 17 major championships.

Many say he is the most exciting player to emerge since Arnold Palmer. Ballesteros says he appreciates such comparisons with the great Palmer, but adds, "I don't think I'm as exciting as Palmer."

Ballesteros has been known to the world for only four years but already has 25 victories, including the British Open last year.

This in itself is remarkable. It becomes even more so when you consider that he grew up as the son of a dairy farmer in

Spain, where only the well-to-do ordinarily play the game and relatively few of those.

But his brother, Manuel, was a professional, and young Seve fell under his influence. When he was nine, Ballesteros acquired a 3-iron.

He sneaked onto a course early in the morning and late in the afternoon to play, using the 3-iron for every shot, and at night he would practice putting in the family barn.

"He had a love of golf you could almost touch," said Manuel, who was here to embrace his brother when he won. "Without a golf club in his hand, he was a man with no legs. It was part of him. Without it, he did not exist. You never saw Seve without that club."

Jack Newton played the final round Sunday with Ballesteros and was one of those who put the most heat on him, once pulling within three shots of the lead when Ballesteros finally faltered briefly on the last nine.

Newton, who tied Gibby Gilbert for second, four strokes behind the champion, said, "Seve's a great player. It seems everybody thinks he's been lucky, probably because of the British Open last year (when Ballesteros hit only 14 fairways in 72 holes and made some miraculous recoveries).

"But this week has driven home the fact that this fellow is a great player. It takes a lot of guts to win a major championship, and he's won two of them."

Guts. Heart. Nerve. Call it what you will, the demand on Ballesteros during these four days was punishing, largely because he led all the way, tying Graham for the front with an opening 66, then moving away alone with a 69 on Friday and a 68 on Saturday that left him leading by seven strokes.

"This was the hardest victory," said Ballesteros. "I had so much pressure all week. At the British Open, I felt more comfortable, maybe because I felt more at home and I had so many friends there."

When he made the nine-hole turn Sunday, he had built his lead to 10 strokes, and the only question that seemed to remain was whether he could break the tournament record of 271 set in 1965 by Nicklaus and tied in 1976 by Raymond Floyd.

But there is an age-old theory here that the tournament is never secured until you've played that dreadful last nine holes, and it held true.

Ballesteros bogeyed the 10th, double-bogeyed the 12th when a gust of wind threw him off and he hit into the water, and bogeyed the 13th when a second shot found water. Newton and Gilbert, meanwhile, were making birdies and, suddenly, his lead was down to two.

Looking back on that stunning turn of events, Ballesteros said, "I said to myself, 'You are so stupid. You were comfortable, and now you must try very hard or you are going to lose the tournament.'"

His tee shot on No. 14 hit a tree limb and kicked far to the left, but he fetched up one of his remarkable recovery shots and salvaged a par. Then he birdied the 15th, and when Newton failed to birdie there, it was finished.

Ballesteros finished with a 72 and was rewarded with $55,000 and the green jacket symbolic of victory in this most glamorous of championships. Gilbert birdied the 13th through the 16th and shot 67, and Newton finished with a 68, each collecting $30,500.

The gloomy day, which held a threat of rain that never fell, was brightened before the title chase began by the pairing of Palmer and Nicklaus, who have fought and won so many wars.

Theirs was a lovely march around the green hills and valleys, not so much for the quality of the golf as for the memories it evoked and the thrills it generated for the galloping, roaring crowd.

Palmer and Nicklaus were applauded at every green and accorded a standing ovation at the 18th as they climbed together the hill where Nicklaus has won five times, Palmer four.

They joked later about playing for last place, but Palmer, who shot a 69 after three 73s, and Nicklaus, who had his second straight 73 after 74 and 71, admitted they were playing each other.

With Nicklaus nodding in agreement, Palmer said, "I don't think Jack and I have ever played together when we didn't compete with each other, whether it was for first in the U.S. Open or last in the Masters. I think we'll always compete—until Jack gets too old."

The laughter died, and the two aging warriors went their separate ways. As he was leaving the press room, Palmer was asked about Ballesteros.

Wistfully, he said, "I used to play like that."

1981

In 1981, Tom Watson was in the fifth year of a six-year run as the best player in the world. From 1977 through 1982, he won 26 tournaments, including two Masters, a U.S. Open, and three British Opens. In the '82 Masters, he fended off the great Jack Nicklaus and the explosive Johnny Miller on the final day.

His record in the Masters has been remarkable. He tied for eighth the first time he played, in 1975, and over the next 15 years, he won twice, had three seconds, one third, one fourth, and finished in the top 10 on 13 occassions. As late as 1997, he had a fourth.

Early in his career, Watson had developed a reputation for being unable to finish when he was in position to win, but after his Masters win in '82, Nicklaus said of him, "The strongest part of Tom's game is mental toughness."

Nicklaus had seen it up close four years earlier in a more memorable battle, when they went head-to head-over the last 36 holes of the British Open at Turnberry in what has been called by some the greatest championship ever. Watson's scores were 65-65, Nicklaus' 65-66. Watson won by one, holing a four-footer on the last after Nicklaus had holed a birdie putt from behind the green.

TALK OF THE MASTERS: JITTERS

What they were saying after the opening round of the Masters:

Lanny Wadkins, 72: "I was totally relaxed all week. Then, walking from the practice green to the first tee, wham, it hit me. I said, 'Hey, I've gotta get hold of myself.' But after I bogeyed the first hole, I came back to reality."

Peter Jacobsen, 71: "This was my first Masters round, and I was nervous for the first few holes, but it was tremendous. I loved it."

Greg Norman, 69: "Just being here is probably the greatest thrill of my life. When I turned pro, my ambition was to play Augusta National. I feel very comfortable. I enjoy playing the course. It suits my game. David Graham told me a lot about the course, and said I have the game to win here."

HIS HEART, GAME THE PERFECT PAIR, TOM SHOWS WHY HE'S A MASTER

Throughout the long Sunday afternoon, smothering tension had lain across the green hills of Augusta National Golf Club.

Tom Watson had begun the final round of the Masters leading by a single shot. He never managed to extend it to more than three—that for only a short time.

Golf's most feared animal, Golden Bear Jack Nicklaus, and the game's most dangerous streak player, Johnny Miller, fired at him, along with young Australian Greg Norman and veteran John Mahaffey.

But Watson stood them off. He shot a one-under-par 71 across greens so slick you needed spikes to walk on them. With that solid round of 71-68-70, he won his second Masters with a 280 total, eight shots better than par and two shots better than Nicklaus and Miller, who tied for second.

Nicklaus, who numbers five Masters among his 19 major championships, summed up what happened out there in this grim drama that unfolded in front of tens of thousands of sun-pinked spectators.

"He never let anything happen to him," said Nicklaus.

"He got himself into trouble at 13 when he hit his second shot into the creek but he made his par. He ran his putt by (about three feet) at 15 and saw me make my putt (a 23-foot birdie putt that raised a roar that shook the pines) on 16, but he made that putt for his birdie and that wasn't easy, I don't care how short it was. Then on No. 17, he made par out of a bunker.

"It's not hard to let things get away from you out there, but he never did.

"The strongest part of Tom's game is mental toughness."

"That's a nice thing for him to say about my golf game," said Watson.

It was sweet satisfaction for the champion.

It brought back memories of several years ago when Watson wore the label of a choker. He crumbled enough times—some of them in major championships—to raise speculation that his heart was a poor companion for his exquisite game.

But Watson has erased that notion. For the last four years, he's been golf's most successful campaigner in a landslide, leading in money winnings and earning Player of the Year honors all four years and three times taking the Vardon Trophy for lowest scoring average. In those four years, he won 20 tournaments, including his first Masters, and two of his three British Opens.

It nevertheless came down Sunday not to whether someone else would win the tournament, but whether Watson would lose it.

He never flinched.

Miller, who has been noted for his spectacular bursts of scoring since he won the U.S. Open in 1973, coming out of the pack the last day with a 64, hoped to crack Watson with his heroics. Playing an hour ahead of Watson, Miller tore off seven birdies (and three bogeys) to get in with a 68 and a 282 total. Watson was still on the 14th hole when he saw Miller's score go up.

"I'm very happy to at least let Watson know I was around, even if I don't win," said Miller. "I wanted to let him know somebody was putting some heat on him besides Nicklaus."

Watson stood a shot ahead of Miller at the time. He said it didn't bother him. He was more concerned with Nicklaus and Norman, who were still out there with him and could do something about their own fate.

"I just said, 'Okay, I've got to birdie the 15th and par in from there.' I felt that way because 15 (a par five) is the last real birdie hole on the course, and I wanted as much cushion as I could get in case one of them got hot," he said.

"After I birdied the 15th, I said, 'Okay, the championship's yours if you just par in." Nicklaus birdied 15 and 16, but I had a two-stroke lead and knew the worst I could do if I parred in was tie."

He stunned the crowd on the par-four 17th, where he plopped a simple wedge shot into the front bunker. Was this where he would blow it? He had bogeyed the hole on Friday and double-bogeyed it on Saturday—from that same trap.

Wasting no time, Watson walked into the sand, blasted out to within four feet of the cup, and knocked it in.

"I never thought about missing that putt," he said.

"And when I made it, I said, 'The championship is mine.'"

1982

When you think of the Masters, you think of beautiful spring days, but there have been some days when even Augusta National looked grim. The weather during the first day of the 1982 Masters was chilly and rainy and some of the players simply couldn't cope with that and the thin fairways and fast greens.

Frank Conner shot an 89, Jim Thorpe an 88, 68-year-old Herman Keiser a 93, Doug Ford an 86.

Dan Pohl opened with a pair of 75s, which often would get you a ticket out of town, but from there, the Masters rookie went on to tie Craig Stadler after 72 holes, thanks in large part to a Saturday streak in which he eagled the 13th and 14th holes and birdied the 15th and 16th en route to a 67.

Stadler parred the first extra hole to win and strike a blow for dumpy guys with short tempers. He's actually a likeable fellow, but he wasn't always, and his habit of showing his emotions when things don't go so well out there make him appear volatile. Curiously, Stadler was one over par on the par fives, which usually means finishing well back in the field, but he did some good work on the others.

WALRUS WOWS 'EM

Well, now we've seen it all.

A man with a weight problem whose nickname is "Walrus" and whose sartorial and behavioral habits had been called into question over the years has won the Masters Golf Tournament.

Not someone with a heroic nickname like the "Golden Bear" or "Tom Terrific." Not someone who models sportswear or does TV commercials or melts the women in the gallery with his smile.

There were plenty of those types hovering around the lead when Sunday's final round started. But Craig Stadler, lumbering along with a pronounced heel-and-toe walk and preceded by a moustache with which you could thatch a hut, beat them all. He built a big early lead, saw it melt in the punishing pressure of the back nine and then recovered to beat Dan Pohl with a par on the first hole of a sudden-death playoff to claim one of golf's grandest prizes.

Our nature being what it is, placing almost as much importance on the appearance as on the talent of our sports stars, it was difficult to envision the beefy Stadler pulling on the green jacket symbolic of the championship, even if he did start the day three shots ahead.

There were the usual sort of jokes that follow Stadler around—"They're tearing down one of the concession tents to make a jacket for Stadler."

All of this, of course, has nothing to do with Stadler the golfer. He may look like a guy who puts in eight hours a day and then sits in front of the TV set with a six-pack, but when he steps to the tee, he can show you some golf that is as elegant as just about anything the glamor boys can manage.

A victory at Tucson and in the Masters and $211,000 in winnings in 1982 attest to that. This year, the flat-bellied blond guys are chasing the fat man.

Shooting 33 on the front side, Stadler, 28 years old, 5-foot-10, 216 pounds, built his lead to six shots over Pohl, Curtis Strange, Tom Kite, Tom Weiskopf, and Seve Ballesteros. Jack Nicklaus and Tom Watson, who collect major championships like add-a-beads, were out of it, coughing in his smoke.

Stadler stumbled with bogeys on the 12th, 14th, and 16th holes, and when he three-putted the 18th from 35-feet for another bogey that left him with a 73, he found himself tied at 284 with Pohl, who had shot his second straight 67.

They went to the 10th hole, a diving, curving 480-yard par four, to settle it. Both drove long and accurately. Stadler hit a seven-iron onto the green. Pohl, who is the tour's longest hitter but had only won $6,000 this year, hit his approach to the right of the green. Pohl putted up eight feet from the cup and, after Stadler had parred, Pohl missed, and the "Walrus" was the champion.

And suddenly the jokes weren't funny anymore.

Stadler's image was built early. When he was playing for the Southern Cal golf team, he sometimes showed up for matches with mixed shoes—one black and one white or two left shoes. His shirttail was always out. Some say he majored in Santa Anita Race Track. He had a temper like Mount St. Helens.

It's been denied, but there was a report that Stadler was left off the 1973 Walker Cup team because he was, how shall we say it, a slob. He showed 'em, though, winning the U.S. Amateur the week after the Cup matches.

He's tried in recent years to clean up his act and succeeded to some extent.

At the insistence of his wife, Sue, he lost 40 pounds but said he felt more comfortable between 205 and 220 and put some of the weight back on. He doesn't throw his clubs quite as hard now when he misses a shot. And while clothing companies aren't fighting for his name on a contract, he no longer looks like something piled on the floor of a laundromat.

He was so disagreeable in the British Amateur one year, his caddy quit on him in mid-round, and the gallery applauded.

"You don't like to read that your husband is a fat man," said Sue Stadler, "but Craig seems to handle those things pretty well. He gets mad on the course, but he almost never gets mad at home."

The Stadlers have, in fact, made the best of the situation. One of the family's cars bears a license plate that reads "Walruz," (Walrus had already been taken). One of their son's playthings is a stuffed walrus.

The nickname comes from his round, slope-shouldered build and his lush moustache.

While others may not take him seriously, Stadler's fellow golfers do. He's won five tour events since turning pro in 1976 and has career earnings of more than $800,000.

His victory here was marked by two distinct aspects —his relatively poor play on the par-five holes—where veterans say you must score to win a Masters—and his late collapse.

Although he's a long hitter, he was one over par on the par fives for the four rounds, a statistic that ordinarily would have eliminated him from the chase. (Pohl, by comparison, was six under on the fives.)

After making birdies on the par-five second, the par-three sixth, and the par-four seventh Sunday, Stadler had what would have been a near-certain victory wrapped up on most other courses. But history shows that the back nine here, which yields a lot of low scores during the first three rounds, can and often does break the back of a title bid.

It got Stadler, just as it has gotten so many others.

After shooting 33 on the front nine with birdies at the second, sixth, and seventh holes, Stadler missed five greens on the second nine, got a lucky break when his second shot to a par-five 13th hung on a bank of a creek, hit his second shot to the par-five 15th into a bunker, and then three-putted the 18th. Not exactly championship stuff.

"On 18 I thought I had hit the putt to within a couple of feet of the cup," said Stadler, "but I was in a slow place on the green, if there was such a thing as a slow place on these greens this week."

The ball stopped eight feet short, and he missed his next putt. Suddenly, all of his lead was gone, and he was starting all over.

When Pohl missed the putt that could have kept him alive in the playoff—an eight-footer that slid just to the left of the cup—Stadler stood looking stunned.

"When he missed it," he said, "I thought, 'Oh, my gosh, he missed,' but it took about 10 seconds for me to realize I had really won."

"On the 18th hole, I still thought I was playing for second place," said Pohl. "Some officials told me to stick around, though, because I might be in a playoff. I went to the practice putting green, and an official with a radio told me what was going on.

"I'd be a fool to say I wasn't nervous in the playoff. It was the first time I'd ever been in a position like that and the first time I'd played in the Masters.

"I played my second shot on the playoff hole to hook from a sidehill lie but it stayed right. I was a little tentative with my approach putt, and then I misread the next one.

"I let him off with a relatively easy playoff win, I guess, but I came here with no confidence because of the way I was playing and I didn't get any until the third round. So, I don't feel I lost. I feel I won because I put on a good show."

1983

Little things sometimes capture our fancy more than the big ones. Seve Ballesteros, whose Hollywood looks, exquisite talent ,and daring play drew large galleries, won the championship for the second time.

But the tournament was also noteworthy for some milestones. Elizabeth Archer, George Archer's daughter, became the first woman to caddy at Augusta National when she carried her father's clubs. The practice range was lengthened, and a 30-foot-high fence was put up to keep shots from going into Washington Road, but Dan Pohl, longest hitter on the tour, cleared the barrier several times. And for the first time, range balls were offered by the Masters. Before 1983, players brought their own practice balls in a shag bag, and their caddies stood out in the range to retrieve them. For safety's sake, the Masters decreed that players must use range balls provided by the club, but gave the players a choice of six brands.

There was one other milestone. Three-time champion Sam Snead, 71, played in his last Masters.

The tournament ended on a Monday because of bad weather.

I was among more than two dozen writers who trailed Calvin Peete into the locker room after he shot a horrible 87 in the third round. Scott Hoch saw us and called us "a bunch of vultures." But it was a big story.

Peete was one of the straightest, steadiest players on the PGA Tour. How could he blow to such a big number?

And he was one of the first black players to make it into the Masters. He had said earlier in the week that the Masters was overrated, that it was just another golf tournament, and now we were asking him if he still felt that way.

Peete handled his disappointment and our overwhelming presence well.

Ballesteros won for the second time. He was quite a bit testier in victory than Peete had been in failure. Seve has always felt he didn't get credit in this country for being the great player that he was. He made that clear in his press conferences, but it was usually couched in a bit of humor and veiled with a smile.

He could be funny, almost as entertaining in conversation as he was on the course.

I thought at the time that he was the best in the game and easily the most exciting. He didn't play enough in this country for Americans to get to know him well—and that was America's loss.

He could play.

NOTES AND OBSERVATIONS

Defending champion Craig Stadler donated the putter he used to win the Masters last year to Augusta National Golf Club for the collection it has on display in glass cases around the clubhouse.

A couple of weeks ago, he borrowed a putter from Ben Crenshaw, and the hot-tempered Stadler said wryly, "It has about 40 less cart-path marks and about 20 less spike marks than the one I was using." In other words, it hasn't suffered being whacked on the paths and stepped on—yet.

This is Sam Snead's last Masters. Nearing age 71, Snead, playing in his 41st Masters, says he no longer wants to "clutter up the field" when he's not a serious contender.

Arnold Palmer says, "Sam still has one of the finest swings in the world and still looks good swinging a club. In the years I've played golf with Sam, I think that swing rubbed off on me. I don't mean I tried to imitate it. It was just good for me to be around that swing."

SUN SHINES ON WHAT COULD BE CLASSICAL FINISH IN THE MASTERS

This has been the most troubled Masters ever. Thursday's opening round was interrupted by a rain delay, Friday was washed out by heavy rains that flooded parts of the course.

Saturday dawned rainy. Jack Nicklaus, a five-time winner here, had to withdraw because of a back problem. Rain pelted the course all day, but the golfers kept going until darkness finally prevented two threesomes from completing play. That canceled plans for a 36-hole Sunday finish, with the final round being pushed back to Monday. The two threesomes completed their rounds Sunday morning, after which the third round was played.

FOR PEETE'S SAKE!

Calvin Peete came walking into the locker room at the Augusta National Clubhouse, trailed by about 30 writers.

Scott Hoch, who had finished the third round of the Masters a few minutes before Peete, looked at the mass of people going past him and said, "What'd you shoot, Cal?"

Peete said, "I didn't play very well. I shot 87."

"Well, what is this then?" Hoch said, looking at the scribes, "A bunch of vultures?"

Hoch doesn't understand. If Peete had shot 87 anywhere, which he said he'd never done in his life until this bright, windy Sunday, it would've been news. When he shoots it at the Masters, it's even bigger news.

Peete, one of the few black players competing at the top level of pro golf, is the very picture of consistency. Read the weekly tour statistics. He hits more fairways and greens than a rainstorm. Tell him to hit it down a sidestreet and he'll ask, "Left lane or right?" He's invariably in the top 10 listings of fairways and greens hit in regulation, usually at the top. He's the straightest shooter since John Wayne.

It all fell apart on him Sunday, though, and from a position of contention at two under par after shooting 70-72 in the first two rounds, he was tied with Bob Shearer for 48th and last place at the end of the day.

The wind, the testy golf course, and the heat of the competition in this grand championship dashed many a hope Sunday. Shearer shot 82 with a 10 on the par-five 13th hole. Gil Morgan, leading after two rounds at seven under par, staggered to a 76. Bruce Lietzke, even par after 36, shot 82. Fred Couples, within four shots of the lead after two rounds, crashed with an 81. Former U.S. Open champion David Graham came in with a blushing 80. And so it went.

Nothing shocking there. On a gusty day, this course will break your heart and your back. But when Calvin Peete shoots 87, that's shocking.

What made the experience even more painful for Peete was the fact that earlier in the week, he had said, essentially, that the Masters is overrated and is just another golf tournament.

A heckler reminded him of that on the 16th hole Sunday. He yelled to Peete, "What are you going to say about the Masters now?"

Peete responded, "I'm glad to know you can read."

Sitting in the locker room now, buried beneath the crush of newsmen, Peete said he didn't mean to suggest that the Masters wasn't a great event, he was just saying the golf course was for spectators and long hitters and he wasn't either of those.

"Asking a black man about the tradition of the Masters is like asking him if he enjoyed his forefathers being slaves," said Peete, one of only three blacks to have ever qualified for the tournament. "I was just expressing my feeling about the course. It's a great golf course for Tom Watson and Jack Nicklaus and all the long hitters who can hit the par 5s in two and hit their drives to all the level spots. But it's too long for me. It's hard to hit a three-wood off a sidehill lie."

That, in golfing terms, pretty well sums up what happened to Peete. Those who play this fickle game know the awful feeling of having the wheels run off, of hitting three-woods from sidehill lies for 18 holes.

Peete, though, is not accustomed to putting such ugly numbers on the board. "I lost count out there," he said, shaking his visored head.

"After the first nine, I wasn't really trying to get it back together. I was just trying to get in without hurting myself."

Peete started the day with a par—hitting a three- wood from an uphill lie on the par-four hole because his tee shot wasn't powerful enough to carry to the crest of the hill, where most of the pros carry it and get a good roll.

Then he double-bogeyed the second, parred the third and fourth, and double-bogeyed the fifth. After that, he said, he thought it would be almost impossible for him to salvage a good round. His iron shot on the par-three sixth landed on the green and backed off, and he made a bogey, and it was a disaster after that.

He parred the seventh, bogeyed the eighth and ninth, double-bogeyed the 10th, bogeyed the 11th, and made a seven on the par-three 12th, hitting two balls into Rae's Creek. He strung together five pars after that but finished with a bogey.

How could this happen to Mr. Consistency?

"This is the only course I've played on the tour that I don't think I can win on," he said. "I came because it's the Masters, and I wanted to be a part of it. But everybody in the field would have to break a leg for me to win here.

"I shot those good scores in the first two rounds because a lot of good things happened to me. My biggest mistake today was trying to play better than I can. I felt I was going to have to play better than usual today because the course was wet, and the wind was blowing, and I had to hit some woods to par four holes. I couldn't even reach the 10th hole (a par four)."

Someone asked Peete if he was thinking of withdrawing after his dismal Sunday.

"No, I'm not going to quit because I shot a bad round," he said. "You've got to take the bitter with the sweet. I'm just anxious for tomorrow to come. I want to go out and let myself know that I'm not an 87 shooter."

Do you think you'll go home and replay all the bad shots tonight, a questioner wanted to know.

"No," said Peete, smiling and standing up to signal the end of the conversation, "I'm gonna go home and get drunk."

HOW GOOD IS HE?
WE MIGHT FIND OUT IF MASTERS CHAMP
SEVE BALLESTEROS WOULD
STICK AROUND FOR A WHILE

With just seven artistic swings of his woods and irons and five brush strokes of his putter in the span of only 40 minutes, Seve Ballesteros won his second Masters championship Monday.

There was still the matter of playing out the round with such giants of golf as Craig Stadler, Raymond Floyd, and Tom Watson in hot pursuit, but the dashing, 26-year-old Spaniard managed that with a minimum of difficulty. The others, who had been expected to make this a memorable finish, fell away on this sunny, windy day, leaving him to march up the last fairway a comfortable four strokes ahead of his closest challengers.

Ballesteros, starting the day in third place, one stroke behind Stadler and Floyd and one shot ahead of Watson, roared out of the gate with a birdie three on the first hole, an eagle three on the second, a par four on the third, and a birdie two on the fourth to lead by three shots. Watson closed to within two shots with an eagle three on the eighth hole, but that was as close as anyone would come to overtaking Ballesteros.

Ballesteros' third major championship and 30th professional tournament victory since 1974, and the manner in which he achieved it, should erase any doubts that might have lingered about his place among the best playing the game today. But his responses to questioning by newsmen after the round hinted that he suspects such is not the case.

On Sunday, when he was asked if he would ever play the U.S. tour full time, he said no, that he was content playing closer to home. When the question was raised again Monday, though, his striking features clouded over and he said, "One year, I will come over here and play full time to see how good I am." Ballesteros plays only a handful of tournaments in this country each year.

He got good breaks on the 12th and 13th holes, but when he was questioned about them, Ballesteros continued a theme that has run through his conversation here. He said, "I just have a lucky week, that's all. Why do you only ask me about my bad shots?"

He smiles when he says those things, but he seems to resent any suggestions that he is lucky. That may date back to 1979, when he hit only 18 fairways in 72 holes—once driving into a parking lot—but won the British Open, and much was made of his good fortune.

He also responds in a condescending fashion to questions about his ability with the driver. He says that only in America is he considered a wild hitter off the tee. "In Spain," he said, "they think I'm a straight driver."

But if Ballesteros is touchy about such things, he needn't be. Players like Ben Crenshaw and Tom Kite—who came from well back to tie for second place at 284, Crenshaw with a 68 and Kite with a 69—hail him as a great player.

Crenshaw adds, "He's the most exciting player. It's unbelievable. He's sorta like the Arnold Palmer of old. And he has shots other people don't know about. He's not as wild as people think. He just hits it so far, he's going to hit a wild shot once in a while."

The cluster of four former Masters champions— Ballesteros, Floyd, Stadler, and Watson—at the top starting Monday's final round presented the likelihood of a roaring battle throughout the bright, gusty afternoon with dramatic twists of fortune. But the Spaniard choked that possibility with his blazing start and his steadfast refusal to come back to the field.

He hit a seven-iron approach eight feet from the cup on the first hole and made the putt for a birdie. He hit a three-wood second some 245 yards to within 15 feet on the long second and dropped that putt for an eagle. He routinely parred the third, then knifed a two-iron 205 yards to within two feet of the hole on the par-three fourth and made that.

"On this course," he said, "the key is you have to wait for the birdies. On the last round, if you try to make birdies, if you play aggressive on this course, it will kill you."

Floyd, Stadler, Watson, and the others had to try to make birdies once Ballesteros had seized his lead and wouldn't buckle. Watson eagled the eighth hole to get within two shots, but Ballesteros quickly answered with a birdie on the ninth, as Watson three-putted for the first of three straight bogeys. And with his five-under-par 31, Ballesteros led the field by four shots.

He could have made a big number on the 12th hole when his tee shot on the watery, windswept par three carried into bushes up a hill behind the green. But the ball bounced backward out of the undergrowth, leaving him a clear chip shot with which he salvaged a bogey.

He drove into trees on the par-five 13th but had an opening through which he could pitch out. He then hit a three-iron about 200 yards to the green. He aimed to the left of the flag, which was set near Rae's Creek, but the shot plopped down to the right of the cup, within a few feet of the water. Another yard to the right, and he might have been in the ditch, but he came away with a par.

From then on, it was smooth sailing.

Kite said, "Ballesteros got off to such a great start, he kind of put a damper on everybody's spirits out there. Birdie, eagle, par, birdie. That's like driving a Ferrari and everybody else out there is driving a Chevrolet. He just blasted us."

With his eagle and three birdies, Ballesteros almost equaled the total output of subpar holes by Watson, Floyd, and Stadler. Between them, they had one eagle and five birdies as they struggled with the course, the wind, and the screeching tires of the Ferrari.

1984

We watched Ben Crenshaw grow up, not actually seeing him, but reading and hearing about him as he came along, winning amateur titles and three straight NCAA titles, winning the PGA Tour qualifying tournament by 12 strokes, and then winning his first pro tournament and finishing second in his second.

A lot of expectations come along with such a fast start. In the ensuing years, Crenshaw proved to be a good player but not a great one. He was always one of the most popular players on the tour and a media favorite, but we had just about decided he would never win a major championship when he proved us wrong and won the 1984 Masters.

He won it on one of those Sunday afternoons when things are exploding all over the back nine. He holed a 60-foot putt on the 10th and then made a two on the wicked little par-three 12th. Larry Nelson's bid died at No. 12 when he hit into the water. Tom Kite fared worse. He hit two into Rae's Creek there and triple bogeyed. Mark Lye, who had also been in hot pursuit, cooled and Crenshaw won by two.

It's safe to say that nobody ever enjoyed putting on the green jacket more than Crenshaw. He loves golf, loves its history, reveres Augusta. And on him, it looked good.

SAD BUT TRUE, NICKLAUS
FACES UP TO REALITY

Jack Nicklaus and Hale Irwin, putting some finishing touches on their golf games in preparation for the start of the Masters today, were standing on the 13th tee in Wednesday's sunshine, waiting to hit their tee shots.

It's nice there, wooded and flowery with Rae's Creek babbling past. But it's also a place where reality steps up to greet you when you are 44 years old, as is Nicklaus, or 38, as is Irwin.

It's a par five that used to be a piece of cake. Now it's a piece of work.

"Jack, see those trees out there?" said Irwin. "We used to hit an easy three-wood around the corner of those trees and hit a little six-iron to the green. Now, we're hitting drivers. We're playing a different game than we used to play."

Sad to say, but true.

Nicklaus related that story late Wednesday to illustrate why he is no longer the dominant player in golf, why he has won only one tournament (the 1982 Colonial Invitational) since 1980, and hwy he has no majors to add to his remarkable record of 19 since the 1980 U.S. Open. And no Masters since he fought off Johnny Miller and Tom Weiskopf in the greatest finish this storied old event has seen to win his fifth in 1975.

It's not outside business interests, not loss of enthusiasm, and not lack of desire that have kept him from adding to his 69 U.S. titles and 87 worldwide. It's age and the growing strength of the competition, he said.

Nicklaus remains the golden god of golf, unchallenged in glorious achievement. He is the standard by which all grand golfing feats are measured.

But he said, "I'm simply not quite as good a golfer as I used to be. I am still capable of winning but not as capable as I was. I don't think I can dominate again. If I could win a couple of majors this year, that would be domination enough for me."

STUNNING PUTT PUT CRENSHAW ATOP MASTERS

On Saturday, Ben Crenshaw had risked the lightning playing around Augusta National Golf Club to get a 100-foot putt on the 13th hole out of the way. Play was being suspended for the day, and he didn't want to face that dragon first thing in the morning.

Sunday, on a fine day when the only thunder to be heard was rising from the throats of the galleries caught up in the drama unfolding around the course, he hurled a lightning bolt of his own. And he rode it to the Masters championship that has been his dream for much of his lifetime.

Crenshaw is one of the best putters on the face of the earth, but when he turned up with a putt on the 10th that was longer than a Texas highway, his only thought was to get it close and, failing that, keep it somewhere on the green.

He caressed it with a putter his father gave him for his 15th birthday, waited, waited, and finally raised his arms in triumph as it fell in. Sixty feet, he guessed, with cliffs waiting on the other side.

"When I made that putt, I thought maybe, just maybe, this was my day," said Crenshaw.

He had come there with a one-shot lead over Tom Kite, the third-round leader, and a two-stroke edge over Mark Lye, who led after two rounds. They were standing on the hillside looking down on the 10th green, waiting to hit their approach shots, when Crenshaw's monster putt went in.

"Boy, when we saw his putt go in on 10," said Lye, "it was like the lights went out. We knew it was going to be tough for him to get down in two. When he made it, you could see it hurt Kite. It broke Tom's back."

Crenshaw didn't seal his victory on the 10th, of course. There was too much peril lurking on those last eight holes, and there were too many people still hot on his heels.

But it made him think, after having lost two U.S. Opens, a British Open, and a PGA championship in the final hour, that his time may have come.

And, when Kite and Lye bogeyed the 10th, it gave him a three-shot edge. Kite triple-bogeyed the 12th to kill himself off, and Lye couldn't muster anything but pars from there in.

The 12th took care of the rest of it, although that didn't become apparent until a while later. Not only did Rae's Creek— babbling in front of the 12th, an innocuous-looking par three of only 155 yards—claim two of Kite's balls, it gulped down one of Larry Nelson's. Until then, Nelson, playing two groups ahead of Crenshaw, was on a roll, four under par for the day and within a shot of the lead. He took a double bogey and didn't seriously threaten again.

Crenshaw, on the other hand, played the devilish 12th in two.

"I was really proud of the shot I hit there," he said. It was a six-iron 13 feet from the hole. "I was determined to make that putt," said the master of the putting game, and that was that.

"No. 12 was the hole," said Nick Faldo, who was paired with Crenshaw. "Oh, that was it."

And so, Gentle Ben Crenshaw, who burst on the pro scene by winning his first tournament and finishing second in the next and then began a one-year journey of dramatic ups and downs, fulfilled his dream. He found himself walking at long last up the final fairway with tens of thousands standing and showering him warmly with applause, a major championship his.

The failures when the big ones were within his reach, the dismal slump that wrecked his game for a year and a half, the questions that have dogged him around the world when he couldn't be what they said he would be, the new Ben Hogan, were gone. In their place, as he walked up that fairway, smiling and waving, were thoughts of his days when he was playing high school golf. Why? He didn't know. But it was a nice thing to think about at that moment.

1985

Some of us media types always make a mental note of what the contenders are wearing when they show up for the final round on Sunday. There was a time when you could attach some significance to that, or we thought there was, anyway. How would that day's outfit look with a green jacket draped over it?

We assumed that the contender had given that some thought, and that those who dressed to accommodate the green coat were the ones who honestly thought they could win.

Bernhard Langer, noted then more for his colorful clothing than, his golf, blew our theory right out the door in 1985 when he showed up in an all-red outfit—shirt, slacks, sweater—and won the championship. When he put on the green jacket, he looked like Christmas.

Langer went on to become one of the top golfers internationally. And he toned down his wardrobe.

MASTERS FRIDAY: FROM CURIOUS TO CURIOUSER

Friday at the Masters began peculiarly.

At the top of the leader board, along with plain old Tom Watson, were a couple of style-setters—Gary Hallberg wearing a fedora-type hat that hasn't been seen on the tour since Sam Snead was a pup, and Payne Stewart wearing plus fours and acupuncture needles in his ears that some doctor told him would aid his concentration. (If Stewart wins, you're going to see more pierced ears on the golf tour than at a punk rock concert.)

At the bottom of the scoreboard, dead last after an opening-round 83, was four-time champion Arnold Palmer. This indignity heaped upon golfing royalty lent more peculiarity to the day.

Palmer had to tee off first, at 9 a.m., five hours before the leaders, to play a round he would rather have skipped. And when they had paired up everyone else in the field of 77 in twosomes, he was left without a playing partner. Charley Coe, a member of Augusta National Golf Club, was appointed to play with Palmer as a "noncompeting marker." Golf poobahs talk like that. What it meant in English was someone to chat with Arnie and keep his scorecard.

Coe wasn't without credentials. He once was one of the best amateurs in the world and in 1961 threatened to become the only amateur ever to win the Masters before finishing tied for second with Palmer behind Gary Player.

But Charley's a little creaky now, and after scraping around the front nine like a club member, he pleaded a pulled muscle and quit. Another member, this one without clubs, took over Palmer's scorecard and, thus unimpeded, Arnie sped around the back nine in one hour flat, finishing with a nice 72.

A CHAMPION IN CRIMSON AND GREEN

There are some who think you can tell how a golfer regards his chances of winning The Masters by what he wears on the last dayt

These sartorial analysts check out contenders' colors when they arrive Sunday to see how well their clothes will go with the green jacket that is the traditional mantle of the event's champion. The assumption is that the players gave some thought to this when they chose their haberdashery for the day.

Most of those who began the chase Sunday in a challenging position wore clothes that would look nice with the jacket—browns, grays, tans.

But the choice of clothing can't be a true test of a man's expectations on Masters Sunday, else why would Bernhard Langer, the West German peacock who heretofore has been noted in the United States more for his flashy clothes than for his golf game, wear a crimson outfit—shirt, slacks, sweater—that with the jacket would make him look like a Christmas present?

It obviously didn't matter one whit to him that he looked like something you wanted to tie a ribbon around late Sunday afternoon when defending champion Ben Crenshaw held the jacket for him to slip into, as is the tradition of this storied old tournament.

1986

For stark drama, the best Masters was played in 1975, with Jack Nicklaus fending off Johnny Miller and Tom Weiskopf down the stretch to win his fifth green jacket. The one I am most pleased to have seen came in 1986, when Nicklaus, at age 46 and presumed to have passed the time when he could win another major title, shot 68 on Sunday to win again.

A clipping of a story written by Atlanta's Tom McCollister was posted on the refrigerator at the house where the Nicklaus family was staying that week. It said Nicklaus was too old to win again. It could well have been a clipping of a column I did earlier that week, in which I said essentially the same thing.

Every Masters Sunday afternoon is charged with emotion, filled with the sound of the great roars put up by the crowds, the best moment in all of sports, but this one may have exceeded all the other Sundays. Could Nicklaus do it, or would the swashbuckling Spaniard, Seve Ballesteros, who had vowed to win before the tournament began, outduel him?

With his son Jackie carrying his clubs, Nicklaus did it, playing brilliantly on the final nine, and when Jackie hugged him on the last green, it was a hug from the heart of a grateful and adoring nation.

Sometimes, fate gets it right.

MOST CRUCIAL SCORES MEASURED IN YEARS

We stand on a lovely slope of Georgia countryside, azalea beds and towering pines at our backs, and look at the figure of Jack Nicklaus standing over a shot in the fairway of Augusta National Golf Club. What a wonderful place to be at this moment.

A sunny day, crowd noises echoing through the valley and up the hills as the second round of the Masters unfolds, and here is Jack, going for the green in two on the second hole, a twisting, diving par five.

Nothing's changed. It's still 1965, isn't it, and Jack is burning the grass off the fairways with a record 271, and Bobby Jones is saying, "He plays a game with which I am not familiar." Isn't it?

No, old friend, it isn't.

That was yesterday.

Nicklaus's second finds the bunker, and he settles for par. He screams a short iron over the third hole and struggles for par. He misses the flagstick on the fourth by a good 60 to 75 feet. And on and on. It used to be so easy.

Now, it is work.

Who is this impostor? Jack Nicklaus never played such a skittish game as this, misjudging distances, pulling the wrong clubs, hitting to the wrong sides of greens, misreading putts, making just one birdie in a round as he did Thursday. Shooting 74-71.

No, old friend, this is not an impostor. This is Jack Nicklaus, only now he is 46 years old.

Age creeps up so softly on a golfer, we don't hear its footsteps until it has already begun to etch its lines in his tan face.

It's just so easy to forget the passing of time at the Masters. Everything stays the same. The majestic pines, the flowering shrubs, the immaculate golf course, the magnolia-lined drive into the club, the thousands on the "patron" list who return year after year, the sound and feel of it all.

Everything stays the same but the players. That is so subtle, it is difficult to accept. Tradition wraps its arms around us on the sweet premises, whispering to us about what has gone before, and we forget that the years, the decades have passed.

We look at the leader board and see names like T.C. Chen, Bob Tway, Greg Norman, Bill Kratzert, Tommy Nakajima, and Danny Edwards. Where are Arnie Palmer, Gary Player, and Jack Nicklaus, who between them won every Masters but one from 1958 to 1966?

The fact is, Palmer, who shockingly flubbed two shots on Thursday the way we might en route to missing the 36-hole cut, and Player, who shot 77-74 and was also dismissed, are simply making curtain calls. Nicklaus is approaching that status, having won no title of any kind in two years. He's not out of it this week, not at all, but he is no longer menacing, just close enough to give us hope that in these next two days he will suddenly find what he has, that he will be young one more time.

Late Friday afternoon, Palmer stood on the clubhouse porch, looked down the hill to the big scoreboard near the 18th green, and said, "I want to look up at the leader board and see a Palmer, Player, or Nicklaus up there, but, as a friend said, when you reach a certain age, a curtain drops. You can play some good holes, shoot some good rounds, but in the end, I guess you know that what he said is true. A curtain drops."

The truth, old friend, is that we have a wonderful golf tournament going. Dazzling golf shots are flying through that blue Georgia sky. Drama is unfolding at every hole.

There's slump-ridden Tom Watson fighting into a tie for the lead through 10 holes, then bogeying the 11th and taking a triple bogey on the watery 12th but answering sharply with a birdie on the 13th. There's the beloved Ben Crenshaw, coming back from a dismal 1985, moving close to the front, faltering, then adamantly shoving back toward the lead. There's the slashing "White Shark," Greg Norman, charging, retreating, then moving forward again.

And there's the dashing Spaniard, Seve Ballesteros, a two-time Masters champion who, enflamed by a bitter fight with the PGA, has said he will win the tournament. He raises a roar from the crowd that bends the trees as he rams in a putt for an eagle three at the water-fronted 15th on his way to a 68.

This is good stuff.

Nothing's changed, old friend, except the players.

A GRAND DAY FOR NICKLAUS, GOLF, US

For a good while now, we've been lamenting what we had lost in professional golf, the true glory of great players battling down the stretch for a grand prize, cheered wildly by people who cared deeply.

And then there was Sunday.

Jack Nicklaus won the Masters again.

They have played this queen of tournaments for 50 years now, but never has there been one more golden than this.

Forty-six years old, without a major championship since 1980 or a victory of any kind since 1984 and in the process of being dismissed as a serious challenger, Nicklaus summoned some classical golf out of his scrapbook to make this perhaps the most glorious day the game has ever known.

It was certainly the greatest achievement in golf of the man generally recognized as the best who ever played.

Six shots behind with 10 holes to play, Nicklaus began a run that crumpled the will of most of his competitors, including the steely Seve Ballesteros, and reached far enough to withstand last-hole threats by Tom Kite and Greg Norman.

Nicklaus birdied the ninth, 10th, and 11th holes, but still found himself three behind Ballesteros, who in recent years has assumed the role of ruler of the game.

But Nicklaus, the Golden Bear, had tasted blood, which, on reflection, may have been what was lacking when his game was on the wane.

When Ballesteros scored an eagle three at the 13th, his second eagle in six holes, Nicklaus was still four shots behind. But then he eagled the par-five 15th himself and followed with a birdie—very nearly a hole-in-one—on the par-three 16th, which he has described as the most exciting place in golf on Sunday afternoon with its huge gallery of fans clustered there in an amphitheater of azaleas and pines.

With the thunder of the crowd echoing in his ears, Ballesteros cracked at the 15th. Going for the green in two from a comfortably short distance, the Spaniard hit a dismal iron shot into the water in front of the green and bogeyed.

Though he left that green tied with Nicklaus, Ballesteros was finished, as his shockingly poor first putt and resulting three-putt bogey on the 17th hole attested.

Nicklaus played those last 10 holes seven under par, despite a bogey on the 12th hole, shooting 30 on the last nine and 65 for the day to win his sixth Masters.

What a day this was, for us and for Nicklaus, crammed with marvelous golf not only by him but, appropriately, by his competitors as well, and teeming with drama and giddy excitement every step of the way. He has now won 20 major championships, 18 of them as a professional, and 89 titles overall, but he said he had never heard cheers like those he heard Sunday.

"The sound walking from green to tee was actually deafening, unbelievable," he said.

Several times in those last few holes, he said, tears came to his eyes as he lived again the sweetness he had known so many times but so rarely in recent years, sweetness so many of us thought was lost forever.

"I got pretty emotional," said Nicklaus. "I sort of welled up four or five times coming in, and I told myself, 'Hey, you've still got some golf to play.'"

A friend had taped a newspaper story on the refrigerator of the house he was sharing with Nicklaus early in the week. It said he was through, and people who are 46 don't win the Masters.

"All week, I kept thinking, done, through, washed up, huh?" said Nicklaus.

Sunday morning, one of his sons, Steve, phoned and asked, "What do you think it'll take, Pops?"

Nicklaus told him 66 to tie, 65 to win. Steve said, "That's the number I had in mind. Go do it."

Another of Nicklaus's sons, Jackie, caddied for him. He said Jackie kept telling him, "You'll get another birdie," and "Get one more," and, aware of his dad's putting problems, "Keep your head still."

When Nicklaus holed out on the last hole, he embraced Jackie and, when he finally got a moment, went and hugged his mother. She hadn't been to the Masters since 1959 and had said she'd like to come back one more time.

It was all so perfect, this grand day for Jack Nicklaus and for us.

As darkness fell over Augusta National Golf Club, Nicklaus mentioned the fast greens, tough pin placements, and emotion, and said, "This is a young man's golf course."

Sunday, he was young again. And so were we.

1987

Almost forgotten in the excitement and astonishment of Larry Mize's miraculous pitch into the hole from beside the 11th green in a sudden-death playoff for the championship with ill-starred Greg Norman was Seve Ballesteros.

But, curiously perhaps, my most vivid memory of that half hour was turning to watch Seve walk back up the 10th fairway after three-putting, leaving Mize and Norman to play for the green jacket. There has been no more dashing figure in golf than Seve but not at this moment. He was inconsolable, weeping, his head bowed, his shoulders slumped. While the crowd raced to watch Mize and Norman play on, Ballesteros trudged up the hill, the loneliest, saddest man in the world.

Just the year before, he had appeared poised to win the Masters, but Jack Nicklaus had played the last 10 holes seven under par and won. Ballesteros had hit a relatively simple iron shot into the water on the 15th hole and then three-putted the 17th to lose to Nicklaus. And the year before that, he had finished tied for second behind Bernhard Langer.

Now, in 1987, he was in a playoff with a chance to win his third Masters title, but he miscued again. I believe those two failures—the watery four-iron on the 15th hole in 1986 and the three-putt in 1987—killed something in Ballesteros. He could have had four, maybe five green jackets, but he would have to settle for two. He wouldn't win another major championship.

As for Mize's lightning-bolt pitch, I regard it as less a stroke of genius for him than one of the many moments of a dark destiny scripted by the golf gods who seem to have delighted in blessing Norman with everything but good luck.

MASTERS ROOKIES GETTING THEIR LEGS

If Billy Andrade could have laid out the way he wanted things to be in his first Masters golf tournament, this is how he might have done it to this point:

Dinner Monday night with old-time great Byron Nelson. Practice round Tuesday with Jack Nicklaus, the defending champion and idol of millions. Being paired in Thursday's first round with another pantheon figure, Arnold Palmer. Andrade, a Wake Forest senior and three-time all-America, wouldn't mind knocking a couple of shots off his score, but a 74 was respectable Thursday, even for nonrookies, on Augusta National's enamel greens. Otherwise, it has gone just about the way a 23-year-old would dream it.

The dinner with Nelson just happened, through a friend of the family. "I found out that in 1945, Nelson was 320 under par for the year. That's amazing," said Andrade. And then he cracked, "I'm two over for the year."

OF MIZE AND MEN: DREAMS DO COME TRUE

On the day before he beat the world's two most fearsome golfers in a sudden-death playoff to win the Masters, Larry Mize, Augusta born and bred, had said:

"I've dreamed of winning it a lot of times. I guess in my dreams I've won it about every way I could."

No, surely not this way. Not even children dream such dreams, do they? Pitching the ball into the hole from some 30 or 40 yards away for a birdie three to beat golf's snake-bitten star Greg Norman and two-time Masters champion Seve Ballesteros in a playoff?

Why not?

"A lot of funny things happen on the last day of the Masters," Jack Nicklaus, the dethroned champion, had reminded us. Conventional wisdom said that sending this boyish-looking 28-year-old out to match shots with Norman and Ballesteros was a waste of what was left of a golden Georgia afternoon for Mize. This wasn't a child's fantasy. Norman is a shark, Ballesteros a panther.

And Mize was the guy who had meekly frittered away the big lead in that TPC Championship and worked himself into some other runner-up situations, earning a reputation as a player who couldn't take the heat.

He was the one who had taken the lead on this tumultuous Sunday afternoon with birdies on the 12th and 13th holes, only to give the shots back on the next two while veteran golf watchers nodded and said, "Here he goes again."

True, Mize had birdied the last hole to get into the playoff, but he had won, what, one pro tournament in his life? Norman won 10 last year alone, Ballesteros half a dozen.

But just when it seemed Mize was coming unraveled, with his approach to the second playoff hole sailing much too safely to the right of the green, away from the pond beckoning at front-left, he killed the shark. The panther had already fallen a hole earlier, when three swings of his putter had sent him walking back to the clubhouse while the other two played on.

Mize also killed the yellow-toothed beasts that have lurked in the corners of his soul since he threw the TPC away in 1985. Smiling sweetly, Mize said, "That loss of the TPC just went right out the window."

No longer would he have to live with the label of a choker. Not after winning the Masters and beating Norman and Ballesteros in the process.

This is getting to be a habit with Norman. Last summer, Bob Tway holed a sand shot to beat him in the PGA Championship. Now, with his ball lying on the fringe of the green waiting to be putted, Norman watched Mize's ball land short of the green, bounce, settle into a roll as the crowd, sensing the possibilities, raised its voice, and then clunk into the flagstick and disappear.

It brought to mind what famed sports columnist Jim Murray once wrote: "Life is rough, but golf is ridiculous."

Reflecting later, Norman said, "That's the way golf is."

If anyone knows, it is this platinum-haired Australian with the heroic bearing who just keeps walking under falling pianos. You know—in 1986, he led all four majors after three rounds, lost three of them, one to Tway out of the sand. And now this. Twice in nine months. Which explained the vacant stare on The Shark's face near sunset.

Mize's pretty little shot and his exultant, semicircle trot to the cup to fetch the ball out in case Norman intended to put his long putt in (it fell to the left) climaxed a day of high drama. The first nine holes meant little. As the challengers rounded the turn and headed for the valley where dragons live and dreams die, the wind was brisk and the nerves tingling. For the longest time, there was no guessing who would win.

The dragons ate Lanny Wadkins, and then Curtis Strange, and then T.C. Chen, but there was still a leader board full of under-par figures, most of them so tightly knotted that they spent the afternoon exchanging positions, with none able to break free. It seemed inevitable that it would require a playoff. We expected the likes of Norman and Ballesteros there, but not Mize. We underestimated the mettle of this young man, though.

And, as Nicklaus said, funny things do happen on Sunday afternoon at the Masters.

1988

It had been 10 years since anyone had birdied the 72nd hole to win a Masters, and there seemed to be little chance it would happen in 1988 after Sandy Lyle, needing a par to tie Mark Calcavecchia and force a playoff, played his tee shot into the fairway bunker.

Lyle had put himself in this position by blowing two shots of his lead with a double bogey on the 12th, and now he was standing in the sand, peering over the steep face, at the green waiting up the hill, ringed by thousands. He took out a seven-iron and knocked the ball onto the green and then made the putt to claim the victory.

It was the first of what would be four straight wins by foreign players and the first of seven out of nine Masters.

CALCAVECCHIA BEATS PRESSURE, LOSES ANYWAY

Mark Calcavecchia, until Sunday just another Honda Classic winner with a difficult name to spell, looked very much like a man who could use a good cry.

But he had been nothing if not manly throughout a Sunday afternoon of pressure in the Masters cauldron. He had strung one fine shot after another and made fearsome putt after fearsome putt, and he wasn't going to crack now.

"I'm still a little stunned," he did say. He looked it, too.

All of us—Jack Nicklaus, Greg Norman, any and all heroes included—would have been stunned by what happened to Calcavecchia as Sunday afternoon turned toward dusk, and another Masters finished with high drama.

Mark John Calcavecchia, 27, has won a tournament each of the last two years and a great deal of money, but we hadn't classified him as a major championship threat until the back nine Sunday.

That's what they all say. The Masters doesn't begin until the last nine holes on Sunday. As he turned toward the valley where dragons and Amen Corner lurk, Calcavecchia was four shots in arrears of Sandy Lyle, the man who would eventually stun him and the sunburned thousands by making a most improbable birdie from a fairway bunker on the final hole.

By virtue of a series of circumstances common to the last nine, Calcavecchia found himself leading when he finished the 13th hole. He never was out of at least a share of the lead after that until the final stroke of the tournament tumbled into the cup.

That was Lyle's downhill putt on the 18th, 10 feet of stark terror. Calcavecchia had posted his 70 and, tied with Lyle, watched from a television studio as Lyle played 18. Lyle hit a one-iron off the tee into a fairway bunker.

"I thought it was over then," Lyle said. "I didn't think I had a chance to hit the ball onto the green."

But he lifted a seven-iron shot over the high-rise lip of the bunker, stood it up against the blue sky, and dropped it well up onto the green. The ball landed on a rise, settled, and began to inch backward down toward the cup, rolling maybe 15 feet before stopping.

"Under those circumstances, it seemed to me it would be easy for him to make a bogey," said Calcavecchia. "But when I saw where he hit the ball, I figured he would make the putt, because he is one of the greatest putters in the world."

Calcavecchia said he's sure he'll look back on this as a great experience. But what will stick in his craw, no doubt, is the fact that in the clutch, he, the guy playing only his second Masters, did everything right, and Lyle, the former British Open champion who is supposed to be unflappable, screwed up and still won.

Bolstered by a telephone tip from his teacher, Peter Kostis, who had observed something Saturday while watching television, Calcavecchia "felt the best I've felt all week."

He felt wonderful when he earned a birdie on the nasty 11th, and Lyle came right behind him and three-putted to reduce the edge to two.

And then, standing on the 13th tee, Calcavecchia had a

close look as Lyle dumped his tee shot on the par-three 12th into Rae's Creek and made double bogey.

Lyle later would call it "annoying," letting the other players "get their tails up" because of his mistake.

"All day, I had been worried about the 12th," he said. "I felt if I could get through Amen's (it's Amen) Corner (the 11th, 12th, and 13th holes), I'd be fine. But it didn't happen."

Calcavecchia, on the other hand, said he thought, "OK, now we've got a new game."

It was a new game. But only for a while.

1989

Lee Trevino won two U.S. Opens, two British Opens, and two PGA Championships, but he couldn't come close to winning a Masters. He played 20 times, made the cut 17 times, but his best finishes were two top 10s, and he made the top 24 eight times. He claimed his lack of success there was because he hit a low fade, and the course favors a high hook, and there was some merit in what he said.

There was more to it than that, though. For reasons never fully revealed, despite a lot of speculation, Trevino was never comfortable at Augusta National. He had some sort of disagreement with Masters officials, and thereafter changed shoes in the parking lot rather than go into the clubhouse, even though Clifford Roberts, who presided over the tournament, took him on a personal tour of the place and tried to better their relations.

Trevino once quit playing in Augusta, but Jack Nicklaus convinced him to come back.

It was a fruitless effort.

At age 49, though, in 1989, ol' Lee Buck, who had shot 81-83 the year before, breezed in with an opening-round 67. It would eventually just add to his aggravation, because he followed with a 74, and then, in a Saturday rain, posted an 83. A closing 69 got him only a tie for 18th.

Up front, Nick Faldo won on the 11th hole in a playoff with Scott Hoch. On the first playoff hole, the 10th, Hoch missed a two-foot putt that would have won it. It was a miss that would sadly always be an asterisk beside his name.

GLORY ELUSIVE TO HOCH

With rain tapping on his shoulders and Sunday night closing in, Scott Hoch, a face appearing suddenly out of golf's crowd, stood two feet from lasting glory.

He told himself, "Well, this is for the marbles." Tap in this little putt and one of golf's grandest prizes, the Masters championship, was his. His playoff opponent, Nick Faldo, had already bungled his way to a bogey five on the long, diving 10th, the first playoff hole.

But Hoch did the unthinkable.

He missed. Three-putted, a sin he hadn't committed in 72 earlier holes on greens that are like ice floes. He had studied the putt, one he could easily have kicked in, from all angles, pacing, kneeling, peering until Ben Crenshaw, watching on TV, blurted, "Geez! Hit it!" All to no avail, because, as Hoch put it, the wires got crossed in his brain, he had a split-second of indecision and yanked the putt ever so slightly.

Given new life, Faldo, a laconic Brit who had already holed several miles of putts in the tournament and had shot 65 to get into the playoff, birdied the 11th hole with a 20-foot arrow into Hoch's heart and claimed the title.

Because he doesn't yet really understand the true meaning of winning and losing the Masters, Hoch gave all this sort of a shrug, saying he was proud of the way he had played all week. Well, he should be, of course, but anyone who can honestly dismiss a wrenching loss in a major championship with a shrug will never win one.

You have to feel the fire inside you, love the battle, cherish victory beyond all reason, and cry in the night when you lose. Only then can you win.

Nowhere in golf is there such drama as this year after year. What happened on this gloomy Sunday was, in its way, as gripping as sports can get. Great players—Faldo, Seve Ballesteros, Greg Norman, Ben Crenshaw, and the like—battling across the killing fields of the back nine with Hoch and Mike Reid, strangers to greatness but interesting elements there among the stars.

If Hoch couldn't convey the pain of defeat, Ballesteros could, with nothing more than the look on his handsome features when he had drowned his chances in the water at the 16th hole. He thought a six-iron would cover the 175 yards, but it covered only 173. His ball spun back off the hillside into the pond, and golf's greatest adventurer was done, all of his wonderful shots from trees and sand wasted with a single swing. "I couldn't believe it," he said. "It was a fantastic shot."

And then he added, "Some people hit a five-iron. I hit a six-iron. That was the difference."

Winning and losing at Augusta cannot be reduced to any simpler terms.

Greg Norman knows how awful losing at Augusta can be. He has done it too many times, in the most dreadful ways. Jack Nicklaus, a man too old to win, shot 65, 30 on the back nine, to beat him once. Larry Mize pitched in on the second playoff hole to beat him once. And then Sunday, he beat himself. He played a cautious iron off the 18th tee, chose a five-iron for his second shot, left it short by what he estimated to be eight feet, and it spun back into the fairway. From there, he bogeyed and missed the playoff by a single stroke.

"I was thinking, 'Nicklaus did it to me, I'll do it to them,'" said Norman, who, crushed, hurried away from the crowd to the locker room, where he slumped with a beer in hand. "I hit a perfect five-iron. It just landed eight feet short. That's the breaks I seem to get on this course. It really hurts."

His legend, or perhaps it is his burden, grows. Norman loses. He thrills us as few can with blinding bursts, but always, it seems, the bursts fade at the end.

Maybe Scott Hoch can shake off the memory of that little putt that didn't go in. We should pray that he does. Ballesteros, a strong man, three-putted the same hole in a playoff in 1987, and it shook him so badly he lost some of his nerve in the year before he could get back to Augusta and fight again.

That's why it's always so good on Sunday afternoons at Augusta. Because it matters so much to so many.

1990

I have covered Raymond Floyd since he joined the PGA Tour in 1963 at the age of 20 and promptly won a PGA Tour event in St. Petersburg, Florida. I saw him win the 1976 Masters by eight shots, win the U.S. Open at age 43, win two PGA Championships, and play on eight Ryder Cup teams. If, late on that Sunday afternoon in 1990, you had told me that this great champion would hit a seven-iron shot into the water on the 11th hole to lose a playoff to Nick Faldo, I would have laughed at such a foolish idea.

Raymond Floyd was made of steel. He might lose, but he wouldn't beat himself. He was noted for The Stare, the look he got in his eyes when he was chasing a title. Raymond Floyd did not hook seven-iron shots into ponds when a major championship was at stake.

But he did. Men often do the unexpected when something as treasured as a Masters jacket is at stake. Scott Hoch missed a two-foot putt. Seve Ballesteros three-putted. Dan Pohl missed a six-foot par putt. All in playoffs such as this. And Floyd hit into the water. He was 48 years old and hadn't won in four years. And it was Sunday afternoon at the Masters. Even men of steel melt sometimes.

FLOYD JOINS LIST OF VICTIMS TRAPPED IN AMEN CORNER

The 11th hole at Augusta National dives 455 yards down a hill toward a green, a couple of bunkers, a pretty blue pond, and a lifetime of regret.

That's where sudden-death playoffs end in the Masters. They begin on No. 10 and, invariably over the years, end on the 11th.

Sunday, Raymond Floyd, once as unshakable as any golfer in the world, went there to lay his heart on the ground where Ed Sneed, Tom Watson, Greg Norman, and Scott Hoch had left theirs in playoffs past.

In the waning sunlight of a perfect day for golf, he hit his seven-iron second shot from 176 yards up the hill into the pond at the left front of the green, handing Nick Faldo his second consecutive Masters championship.

Last year, Hoch had missed a two-foot putt on the 10th hole to keep Faldo alive and then lost to the Brit's long putt on the 11th.

All of them are punishing, but this one almost brought a 47-year-old man to tears. He had led by four shots with six holes to play, and at that point, he would say later, he didn't think he could lose. But Faldo birdied the 13th, 15th, and 16th, and Floyd, noted as a splendid putter under pressure, three-putted the 17th for a bogey.

Choking back his emotion, Floyd, who has been playing pro tournament golf since 1963, said, "You cannot imagine the disappointment I feel. I've never felt like this, ever. I've never had anything affect me like this.

"A victory could have meant so much to me. It would have been a wild dream come true. At this stage in my career, how many chances do I have left? When you're 25 or 35, you think you have another chance."

You suspect that his regret will be deepened by the realization that he didn't play the way he has played all his life, with homicide in his heart and blood in his eye.

He didn't go for the throat. He's been coming here all of his adult life, has played in 26 of these Masters and has won one of them. He knows what can happen on the back nine on Sunday afternoon. And still he played prey instead of hunter.

Maybe it was his age. He would have been the oldest ever to win a major championship.

Lanny Wadkins, as gutsy as anyone with a club in his hands, finished early Sunday, looked at the scoreboard, saw that Floyd had a three-shot lead over Faldo with four holes to play and said, "He'll try to build his lead. He wants them to see smoke.

"He wants to birdie 15 and maybe 16 and enjoy the last two. When you have a three- or four-shot lead, you can enjoy it. It grinds your guts to play the last three holes with a one-shot lead."

But he misjudged his man. Floyd didn't attack. He had

been lulled into playing cautiously when nobody made a hard run at him in the early going.

"I think what happened," Floyd said, "it was a round when nobody made a run at me, and that dictated play. I started playing for pars, and I don't think I do that naturally."

He didn't try to reach the short par-five 13th hole in two and said he probably wouldn't have tried it with a longer tee shot. On the par-five 15th, he said he could have made it home with a four-iron or three-iron but chose to lay up and settle for par, where several of his closest pursuers were making birdie or eagle.

"I think it was the right decision, not to go for it," he said. "I'd defend what I did, even though it's not my nature."

Floyd said it was only after the 17th hole, when all of his lead was gone, that he thought the game was on. He responded with a tying par on 18 that had a lot of his old steel in it. His swing betrayed him there, as it had several times earlier, dumping his tee shot into a fairway bunker. His next hit a green-side bunker. He blasted to within six feet and made it, knowing if he missed, it was over.

He almost birdied the first playoff hole. Faldo, showing steel of his own, came out of a bunker there to tie him.

And then came the fateful swing on the 11th. Ben Hogan once said of the 11th, "If you ever see me close to the pin there, I've made a mistake."

Floyd said he didn't know if he had pulled the shot ("It didn't feel like a pull, but when I looked up, it was going left") or just lined up wrong.

"I'll never know," he said.

But he will always carry the burden of it. Regret. It's always waiting down there on Amen Corner.

1991

Tom Watson was 41 years old, had won only once since 1984, and had begun to struggle with his putter, but he stole the show in the 1991 Masters. He didn't win. Ian Woosnam did, and José Maria Olazabal finished second, but Watson, who had won five British Opens, two Masters, and one U.S. Open, brought the thrills to the back nine on Sunday.

He double-bogeyed the 12th to fall four shots behind Woosnam, but after a 20-minute wait on the next tee, he eagled the 13th and 15th holes and came to the last tied for the top but drove into trees, three-putted, and finished third, bitterly disappointed. He had won his last major.

CHILLS! SPILLS! FRIDAY ROUND FULL OF THRILLS

Mark McCumber had been out in the thick of some of the finest drama the Masters has seen in years Friday, and someone asked him how it had felt out there.

He said, "It is always a special day at the Masters. Dramatics happen here. Train wrecks. Apollo launchings. Roller-coaster rides. It's amazing."

We had all of those on this warm, overcast day at Augusta National, a day that tossed emotions around like azaleas in the wind. It was truly amazing.

There were three significant train wrecks, followed by Apollo launchings. Jack Nicklaus, of all people, was involved in one of those wild and wonderful series.

Nicklaus had told us he could win this tournament for the seventh time at age 51 and had opened with a 68 on Thursday, in case we weren't listening. He had followed with a neat 36 on the front nine Friday, and then a couple of pars. But on the 12th, a diabolical little par-three across Rae's Creek that bears the disarming name of "Yellow Bell," the great man did the unthinkable. He did what we mortals might do.

With the flag hanging limp, taking out the guesswork, the Golden Bear hit an eight-iron into the water. He walked to within 60 yards of the hole, dropped, and plopped another into the drink.

"I started thinking, 'What am I going to make, a seven, a nine, an 11?'" said Nicklaus, sounding like the rest of us. "I'd better get this next one on the green and get out of here."

He did, leaving with a seven that erased all of the red numbers he had worked so hard to put on the scoreboard.

Gathering himself up for the 13th, he said, "OK, dummy, you've done this, but no matter; you're still only six shots behind. Get your composure together, and go play golf."

And he did. He birdied the next four holes, lofting lovely shots through the sky and holing one long, long putt. And when night fell, he was only four shots off the lead held by his playing partner, Tom Watson.

Nicklaus was so pumped up, he hit a six-iron second shot on the 500-yard 15th. Only once before, 18 years ago, had he hit anything that short to that green.

"He was really proud of that," said Watson, who, amused, had turned to the gallery and said, "Know what Old Folks here hit to that green? A six-iron."

WATSON MAKES THIS MASTERS MEMORABLE

Ian Woosnam, a wee Welshman, won the Masters Sunday, but it was Tom Watson who made it a Masters to remember. In a week marked by spectacular golf and stirring drama, Watson had been at center stage. And there he stood again Sunday, when it was all on the table.

Watson, a man with a closet full of championship trophies, had just made a rookie's mistake. His lovely swing had come a bit unhinged, and he had hit a seven-iron into Rae's Creek, which ambles just in front of the 12th green at Augusta National.

As soon as he hit it, Watson blurted, "Darn it," and started walking. He had been within two shots of the lead in Sunday's final round, but this shot drifting into the water and the ensuing double bogey would leave him four behind Woosnam.

You felt Watson would fade into the scenery at some point, and here it was. He has 41-year-old nerves, only one victory since 1984, and a putter that has betrayed him shamelessly in recent years. All reasons to think he couldn't handle the pressure on that back nine that on Sunday afternoons examines the mettle of a man as no other nine in golf can.

A nine about which Ben Crenshaw, who narrowly missed winning again, as has become almost a custom with him in Augusta, said, "There's no other nine like it, never will be. It works on players' emotions. There is constant psychological warfare between you and the course."

Watson knows. He dragged his broken heart up to the 13th tee and then had to wait 20 to 25 minutes before teeing off. There was a traffic jam in front of him.

"That was a lot of fun," he said, sneering, "waiting 25 minutes when you've just knocked your ball into the stupid water."

But Watson didn't win five British Opens, two Masters, and one U.S. Open by sitting around pouting or knuckling under to pressure. While he waited on the tee, he lectured himself: Get an eagle on one of the par fives—13 or 15—and you can get back into this thing.

He didn't eagle just one. He eagled both, setting off some of those incredible thunderclaps of noise that are unfailingly a part of Masters Sunday. Driver, five-iron 195 yards, 15-foot putt on 13. Driver, five-iron 205 yards, eight-foot putt on 15. Dazzling, heroic golf that only the great ones can manufacture. And from near oblivion, he was back, tied for the lead.

Amid these wonderful heroics, he took time out to help his playing partner and the man who would eventually beat him for the title, Woosnam. Some ugly American in the gallery at the 14th tee had tried to ruffle Woosnam, telling him, "This is not a links course. This is Augusta National." It upset Woosnam, but Watson took him aside and said, "Hey, cool it. Let's think about what's in front of us, not what's behind."

And he told Woosnam how Don January would respond to negative remarks from the gallery by turning to them and saying,

"Thank you very much," with a little twist of profanity thrown in that can't be repeated here.

Woosnam drilled his tee ball on the 14th, then turned to the galleryite and said, "Thank you very much," with a twist.

Watson went stroke for stroke with Woosnam and José Maria Olazabal in a three-way tie through 15, 16, and 17.

But on the last hole, while the young Spanish star—and future great—Olazabal was spoiling his bid with a bogey up front, Watson pushed his three-wood tee shot into the trees. This time, it wasn't "darn." It was "damn."

He sawed a three-iron out into a bunker fronting the green, blasted 25 feet by, then tried to ram the putt in and three-putted. ("I was just trying to put the durn thing in the hole," he said.) The last two didn't matter. By then, Woosnam had parred and won it. He's worthy of that green jacket—a 40 short, by the way.

Watson was bitterly disappointed, and so were we who had hoped he might live the glory once again. But he has our applause, because he as much as anyone made this Masters one for the scrapbook, one to pull out from time to time and admire and relive.

1992

When Fred Couples won the 1992 Masters, highlighting a 12-month span in which he won six times worldwide, we rushed to proclaim him the next great player. Greatness eluded him, though. He was at or near the top of the world rankings for a long time, but back problems and a shortage of passion for the game left him just outside the door to greatness.

His victory in the Masters is remembered more for a nearly disastrous shot than for anything else. His tee shot on the par-three 12th landed just short of the green and started to roll back into Rae's Creek, as all balls do that don't clear the creek bank. His ball stopped, hung perilously on the little hillside just two feet short of the water. He played it up and made his par.

DALY SHOWS GOOD SIGN AT MASTERS

The Masters has a rule against fans asking for autographs except in designated areas, but minutes after he finished his first round ever in this spring classic Thursday, John Daly was signing for some guys beside the practice green.

Daly does this because he's a nice guy who's not too interested in such constraints, but this is not a good habit for him. A day earlier, during a practice round, Daly had signed between the ninth green and 10th tee, and it turned out the guy getting the autograph was a process server. Daly's old girlfriend had hit him with a paternity suit.

When Daly realized what had happened, he handed the papers to his caddy, and the caddy stuck them into the golf bag to be turned over to an attorney at a later date.

DRIFTING DAYS THING OF THE PAST FOR COUPLES

When Freddie Couples had holed the last putt in the soft twilight Sunday and walked off the green as the Masters champion, Raymond Floyd was there to hug him.

Floyd is a tough, old warrior who had hoped to win another Masters himself and gave it a gallant effort, but he finished second in this one by two shots. As tough as he is, though, he has a soft spot in his heart for Freddie Couples, probably because he sees some of himself there.

Like Couples, he blithely frittered away talent until someone—in his case, Arnold Palmer—convinced him to grow up and quit wasting his gift.

Floyd settled down, got serious, and became a U.S. Open and Masters champion, one of the best players of our time. Couples, 32, has stopped his hazy drift, given some direction and some effort to his career, and become far and away the dominant player in the world.

With a slender lead and with Floyd and about a dozen others just waiting for him to make one mistake Sunday, Couples came to the heart of Amen Corner, the 12th, a baffling, terrifying, watery par three that many golfers rank the best in the world. Couples would later say he had never been as nervous as he was playing that hole.

His tee shot landed on the steep bank fronting the green, bounced back and magically stopped two feet short of the water. Balls don't stop there. They go on into the water and die, taking hopes with them. But Couples' ball stopped, and he made his par.

He said it was the best break he ever had in golf, but it wasn't. The best break he ever got was a ball that did go in the water, a nine-iron shot on the last hole of a Ryder Cup match in 1989. Couples could have won the cup for the United States, but he hit into the water. He choked, and he knew it.

Floyd was captain of that team. Sunday, sounding like a proud father despite his narrow loss, he said, "Winning this major was easier than Fred trying to hit that shot in 1989, but he took it very hard. He felt he lost the Ryder Cup, but that wasn't true. We had 12 guys out there.

"I told Fred, 'That shot is going to make you a much better player, you won't believe it. You don't think so now, but someday you're gonna come to me and say, 'Dammit, you were right.'"

Couples was so grieved by that shot, he became almost fanatic about making the team the next time, last September. He worked harder, concentrated more, played more and, for the first time, had a real purpose.

He talked with Floyd and Curtis Strange and spent a week in Tom Watson's home talking. Then, with Floyd as his partner, he was the star of the Ryder Cup matches, and he hasn't stopped starring.

Since last June, Couples has played in 25 tournaments worldwide and has finished in the top six 20 times, winning six times. (He won only three times in his first nine years on tour.) He has already won more than $1 million this year. The talent was always there. Everybody said it. But Couples coasted along, not seeming to care a great deal, not working hard enough, not even playing enough. He had a reputation as a flake, sometimes forgetting to enter tournaments, and sometimes saying things that other golfers found outrageous.

Couples was just a good-looking guy with a gorgeous swing who hit it a long way and was called "Boom Boom." People shook their heads at the waste. Tom Weiskopf once said of him in a magazine article, "Great talent. No goals in life, not one."

Now, the sky's the limit. Floyd says Couples has the game to win as many Masters as Arnold Palmer or Jack Nicklaus. He says if Couples wasn't great before he won the Masters, "he's about to be."

A thought echoed by Corey Pavin, who finished third. "He's starting to get great," said Pavin.

Floyd even helped Couples around that dreaded back nine Sunday. Freddie said he relaxed back there because —you'll laugh at this—he knew if he slipped, his pal Raymond would be the beneficiary.

1993

One of the best places to watch play in the Masters is at the elbow of Amen Corner, where you can see the approach shots on No. 11, everything that happens on the 12th, and the tee shots on the 13th. There's a leader board there and a concession stand and some facilities and the potential for a few train wrecks.

Over the years, I devoted columns to the 12th hole several times. On Friday of the 1993 tournament, I spent a lot of time there and saw the then-unflappable Nick Faldo make a quadruple seven and several others thrash about trying to get it over with and be on their way. The restless, changing wind, the water, the thin green, the bunkers, the dark history of hopes drowned there, and the importance of the event can terrify the best.

Probably no hole anywhere has ever had as much to do with determining the winners of a major championship than the 12th at Augusta. It is called, with deceptive sweetness, "Yellow Bell."

GOLF'S BEST FALL OUT OF THEIR ELEMENT

Until Friday, if you had asked Nick Faldo when was the last time he made worse than a bogey on a hole, it's a good bet he couldn't remember. The beeline Brit has a disaster hole maybe once a year. He'll make 17, 18 pars a round easy, or so it seems.

But Friday, down at Amen Corner, there was the two-time Masters champion, the man generally thought to be the best playing the game right now, looking like some 24-handicapper from your Saturday-morning foursome.

Nobody can figure out the wind on the 12th hole, a watery par-three in the elbow of Amen Corner. Wind comes from so many directions there, it could be a game show.

Faldo guessed wrong, and his tee shot plopped into the creek in front of the green. He dropped another and hit that one plenty long enough, into a bunker behind the green. He blasted out long, and the ball rolled across the slender green and back into the drink. He dropped another in the bunker, knocked this one close and tapped in for a (blush) seven.

Still, it was considerably better than the 13 Tom Weiskopf had there several years ago.

Along came poor Bob Gilder. On 10, his birdie putt from about five feet grazed the cup. Had he made it, he would have been the sole leader.

Two holes later, he was just another guy named Bob. He bogeyed the 11th, then did a Faldo on the 12th, plopping two into Rae's Creek and crawling off with a seven.

Nick Price, one of the hot favorites in the Masters after having recently won the Players Championship, set a record of which he is not proud.

He made eight on the 14th hole, a fairly routine par-four. That's the worst score ever recorded there.

There was a tree root, and a pitchout, and an iron that bounded over the green, and three putts, and before you knew it, it added up to eight.

Price trudged in with an 81 and went looking for an airline schedule.

FORSMAN FINDS MISFORTUNE
IN RAE'S CREEK

It wasn't like Dan Forsman didn't know despair lived down there in the valley where Rae's Creek flows muddy through Amen Corner.

He had seen it on TV, all the times he didn't make it to Augusta National in the spring, and once, after failing to make the cut in the Masters, had walked around as a spectator and seen firsthand the peril that waits on that pretty little par-three 12th hole with the brook in front.

He knew, and still it didn't make any difference, and on an Easter Sunday afternoon golden with sunshine and opportunity, he knocked his dreams into the brown water where hopes go to die. Not once, but twice. Seven. Quadruple bogey.

With two swings, Forsman went from one stroke out of the lead in the final round of the Masters to also-ran.

The stoic German, Bernhard Langer, stood nearby at the 11th green and watched. The crowd was reacting so loudly to Forsman's travails, Langer decided not to putt until things quieted down.

With his closest pursuer out of the way, Langer then played on in to his second Masters championship.

There are so many dead challenges lying in that creek bed. They had been refreshed in Forsman's mind a week earlier when, in anticipation of his third trip to Augusta, he had rented a video of past Masters tournaments. He saw film of one player after another, many of them great players, drown golf balls down there on 12, where the wind plays baffling tricks.

Forsman had watched all that. And he had heard the veterans say never, ever, hit for the flag on No. 12 if it's on the right side of the green. It's too easy for the ball to drift a fraction to the right, into the creek where it tucks back in there, especially if the wind helps it.

His playing partner Sunday, Lanny Wadkins, says he never looks at the pin on 12, just gets his yardage, hits for the middle of the green, and starts walking. He looks for the hole when he gets there.

Forsman had heard all that. But . . . .

When he walked to the 12th tee, the huge crowd gathered on the hillside there cheered and clapped. He had just saved par from a bunker on the treacherous 11th and was keeping the heat on Langer and the gallery appreciated it.

"My spine was tingling," said Forsman, a tall, likable fellow who has won four times on the PGA Tour. "It was feeling the pride, the aura that's such a part of this event. I tried not to get caught up in it, but it's hard not to. The people know the pressure involved, and I think deep down they all would like to see a guy do well.

"It's a beautiful setting. There's such excitement there. And 12 is such a great hole. My mind was racing. I wasn't able to calm down."

He lined up toward the left edge of the bunker fronting the middle of the green, where champions aim when the flag's on the right, but his subconscious made him shove the shot a little to the right, and he knew immediately it was gone.

He dropped 100 yards from the cup, for a full sand wedge that he could spin and stop on the thin green. "I figured I could get a five out of it," he said. But he mishit the ball, and it landed on the far bank and rolled back in.

"It's kinda embarrassing, really," said Forsman, manfully trying to tell us how he felt at that awful moment. "You're in the Masters, you're playing well, you're in the hunt, a lot of people are pulling for you. You're a professional. That's the hard part.

"I just wanted to get out of there, wouldn't have minded (before teeing off) even bogeying the hole. You think it's easy to make a four, but it just wasn't that easy."

At the end of the round, Wadkins told him, "Hey, you played great. You were right there. You tasted it. You'll have a chance again."

Forsman said he will think about this for a while, then make it a positive thing, being in the hunt and tying for seventh.

But, he said, "I wish I could have had a mulligan."

1994

José Maria Olazabal won the 1994 Masters and became the seventh foreign winner in eight years, but the most engaging figure in that tournament was unheralded Tom Lehman, who had knocked around minor-league golf and foreign tours for years before finally achieving stability on the U.S. tour.

Lehman was tough, as he proved that week and would prove in the ensuing years with a British Open win and berths on Ryder Cup teams, but we didn't know it until Sunday afternoon, when he and Olazabal went head-to-head down the back nine.

One of the most memorable moments in Masters golf for me occurred on the 15th hole that day. Lehman and Olazabal were tied for the lead going to that hole. Both hit the par-five green in two, and as they prepared to putt—Olazabal a 30-footer, Lehman a 15-footer—the silence that lay over the thousands down there in the valley was like that in a cathedral. There was more drama packed into that hole than there is in most week-to-week PGA Tour events, total.

Olazabal made his putt, and Lehman's lipped out, and that would prove to be the difference.

Olazabal would win the Masters again in 1999, after overcoming a problem with his feet that threatened to end his career.

THIS LOVE AFFAIR WITH MASTERS AN UNDYING ONE

This will be my 40th Masters. I figure I've written close to 250,000 words on these premises, walked about 1,000 miles along these fairways, and spent the equivalent of a week waiting for a table at Augusta restaurants.

Forty years. And I still love it like the first day I walked into the place and thought I'd died and gone to heaven.

Take away every sports event but one, I'll keep the Masters. I'm a hopeless fan, and I make no apologies. Writers ought to pay their papers to let them cover this tournament.

How can you not love a place where, on a gorgeous Tuesday afternoon with a light breeze stirring the great old trees on the Augusta National clubhouse lawn, you see Byron Nelson leaning on a cane, talking with Billy Casper and Tom Fazio?

Where David Graham, a former U.S. Open champion, is a member of the committee that sets the tees and pins for the tournament?

Where you cannot find a weed—not with a microscope—and where the fans aren't gouged every time they reach for their wallets. You can buy a sandwich for a buck, a beer in a souvenir cup for a buck fifty. They give you your pairings sheet free, and parking doesn't cost you a nickel.

Where great shots and great moments are memorialized on the clubhouse walls with the clubs that were used to produce them, and if you want history in the flesh, Gene Sarazen and Sam Snead and other legends are hanging around, and Arnie and Jack and Gary are out there trying to win another one.

Forty years, and I'm still passionately in love with this place and this event. I think that's because I've never looked under the carpet to see if there was dust there. I don't want to know what makes the Masters tick. Club politics, fusses over invitation lists, money, stuff like that, I've avoided.

Every year the club president has a news conference. I skip it. It's not about golf shots and shining moments and green jackets.

And so I have managed, after all these years, to retain a certain awe for where I am and what I am seeing.

Every year, I set myself up for the week by walking down the back nine, first thing.

The back nine at Augusta National is Eden with flagsticks, all pines and azaleas and dogwoods and rambling creeks and little ponds and memories and promises.

This is where you go to feel the embrace of the Masters before the battle starts, to see the beauty, to know the peril, to look for ghosts, to listen for echoes.

Walk down the 10th hole, twisting and diving, a spectacular and inviting pathway to Amen Corner. Walk past Ike's Cottage and Bobby Jones' Cottage, down through the trees toward the green set on a ledge. And from there on down to the corner, where all those hearts have been broken and all those heroes have slain the dragons. Then wind your way back up the hill to the clubhouse, remembering the dramas that have unfolded on the 18th.

My fondest memory of the Masters? Nicklaus winning his sixth in '86 was one. Nicklaus beating Weiskopf and Miller in '75, the greatest Masters of them all, is another. Palmer beating Dow Finsterwald and Gary Player in a playoff in '62 qualifies. Ben Hogan burning down the back nine in 30 shots long past his prime, Larry Mize's pitch-in. So many.

But the fondest had nothing to do with a shot or a score. It was the first time I drove down Magnolia Lane, back when they let the working people come in that way, parked, walked around the clubhouse and saw the golf course spread before me. I had never seen anything so green.

Tuesday, everybody was loose, relaxed, renewing acquaintances, feeling out the course, talking about what great shape the fairways and greens are in this year. Every year now, they say the course is in the best shape ever.

Thursday, the battle starts, and Sunday afternoon, something wonderful will happen. It always does. At least it has for the last 40 years.

TOM LEHMAN FINDS HEART, LOSES MASTERS

Maybe Tom Lehman wasn't the best guy to send out there to turn back the Spaniards and Australians and South Africans and other invaders who are making a habit of stealing away with our green jackets.

Tom Kite, maybe. Tom Watson. Even Larry Mize. At least he had won the Masters once. Somebody who had some credentials to flash. But those scarred warriors fell away Sunday, leaving Lehman to fight young José Maria Olazabal for the Masters championship.

Left there, where he had never been before, he lost, but he fought like a lion.

In the aftermath, some insolent inquisitor broached the subject of choking to a man who had never won on the PGA

Tour, but who went out there and shot even par in the hellish heat of Sunday afternoon at the Masters, where doomsday seems to hang on every swing.

Choking?

"Choking is when you don't go for it," said Lehman, who went for it. Lehman has a thick waist, thinning hair, and everyman's face, and his victories have all been won off Broadway, on the secondary tours. You look for him to win Albuquerque Opens, not major championships, but he went the distance with his heralded rival, something nobody else could do, and came away a hero.

Olazabal shot a 69 on an Augusta National course that snapped and snarled all week, and became the seventh foreign winner of the Masters in eight years.

Lehman shot 72 and finished second, two shots behind. "I feel like he won it, but I also feel I could have won it, too," said Lehman.

They stumbled over each other at the last hole, trying to see who could hit the worse shots. Lehman's one-iron off the tee, a sensible play for a man who has problems fading the ball around that corner, went about 25 adrenaline-driven yards longer than he normally hits it, into a bunker, and he bogeyed. Olazabal hit over the green and played back short but holed the putt.

But the decisive blow had been struck earlier, on the watery par-five 15th. Lehman awoke Sunday as the leader of one of the world's great tournaments, but he had the look of a man who would fade into the scenery in Sunday's inferno while the heroes fought over the trophy. They always do, the Tom Lehmans of the world. But Lehman got up early, spoke at a local church, then went out and played well enough to be tied for the lead going to the 15th.

Olazabal spun almost out of his shoes, hammering his tee shot there, then hit a five-iron across the water, onto the front of the green. Shots hit there often spin back into the water. The crowd oohed as it watched Olazabal's ball roll back, but then settle on the fringe. Another foot of backspin, and it would have been wet.

Undaunted, Lehman fired his second at the flag. It rolled 15 feet past, and the roar shook the trees.

Sometimes it gets so quiet down there on the last nine holes at Augusta National on Sunday afternoon, it's eerie, and there is electricity in the air, a sense something is about to happen.

So it was as Olazabal stood over his putt, a 30-footer uphill, breaking right to left about a foot. Quiet, then a murmur, as he hit the putt and it began to roll, the murmur getting louder, then the explosion. The ball went in. Eagle three for Olazabal.

Lehman would later say, "I wasn't the least bit surprised he made that putt. He's a great putter. It motivated me."

Too much, maybe. Lehman worked over his putt, the 15-footer for an eagle of his own, then settled into the silence and rolled it. It kissed the right edge of the cup but stopped, refusing to drop. Lehman leaped, spun, fell to his knees, and pounded the grass. "I put my whole heart and soul into that putt, but it just didn't go in," he said.

He put his whole heart and soul into the round, too, and that one he won. Not the green jacket. Something more valuable.

1995

Tiger Woods, only 19 years old but already celebrated as a future great, made his Masters debut in 1995 and drew rock star attention along with high praise from fellow competitors. But he shot 72-72-77-72 and tied with Seve Ballesteros for 45th. As was his nature at the time, Woods was almost defensive when talking about Augusta National and the Masters, attempting to dismiss it as just another golf tournament.

As he matured over the next few years, he relaxed, became more personable, and one result was a record-setting performance to win a green jacket in 1997.

Ben Crenshaw, one of golf's most genial personalities and a man who treasures the history and tradition of the game, won for the second time and dedicated his victory to Harvey Penick, his longtime friend and teacher, who had died a few days earlier.

This year was also marked by the failure again of two of the game's brightest stars, Davis Love III and Greg Norman, to win the title. They were paired on the final day and waged a gripping head-to-head battle, but Crenshaw rushed in to beat both.

GOLF'S PRODIGY SINGLE-MINDED
OF PURPOSE

Early Tuesday afternoon, Augusta National's Amen Corner was so full of neon names, even the azaleas paled under the glow. You could stand on a hillside and watch a foursome of Paul Azinger, Lanny Wadkins, Tom Watson, and Phil Mickelson hit their tee shots on the 12th hole, while Raymond Floyd, Fred Couples, Greg Norman, and Tiger Woods putted on the 11th green.

Notice how smoothly Woods' name slides in there among the great and the grand, with whom he was keeping company during practice for the Masters that opens Thursday. We don't even pause to ask what he was doing there.

He's only 19, an amateur, a freshman at Stanford, but already he has so intrigued the golf world that Watson has labeled him "potentially the most important player to enter the game in 50 years." Someone else has compared him to another notable prodigy: Mozart.

While those thoughts may be a bit overcooked, given what Arnie, Jack, and Wolfgang did, it is a fact that no one has been so eagerly awaited at Augusta since the young Nicklaus.

What has made Woods even more fascinating is the color of his skin. He is only the fourth of his color to play in the Masters. He was going to be the greatest black player ever. That was the deal: finally, a black who could win golf's big ones.

Lately, though, he has corrected those who refer to him as black or African-American. He is, in fact, only one-fourth black. He's also one-quarter Thai, one-quarter Chinese, one-eighth American Indian, and one-eighth white.

"I'm Indian, black, Asian, and white," he says. "It's an injustice to all my heritages to just single me out as black. It's just unfair."

Whatever, he cuts a striking figure. Tall, slender, handsome with a megawatt smile that he doesn't use often enough. His swing is a symphony, his power shocking. He hits it Greg Norman long, Fred Couples long. And he can do the rest of it.

"And charisma," Jim Dent, an African-American playing the PGA Senior Tour, told the *Augusta Chronicle.* "He could be like the Jackie Robinsons, and the Willie Mayses, and the O.J. Simpsons, and the Jim Browns, and the Michael Jordans in their prime. Believe me, he will be an asset to golf. Tiger doesn't mess around."

We've seen Eldrick Woods grow up beating everyone, winning all the junior championships and then, last year, at 18, becoming the youngest ever to win the U.S. Amateur. Now, we want to see him play with the pros, in a major championship, on a golf course as whimsical as the restless wind that blows through its valleys and around its bends.

We look forward to this week and to decades of Tiger Woods, whistling his tee shots down the fairway, as he did

Tuesday on the 15th hole, a 500-yard par five, where he had only 154 yards left to the green, a nine-iron.

And to the iron shots that lock on the pins and dance on the grass, as his approach did on the ninth Tuesday, where Norman missed the green, and Couples and Floyd were 30 feet beyond the flag.

Or on the par-five 13th, where Woods had driven into trees and pine needles but whistled an iron out around a limb and drew it back, onto the green, 20 feet from the hole, while Floyd laid up short of the water, Couples hit way past the flag, and Norman hit into the creek. We're captivated.

Woods, on the other hand, would have us believe he is not, and that's too bad. He's only 19, but his idea of the Masters, as expressed Tuesday, is "Magnolia Lane is a short drive," and "the clubhouse is smaller than it looks on T," and the Masters "is just another tournament; it just happens to be a major, and you have to treat it that way. At least I do."

You aren't thrilled to be here?

"I'm thrilled, but my main focus is on my game, not the atmosphere."

Ah, too bad. He should smile more and look at the flowers and hear the ghosts of great players who have done great things telling him what Augusta and the Masters are really about.

There's plenty of time to worry about the game. There will never be another first time at Augusta for him.

PENICK'S SPIRIT IS EVERLASTING, FOREVER TEACHING

The ghost of Harvey Penick is walking the fairways of Augusta National Golf Club this week, his presence almost as real as the sunshine and the dogwoods.

He walks with Ben Crenshaw and Tom Kite—to whom he taught the lessons of golf—and occasionally looks in on Davis Love III, who used to come by to visit and talk golf.

Penick died last Sunday at the age of 90. He had been the teaching pro at Austin (Texas) Country Club for 48 years. Although he had taught Crenshaw and Kite and thousands of others, he never achieved fame until recent years, when a collection of his wisdom appeared on bookstores under the title *The*

Little Red Book. It was essentially Penick's homespun instruction like, "Take dead aim," but it became the best-selling sports book in history.

Davis Love thinks often about Penick this week. He used to go by to see the old gentleman from time to time, not for lessons—his dad was his teacher—but just to visit, and Penick would always insist that he get his clubs out or show him his grip or talk golf with him.

Last Sunday, on his deathbed, one of the last things Penick did was clap his hands three times when someone told him Love was winning the tournament that would qualify him for the Masters this week. Friday, Love shot his second straight 69 and is only three shots out of the lead at the halfway point of the Masters.

Crenshaw and Kite flew to Texas on Tuesday to be pallbearers. Kite missed the cut Friday, but Crenshaw is only two shots off the lead. Ben credits Penick.

"I had one last lesson with him," said Crenshaw. "I went in to see him the Sunday before New Orleans (Sunday before last) and he said, 'Can you please get a putter and show me how you're stroking that ball?'"

"And he said, 'Now, I want you to take two good practice strokes, and then trust yourself and don't let that club get past your hands on the stroke.'

"And I've thought about it quite a lot. Any good stroke that you see, any good putting stroke has those complements in it."

Crenshaw had his first lesson from Penick when he was about seven years old. "He put my hands on the club," said Crenshaw, "and my grip hasn't changed. One of his friends gave me a little blade putter and a mashie, so those were the two clubs that I had. He said, 'You go off to the side of the green, and you chip this ball up on the green, and you putt it into the hole. That's golf. You're playing golf.' So that's what I did for a good while. He'd be watching me always. There were always a few words.

"Just before my teenage years, I started to know what a man and what a teacher he was, because I kept seeing these incredible players coming in for lessons. I think there were three people whom he would not tell anything further about their swings, and they were Mickey Wright, Don January, and George Knudson."

Penick got no fancy fees like today's top teachers do. Crenshaw swears this is a true story:

"Michael Jordan called Harvey. Helen, his wife, answered the phone. She said, 'It's Michael Jordan from Chicago.' He said, 'Who?' She said, 'It's the basketball player, Michael Jordan.'

"So he got on the phone. Michael said, 'Can I come to see you? And what do you charge for a lesson?'

"Harvey said, 'I'll be happy for you to come see me. The charge is $5 and you've got to hit your own balls.'"

After Kite won the U.S. Open in 1992, his wife, Christie, took the trophy to the practice tee where Penick, sitting in a wheelchair, was giving another lesson. "Here," she said, putting the trophy in Penick's lap, "Tom said this was for you."

Now, Crenshaw is taking dead aim on another trophy for Penick. If he is standing out on the lawn Sunday afternoon with a green jacket being pulled around his shoulders, holding the jacket will be the 1994 champion, José Maria Olazabal, but Crenshaw will know who really put it on.

LOVE, NORMAN GAVE MASTERS
A FINAL SPARK

They walked down into the valley, shoulder to shoulder, throwing lightning bolts, and you sensed that if anyone else was going to win the Masters, it would be over their fallen bodies.

It was Sunday afternoon, and this was the back nine at Augusta National. That's when, and where, this tournament begins. Davis Love III and Greg Norman had begun the day three strokes out of the lead—but at the turn, Love was within a stroke of the front-running Ben Crenshaw, Norman was within two, and now they were turning toward Amen Corner, fire in their eyes. A two-stroke lead is so thin, it can be blown away on that back nine by a puff of wind.

Love and Norman had the advantage of playing well ahead of Crenshaw, out where they could give him something on the leader board to chill his blood.

They got right to it. On the 10th hole, a 485-yard Rembrandt diving down and around into the pines and azaleas, a hole that has tormented him over the years, Norman chipped in from 40 feet. Love responded with a 10-foot putt for a birdie of his own.

They parred the next two and then ripped huge drives around the corner to perfect position on the par-five 13th. Framed by a little creek and the dogwoods and the greenery, with thousands of people straining against the ropes, they had the chance to strike decisive blows right there. Eagles would have been golden. Love pulled his seven-iron to the left fringe and three-putted. Norman hit the green but two-putted. Love birdied the 14th, spinning his approach backward, grazing the cup. Norman parred.

As they waited for each other to hit or to putt, you wondered what they might be thinking. Love has for a few years now been regarded as one of the best players in the world—but he had never shown it in the majors, never contended. Norman's career has been chapter after chapter of contending and losing. Sometimes it has been bad luck, sometimes it has been bad shots. Now, both were within a swing or two of erasing the past.

At the par-five 15th, they killed their tee shots and they knocked their second shots on the green, and the crowd stood and applauded them every step of the way for the last 100 yards or more. But putters, always treacherous things, become writhing snakes on Sunday afternoon. Love and Norman missed the eagle putts, settled for birdies, and later would believe that was where it might have been lost.

"If I'd made the eagle at 15," Love said, "that would have been the killer. Not just because of the stroke, but because of the noise. Same with Greg's putt. I was ready to hold my ears. If Greg or I could have got the noise going (for Crenshaw to hear), maybe it would have been different, but it was kinda quiet down there."

Love three-putted the 16th, down a slippery slope where Crenshaw would make a birdie to seize the lead for good. Love birdied the 17th, almost holing his approach, but Norman hit a horrible sand wedge shot about 40 feet left of the flag and three-putted. Sometimes it has been fate. This time, it was a hacker's stroke that finished him off.

They parred the last, but it didn't matter—because Crenshaw would also birdie the 17th before bogeying the 18th to beat Love by a shot, Norman by three.

Love watched Crenshaw wrap up the victory and then double over in tears of relief and joy and memory of his beloved teacher and friend, Harvey Penick, who died last Sunday. Crenshaw had interrupted his preparations for the Masters to fly to Austin to be a pallbearer.

But first he had called Love, who had also been a dear friend of Penick's, and told him not to come to the funeral, but to stay in Augusta and rest and get ready. Love had kept a torturous schedule trying to qualify for the Masters and had just gotten in by winning last Sunday. Crenshaw knew he needed time to prepare.

"If I'd been beaten by any other player, I'd be more disappointed," said Love.

"I wish it wasn't him who is second place," said Crenshaw.

1996

After Greg Norman had built a six-stroke lead through three rounds, an unthinking acquaintance said to him, "Not even you can lose that lead."

That night, I wrote that Norman, who had been runner-up in seven major championships either as a result of his own failing or the astonishing feats of others, would surely win this time. People could pitch the ball into the cup or hole from a bunker or knock one in from the fairway, but it would make no difference, because this time the Shark had a lead that could withstand all their heroics.

I was wrong. Norman, no doubt burdened more by the fear of failure than what his rivals might do, collapsed. It was painful to watch. It would have been painful had it been anyone else, but it was especially so because it was Norman, fate's plaything.

Nick Faldo won, playing championship golf with a closing 67, but his joy was tempered by Norman's distress, and when the champion hugged the fallen man, both had tears in their eyes.

MEMORIES CROWD HALLOWED
IIALLS OF AUGUSTA

Along the walls of the Augusta National clubhouse, encased in glass, there are golf clubs that helped fashion some of the game's richest lore. Dead steel and leather and wood, but immutable if you listen with your heart.

Larry Mize's wedge that stunned Greg Norman and the world in the 1987 Masters. Raymond Floyd's five-wood that helped him tie the untie-able 72-hole record of 271 set 11 years earlier, in 1965, by Jack Nicklaus. When Nicklaus did it, Bobby Jones said young Jack played a game with which he was not familiar.

Gary Player's two-iron, Cary Middlecoff's hickory-shafted putter, Ben Hogan's four-wood, Billy Casper's sand wedge. Last year, during his first Masters, the amateur Tiger Woods lived upstairs in the clubhouse, and at night, when everyone was gone, he would go downstairs and look at these things and feel the Masters putting an arm around his shoulders.

And perhaps telling him, "You should have been here in 1967, the year Hogan shot 30 on the back nine" or "Now, son, let me tell you about 1975, when Johnny Miller shot 65 on Saturday and 66 on Sunday, but it wasn't good enough. He only tied for second with Tom Weiskopf, one shot behind Jack Nicklaus. Now that was a golf tournament . . . ."

They are all golf tournaments, these Augusta Masters. Something dramatic always happens, and it will this week when they play it again. Ben Crenshaw, who won it for the second time last year, says it's almost eerie how things work out in the Masters.

"Unexplainable" is the exact word he used. He was thinking of many things, including his victory last year less than a week after he had buried his beloved mentor Harvey Penick. He had wanted desperately to win again, when he could dedicate it to his old friend, and it happened.

Crenshaw also mentioned Nicklaus' sixth Masters championship in 1986, when the Golden Bear was 46 years old and no longer regarded as a serious threat.

Nicklaus was five strokes behind after eight holes on Sunday but played the last 10 seven under par to shoot 65 and win.

"It had all the elements of drama that anyone could hope to see in a golf tournament," said Crenshaw. "It was just magical."

Magical, too, was Hogan's 30 on the back nine on Saturday in 1967, when he was 54 years old and long past his prime. Gray hair showing from beneath his white snap-bill cap, bronzed face set in that enigmatic smile, he turned in 36, then birdied Nos. 10, 11, 12, 13, 15, and 18.

He didn't win, but he did give us something to remember him by, his last great round. He chose the perfect place to play it, here where it would be treasured and dusted off and admired and where it can send chills down the backs of future Tiger Woodses when they pause in the night to listen to the echoes.

Gene Sarazen started it all back in the misty past with that four-wood for a double-eagle on the 15th. Wonder has followed wonder ever since.

But we remember the failures, too, of course, because they are so often spectacular. The little putt Scott Hoch missed. Seve Ballesteros' four-iron into the water on the 15th when Nicklaus was chasing him in '86. The steely Raymond Floyd's iron into the water on the 11th that killed his chances in a playoff with Nick Faldo. The golf course and the prize conspire year after year to offer us as good as the game can give.

"Pure golf," Greg Norman calls it, and he speaks of "traditions that you really love to play with and understand.

"There's no other golf tournament anywhere in the world that generates that type of feeling," he said. " . . . It's just the wonderful mystique that this tournament can create . . . . "

This weekend, someone will do something wonderful, and another club will be added to the walls, and another memory will take its place.

WOODS' SPOTTY 75 SHOWS THE FUTURE NOT NOW, NOT YET

Golf's future was three over par when the sun went down Thursday.

This was not what we in this horde of thousands had tramped across hill and dale to see on this gorgeous opening day of the Masters. We came to see wonders.

On Wednesday, Jack Nicklaus had told us Tiger Woods might win more Masters jackets than he and Arnold Palmer had between them, which is enough to start a haberdashery. Ten of them.

Nicklaus had anointed the 20-year-old Woods as "your favorite for the next 20 years" of Masters tournaments, declaring him the most fundamentally sound young player he had ever seen.

And so we wanted to have another look at Tiger Woods, to watch him grapple with the subtleties of Augusta National and with the wind and with the burden of being himself. No player since Nicklaus has come out with so much expected of him and so many watching, but Nicklaus' remarks made us look with an even more curious and admiring eye.

But by the time Woods reached the turn, he was two over par and already seven shots behind Phil Mickelson, the early leader with a 67. Amen Corner awaited.

Down into the valley we went with him and defending champion Ben Crenshaw, to see the kid get his strokes back and then some.

He had played the front nine like a scared 20-year-old amateur, misclubbing, missing little shots, missing putts. But he would settle down, kill the two par-fives and show us what Jack was talking about.

It never happened. He shot 75. And get this—it was the best driving round, for distance and accuracy, I've ever seen. He is John Daly-long, and he hit every fairway. He doesn't look like he swings hard, but he has crushed or cracked five driver heads in the past six months. He can kill it and keep it on the sprinkler heads.

He took our breath away with his tee shots, but he hit only 10 greens, three-putted two or three times, and shot 75. Scott McCarron beat him. Ted Tryba beat him. Fred Funk beat him. Arnold Palmer, 66 years old, beat him.

For any other amateur in the world, a 75 in the opening round of the Masters, playing with the defending champion, with every living soul in the golf world watching and Jack Nicklaus' praise echoing around the place, would be a good day's work. But when Woods did it, we gathered around to do an autopsy.

He's not old enough to buy a beer. The only jacket he has is a blue blazer.

But if he doesn't dazzle us and beat all those legends out there, we want to know what's wrong.

"Overall, it was a good round," said Woods, 6-2, 155 pounds, a Stanford sophomore who was carrying his own bag in a collegiate tournament a week ago.

"I hit some good shots, and I was pleased with my play overall, but I was disappointed in my putting."

Some of those shots surprised him, as they did us.

For example, he airmailed the second green from 221 yards out with a four-iron. He thought it was a good shot until it scattered the spectators. He chunked his pitch shot, a really tough one, and made bogey.

Crenshaw explained it all to us, though. "Tiger's incredible," he said. "He's unbelievable. His talent is out of this world. But he'll get better."

"He'll learn to use the wind to his advantage and to club himself better. I think he'll find the small shots are where he needs to make the major improvements. He's just learning the game, but with the littlest of help he can do anything."

In other words, Woods has the talent but still uses it at times like a 20-year-old amateur. He finished the day 12 shots behind Greg Norman.

"I'm still in it," he said, and you have to like that, but he'd better hold on to that blue blazer for a while.

LOSS AT AUGUSTA MORE TORMENT FOR A TORTURED SOUL

Standing on the 18th green of Augusta National with the sun going down on an amazing day of golf Sunday, Nick Faldo, the Masters champion for the third time, put his arms around his longtime rival Greg Norman and said what a lot of us were feeling.

With tears in his eyes and in the eyes of Greg Norman, he said, "I just want to give you a hug."

Faldo knew that if ever a golfer needed a hug, it was Norman on this Sunday when he suffered the worst collapse by a third-round leader in the history of the game's major championships, the biggest disappointment in a lifetime of golfing disappointments for the man they call Shark.

Shark. How inappropriate that nickname seemed Sunday. There was nothing of the killer in him on this pretty, sunshiny day. He went down without a fight as ingloriously as a carp on a cane pole.

Still, it's hard to feel scorn for Greg Norman. His soul is a montage of scars from championships lost. Some of them he threw away, as he confessed he did this one. Some were robbed from him. No matter how it happened, it did happen, and it is a burden no man should have to suffer playing a game.

Norman began the day with his hands on the Masters title that he has coveted so passionately for so long. He had a six-shot lead. Duffy Waldorf could probably have won with that, but Duffy Waldorf doesn't carry history around on his shoulders, doesn't have a devil whispering in his ear about all the championships he has lost when they were there for the taking.

Norman is cursed. He is golf's most glamorous figure, wonderfully talented, devilishly handsome, extremely rich, and he has won dozens of titles around the world, but when it comes down to the last holes in the big ones, none of that helps. He loses. Eight times now he has been a runner-up in one of the four majors. He has won only two, both British Opens.

He wants us to believe that he can shake it off, that after a good night's sleep and perhaps a stiff drink or two, he can put it behind him and be on his way. But how can we buy that? Everyone who knows him well will tell you he's a perfectionist, but he has all these imperfections in his career. He's trying to win the tournament he says is the greatest in the world, and he chokes his guts out with millions watching. He can just shrug that off?

"Watch," he says, and smiles at you when he says it.

"For me," he continues, "there's not a whole lot of anguish. Sometimes things work out for you, and sometimes they don't. It's not the end of my world. My life will go on. I'll enjoy my life.

"I'm very philosophical about it, that's one of my strengths. I'm not a loser, I'm a winner. And I will win again."

He believes "these hiccups," as he calls them, are happening for a reason. He is being tested, he said, and "there's something great down the line waiting for me."

Perhaps. But it's getting late. If he was ever going to kill the demons, it should have been Sunday. He had six shots on the field, a perfect day for golf and three days of good shooting behind him.

Norman couldn't handle it, though. He claimed there was no tension in his body or his mind, but he shot 78 to Faldo's 67. At the precise moment when he needed greatness, at the wicked par-three 12th hole after he had blown all of his lead, he flinched. He pushed a seven-iron shot into the creek at the 12th and double-bogeyed, and, suddenly, he was two strokes behind

Faldo. And when he still had breath, at the 16th, two behind, he hooked another ball into the water with a six-iron.

Those are the strokes of a frightened man.

But he had so much more to lose than the rest, and he was afraid of losing it. So much to win and so much to lose. It was too much for him, and everyone saw it and knew that it was not Faldo's lovely shots but Norman's betrayal of himself that beat him.

And everyone knew he needed a hug.

1997

Tiger Woods had played in the Masters before, but when he arrived in 1997, he did so as a rookie professional who had gotten off to a sensational start and heightened the intrigue that had surrounded him since he had been a child star.

With no Palmers or Nicklauses or Trevinos or Watsons to dominate with their enormous talents, tournament golf in the United States had become a ho-hum affair. No exciting new players had emerged. Davis Love III and Fred Couples were superior players, and we thought they might dominate the game for years, but they have never quite gotten over the final hurdle to greatness.

Then along came Woods, with his enormous distance and his wealth of talent and his fine looks and his multiethnic background, and we couldn't get enough of him. And then he won the Masters and set a scoring record doing it.

I called it the most significant victory by anyone in golf since Arnold Palmer won his first Masters in 1958 and triggered an explosion of popularity for the game among the masses. I still believe that, because Woods attracted the attention of an element of society that is not usually drawn to golf, and in addition, he excited us and restored what had been lost in tournament golf.

Woods was edgy, defensive, sometimes abrasive, and not a little bit arrogant along about that time, but over the next couple of years he grew more comfortable with the attention, relaxed, and seemed to enjoy his life much more, and as he did, his following grew even larger. He changed his swing to gain more control, and he rid himself of most of the impetuosity that had resulted in tournament-losing triple bogeys where a pitchout and a bogey would have served him well.

Woods is capable of wonderful things, perhaps more wonderful than we've ever seen, although that 1997 Masters was pretty wonderful.

MASTER OF HIS DESTINY

He is the golfer for whom we've been waiting, and this is the moment.

Tiger Woods in the Masters.

He tees off Thursday. The world will be watching.

He has played the Masters before, but this one is different. We see him differently. He is different. He can win this time.

If he did win—and Arnold Palmer and Jack Nicklaus say he will win more than their combined 10 Masters green jackets—it would be the most significant golfing victory since Palmer won the 1958 Masters. Perhaps as the years passed, Woods' would become the most significant of them all.

Winning would undergird the common belief that Woods, 21, has the talent for unprecedented greatness. It would enhance his Michael Jordan-like attractiveness, which is already drawing record crowds wherever he plays. And it would be the first major championship for an African-American, won in a tournament for which no black qualified until 1975.

The Masters has received over 500 more requests than usual for media credentials. And if there were enough tickets available, and room on the course, there would be hundreds of thousands of people lining these green, flowing fairways at Augusta National Golf Club every day this weekend, partly because it is the Masters and partly because Woods is playing.

What they would see would be a lean-looking young man with skin the color of coffee with cream, walking with an easy gait, flashing a smile that looks like a snowy mountain range, or beating the ground with an offending club after an imperfect shot.

They would see Woods hitting shots distances that make PGA Tour veterans just slump their shoulders, drop their heads, and laugh. Three hundred and thirty-six yards is how far he hit his first tee shot as a professional. Two hundred and sixty-seven yards is how far he hit a three-wood second shot on the par-five 18th at Pebble Beach when he needed an eagle. On a 576-yard par-five in Phoenix, he drove the ball 351 yards, hit a two-iron 225 yards to the green, and holed a 12-foot putt for an eagle. He'll kill the par fives at Augusta.

If the crowd followed Tiger, they would see all of the kids and all of the African-Americans and most of the Caucasians who have the prized tickets to the Masters moving around with him. He is a remarkable golfer, but there is something else almost mystical about him, something Michael Jordan has, Colin Powell has, Jackie Robinson had.

Woods has played the Masters with relatively poor results, never shooting lower than par-72 in six rounds. But that was as a collegian who had to finish term papers at Stanford before he could leave for Georgia. Before he had finished with a swing adjustment that would allow him to shoot 61-65 in the Pac-10 Championship a week after he missed the cut with a pair of 75s in last year's Masters.

Before he won his third consecutive U.S. Amateur, coming from two down with three to play, and turned pro late last season. Before he won two of the eight PGA Tour events he entered, beat veteran Davis Love III in a sudden-death playoff in one, shot in the 60s 22 times in 31 rounds, and won $790,594, signed endorsement contracts worth an estimated $60 million.

Before he opened this year by winning again in the Mercedes Championship, his third win in nine starts as a pro, knocking the stick out for a birdie to beat British Open champion Tom Lehman in a playoff.

Before he shot 63-64 on the weekend to finish second in the AT&T Pebble Beach National Pro-Am and growled, "Second sucks."

Before he notched 10 more rounds in the 60s in 23 attempts this season, drawing record-breaking crowds wherever he played, and winning $480,350 more.

Before he was named Sportsman of the Year by *Sports Illustrated*, appeared on the cover of *Newsweek* and in feature stories in *People* and *Time*. Before he received a royal welcome in Thailand, home country of his mother.

Before he became, at 21, a man. And The Man.

We've sat around and mused that someday a player would come along who could hit it a mile, had a swing like the pictures but more powerful, had the touch of an angel around the greens, could handle the putter, had unshakable confidence, and had about him a charisma that would bring thousands trailing after his every step.

Unless a lot of discerning people like Jack Nicklaus, Arnold Palmer, Tom Watson, Curtis Strange, and Ben Crenshaw are wrong, Woods is that golfer who existed for so long only in our minds and hearts; the golfer who would change the landscape of the game, the crossover star who would play the game as no other had played it and draw people to him who knew little about golf but wanted to be in his presence. Like Arnie in the '60s.

Woods' father, Earl, thinks his son is even more, that he will impact nations in ways other than golf, that he will be more influential than many of the great men of history. "He is the Chosen One," said Earl.

Others may not share that lofty opinion, but they do see something special there. "He's come along at exactly the right time," tour veteran Loren Roberts said. "He's like Arnold Palmer, a guy who is going to popularize the sport to a bigger audience, to reach out to areas where maybe golf has been slow to reach."

"He's got every gift," said Crenshaw.

"I didn't think that anybody coming in today would have the career, the numbers, that I had, just because the competition is so great today," said Nicklaus, who won 20 major championships and is generally regarded as the greatest of all time. "But he might. He's got a pretty good head start."

Neither Nicklaus nor Palmer nor anyone else came out with the trumpets blowing and the flags waving the way they have for Woods.

There is a risk in that, of course, in proclaiming a golfer the "next Nicklaus" or the "next great." The list of them is long, among them Scott Verplank, Phil Mickelson, Hal Sutton, Bob Tway, Robert Gamez, Bruce Fleisher, even Gary Nicklaus, Jack's son, before Gary was shaving. They've had mixed success, but none has approached greatness.

Pressure, burnout, bad advice, any number of things can waylay a career. Woods could get waylaid this week by the expectations—his and others'—and by a golf course that must be understood to be played well. He has studied film of how Nicklaus and Faldo play it, has talked with many of the top players during practice rounds, has refined his swing and softened his putting stroke. And has said of Augusta, "The place was made for me."

He says the expectations of a world won't be a problem, because his expectations are just as high or higher. Dealing with the mental chaos of Masters week, especially on Sunday when you're in contention, can make a strong man cry. But Woods has been trained in mental strength by his father, Earl, a military man, and Earl says his son will never meet anyone mentally tougher than Tiger himself.

But golf and Augusta and the elite field and the magnitude of the occasion can conspire to crack the strongest. None was braver than Raymond Floyd, but he whipped an iron shot into the water on a playoff hole and lost. Seve Ballesteros did the same on the 15th hole on a Sunday when it appeared he was going to win. Scott Hoch missed a two-foot putt that would have won him the green jacket.

You can't call your shot when it comes to winning golf tournaments. That is so true; many players say a tournament wins you. In this first one as a pro, then, Woods will have to wait and see. Someday, though, barring injury or illness or early burnout, he will win it. And win it again. We all know that. And he has said so himself. When he was 19, he looked at pictures of Masters champions on the Augusta National clubhouse wall and said, "Someday, I'm going to get my picture up there."

TIGER'S MASTER STROKE

At every hole throughout the afternoon there had been a standing ovation for him. But the greatest, clearly the most heartfelt, came at the last for Tiger Woods Sunday, and it will echo forever.

Up the hill toward the Augusta National clubhouse and a place in golfing history he climbed under an overcast sky, with a chilly breeze moving the pinetops and rippling his red shirt. The electric smile that had been absent so much of this grueling day glowed on his brown face.

At age 21, in his first year as a professional, Tiger Woods had won the Masters and become the first player of African-American descent to claim any major golf championship. It was the most significant victory anywhere in golf since Arnold Palmer won the 1958 Masters.

Lee Elder, in 1975 the first black golfer to play in the Masters, had flown in to be on hand. He said, "No one will ever turn their head again when a black man walks to the first tee."

When Woods had knocked in his last putt Sunday on the hardest round he had ever had to play in a lifetime of hard rounds, he embraced his dad, Earl, and showed us that he is not all steel and stare. He cried on his dad's shoulder.

Under pressure beyond our imagination, the 21-year-old Woods shot 70-66-65-69, a stroke better than anyone had ever done it, and that would include the likes of Bobby Jones and Gene Sarazen and Ben Hogan and Byron Nelson and Arnold Palmer and Jack Nicklaus.

He crushed the elite field by 12 shots, the widest margin in a major championship since Young Tom Morris won the British Open by that number in 1870. In his 18 major professional victories, Nicklaus never won by more than nine. In his seven, Palmer never won by more than six.

Sunday was tough, tougher than the 66 Woods shot on Friday or the 65 on Saturday, because Woods took a nine-shot lead to the first tee and had to fight off the demons that came swarming. Memories of Greg Norman's collapse last year were there among them. Thoughts of all the years of planning and working for this moment, they were there, too. The hopes of kids who have taken to him and of racial and ethnic minorities, of Elder and Charlie Sifford, and all those other old black campaigners who cut a path for him.

He got a little nervous, he said.

His dad told him, "Son, this will probably be the hardest round you'll ever have to play. Go out there and be yourself, and it'll be one of the most rewarding."

And it was. Especially so, said Tiger, because of what it might mean to minorities and to kids.

"I think now kids will think golf is cool, really, and start playing," said the new Masters champion, who makes frequent trips to Taco Bell and McDonald's, pitches an occasional youthful fit, likes video games and sleeps the sleep of the innocent, even on the night before he wins the Masters.

Now that we have seen that Tiger Woods is what we thought he would be and hoped he would be, we turn our eyes to the future. What's out there for this remarkable talent who fears nothing but failure? The Grand Slam, perhaps? Is it realistic to suggest that he might win all four majors (the Masters, U.S. Open, British Open, and PGA Championship) in the same year?

"Whether it's realistic or not, I couldn't really tell you," said Woods, "but I think it can be done. Phil Mickelson won four tournaments last year. You just have to win the right four.

"You're competing with the best players in the world under extremely difficult conditions, but if you can peak at the right times, and have a lot of luck on your side, and play well, who knows?"

The other major championship courses will not necessarily suit Woods' game the way Augusta National does, with its wide fairways and forgiving rough. His huge tee shots allowed him to play a course the others weren't playing. He was hitting soft shots into the greens with short irons while others were whistling longer irons at surfaces that showed no mercy for them.

But is there a course Tiger Woods can't play? He's won junior titles in bunches and three U.S. Amateurs and already has four wins in half a year as a pro.

Today, nothing seems impossible.

1998

*The Masters is about more than just golf. It's about renewal,
emerging from the gray of winter into the sunshine.*

*The grass and the azaleas and the dogwoods provide a glorious
backdrop, but not even they can add more of a sense of returning
than the old gentlemen of the game who come and stand under the
great trees on the clubhouse lawn like monuments to tradition. Gene
Sarazen came every year until his death in 1999. Byron Nelson
came on a walking cane. Sam Snead came.*

*In 1998, Snead, 85, gave Sarazen, 96, a quick tune-up lesson
on the practice tee before they and Nelson went out to hit the ceremonial opening shots of the tournament, and then Snead, who has
always seemed to be in a hurry, stayed around long enough to talk,
to tell us that just about any pro will tell you he would rather win
the Masters than any other event.*

*The Masters is what it is in great part because the Sarazens
and Nelsons and Sneads never leave, even if they die. They are
always out there in spirit. Here, you think, this is where Sarazen
must have been when he had his double eagle in 1935. Here, down
in the valley, remember when Nelson played Nos. 12 and 13 in 2-3
to pick up six strokes on Ralph Guldahl and win the 1937 Masters?*

DEMONS FOLLOW ZOELLER,
DALY AROUND AUGUSTA

This was no place for clouds, this sunlit Tuesday at Augusta
National Golf Club, where the flowers bloomed and the trees did
a slow dance in the breeze, but shadows lay across two familiar
figures out there, wherever they walked.

A year ago this week, Fuzzy Zoeller, hanging out with some
media people on the clubhouse lawn, joked about Tiger Woods
serving fried chicken and collard greens, "or whatever they
serve," at the champions' dinner this year.

He meant no harm, but it ruined his life.

A year ago this week, John Daly was in the Betty Ford Clinic being treated for alcohol abuse.

Tuesday, they were out there in golf's grandest theater, playing a practice round together, as they often do, getting ready for the Masters. Each has won two major championships. Both have been extraordinarily popular with the galleries. But both have demons that won't go away.

And so they have a kinship. When Daly went on a 14-hour drinking spree last March, it was Zoeller who was awakened by a phone call from Daly's wife, asking for help.

And when this new Masters approached, and the Zoeller-Woods thing would not go away, it was Daly who suggested that Woods and Zoeller play a practice round together to show the world the incident was dead. But Woods said it would just be a public relations thing, and he was going to be busy preparing for a major championship.

Zoeller, who has won a Masters and a U.S. Open, whistled his way around Tuesday, as he always does, and cracked some jokes. He thrilled the gallery with a hole-in-one on the sixth hole. He autographed the ball and gave it to a kid. That's his way. Whistling, relating to the galleries, taking life one sunbeam at a time.

But the comment won't go away. The *Augusta Chronicle's* blackest headline, front page, Tuesday was "Zoeller Arrives Quietly." He didn't do anything but show up, register, and leave, but he got the headlines. It's no wonder, then, that the ordinarily loquacious Zoeller brushed past the media trying to interview him after his round Tuesday. He did it pleasantly, but wouldn't stop to talk.

Fuzzy and Tiger would meet face-to-face Tuesday night at the traditional champions' dinner at the club. Asked what might transpire there, Woods said, "It's done, it's over with. We've talked about it, made a statement about it. It's sad it did happen, but it's over with and we've moved on."

No slack. No public relations. Tiger says he's not the sentimental type. If he were, if he would let him up for air, he would enjoy the company of Fuzzy Zoeller, and Fuzzy would enjoy life more.

Daly has battled alcohol since he came to our attention with a huge bang, winning the PGA Championship in 1991 with his mammoth drives and his delicate short game. He has been in trouble with cops, had a couple of divorces, and fallen off the wagon with a loud thud a few times, interrupting his soap opera to win a British Open.

Now, he takes it a day at a time, a swing at a time. He attends lots of AA meetings and marks his ball with coins given to him by well-wishers, coins with messages on them. He has inspirational words printed on his golf bag, and he feeds his demon with candy. He has put on a lot of weight, but that's a burden that's a lot easier to carry.

Zoeller, 46, and Daly, 31, both lost big-money sponsors because of their problems. Gradually, though, they have replaced them. Gradually, they've brought their games back to a higher level.

Still, though, they walk in shadows that won't go away.

SLAMMIN' SAM STILL GOING STRONG AT AUGUSTA

Thursday, the first day of the Masters, came up fresh and sweet, scrubbed by thunderstorms that had rumbled through during the night. It was a day that would belong to players like Tiger Woods and Fred Couples and Paul Stankowski and to the wind that whipped around their ears, but this soft morning belonged to legends.

Gene Sarazen, 96 years old, Byron Nelson, 86, and Sam Snead, 85, three whose names are always mentioned when there is talk of golfing greatness, hit ceremonial tee shots to begin the tournament.

Sarazen hit one about 125 yards, his best in years, after having had a lesson from Snead on the practice tee, an 85-year-old instructing a 96-year-old, "Try to get your left shoulder under your chin." Sarazen listened, took three swings and said, "OK, that's enough."

Nelson, whose swing was once elegant but who walks with a cane now, pushed a 175-yarder to the right. Snead, grinning and doing a little dance step as he moved into position, familiar straw hat covering his baldness, caught one right in the screws and smacked it down the middle about 220 yards.

Still Slammin' Sam.

Three Masters, three PGAs, one British Open, 81 official tour wins, 135 wins overall, 163 course records, 37 holes-in-one in competition, one of them left-handed. That's a quick résumé on Sam. There are no U.S. Opens there, you'll notice. He never won one. He didn't play well in June, U.S. Open month, for some reason. Had he shot 69 in the final rounds, he would have won nine of them.

"He'll lie in bed and think about things like that," said his son, Jack.

Snead had worried us Tuesday. He had been hospitalized by what reports said might be a stroke. Turned out it was just fatigue catching up with him. He's been flitting around the country promoting a new line of clothing and working on other money-making enterprises.

Snead tried to get out of the hospital to go to the champions' dinner on Tuesday night, where he annually regales the past winners with off-color jokes, but Jack (he's really Sam Jr., but goes by Jack) wouldn't let him.

"He's tough," said Jack. "He had his tonsils taken out in a dentist's chair. And when he had a wreck down here a few years ago, he went to the champions' dinner that night with a dislocated shoulder, a busted leg, and stitches in his head."

It was comforting to see Snead clowning around on the first tee Thursday morning. He stayed young longer than anyone in sports ever has, shooting a 60 when he was 71, shooting a 67 when he was 84, finishing third in the PGA Championship when he was 63, kicking his leg so high he can touch the top of a door frame to this day.

We lost Ben Hogan a few months ago, but losing Sam would be different. He gives all of us hope for immortality.

Life has had some dreadful moments for him in recent times. His wife died. He was responsible for an awful accident in Augusta a few years ago that severely injured a passenger in another car. His eyesight is failing. His dog "Meister," a pal for 14 years, died recently. And then Sam had to fly to Texas to help bury his old rival Hogan.

Ben Hogan. Sam's son Jack said, "They were great rivals, but neither could tell a story without mentioning the other. When Ben died, my dad was playing golf with some friends back home in Hot Springs (Virginia). I went over there and said,

"Pop, somebody you know passed away. Ben Hogan." He kinda turned away, and when he turned back around, he had a tear in his eye and he said, 'Boy, we had a lot of fun together.'"

Snead doesn't play much competition anymore, but he does still play a lot of golf.

"He won't just go out and play," said Jack. "He has to have somebody he can play for money. You wouldn't believe how many people one-third his age lie about their handicaps so they can say they beat him out of some money."

Sam paused outside the Augusta National clubhouse Thursday after his ceremonial shot and said, "I asked Bobby Jones one time which was the greatest Masters of them all, and he said the one when Hogan and I were in a playoff (1954, Snead won). That was nice of him to say that."

On the other side of the clubhouse, the tournament had begun. Sam would like to have been out there.

"Ask any pro what tournament he would rather win," he said, "and he'll say the Masters. I'm pretty sure of that."

His car was waiting, to take him to a plane that would fly him home.

"Gotta go," he said. "See you next year. I hope."

AZALEAS SHAKE AMONG THE ROARS FOR NICKLAUS

Who would have imagined that on a golden Easter Sunday at the Masters, the cheers for a limping 58-year-old man would move Tiger Woods to pick up the pace and try to get away where the noise wouldn't be so deafening?

But this was a Masters more magical than any in many years, with compelling stories as abundant as the azaleas, and none was more compelling than that of Jack Nicklaus, who for four days was like the Golden Bear of old.

No man older than 52 has ever won a PGA Tour event, but Nicklaus, 58, walked down the 15th fairway Sunday telling his son Steve, who was caddying for him, "If I can eagle here and get a couple of birdies going in, I have a chance." He managed one birdie out of the lot, shot four-under-par 68, and tied for sixth, four shots behind champion Mark O'Meara. And he was disappointed he didn't win.

It fell short of a title, but it was one of the most remarkable performances ever in this place where the extraordinary is commonplace.

This was Nicklaus' 40th Masters. He has won six, to go along with his 14 other major championships, but he hadn't had a top-10 finish in a major since 1990.

Sadly, Nicklaus is now at a stage where every tournament might be his last.

He has a problem with his left hip, a severe loss of cartilage, that could finish him at any time.

"I'd love to play until I'm 100, Lord willing," he said, his voice getting a little husky, "but I think there's a reasonable amount of time. I'm having an awful hard time walking, and after about 14 or 15 holes, my hip has about had it.

"You know, how long that will last, how long my exercise program will hold off what might be inevitable for my hip, I don't know.

"If it is my last round at Augusta, I couldn't have had a nicer way to go out. Obviously, I would have liked to have shot a few strokes lower, but that's still a pretty nice way to go."

The cheers that erupted when he almost eagled the second hole and chipped in for a birdie on the third and holed a birdie putt on the sixth and another on the seventh were perhaps as loud as any ever heard in this place where the roar of the crowd is uniquely thrilling, not just to the players but to those who hear them echoing around the hills and valleys.

They were so explosive that Woods and playing partner Davis Love, in the group ahead of Nicklaus and Ernie Els, were bothered by them early in the round and made an effort to speed up, put some distance between themselves and the Bear's thunder.

As they crossed paths with Els at the eighth green and ninth tee, he told them, "I need some earplugs."

Woods said, "It was pretty neat to see Jack right there on the leader board where he used to be. I don't know about you, but I thought it was pretty nostalgic."

Tiger, who killed this course last year, shooting 18 under par and winning by 12 shots, shot 70 and finished at three-under-par 285—three shots behind Nicklaus— and said, "I could've won today if I had gotten the start Jack got."

If the kid could've started like the old guy.

Woods, 22, never got going, never broke 70, never had the sizzle that had rocketed him to stardom and had moved us to anoint him as the next Nicklaus.

After he abused the course last year, there was talk of "Tigerizing" it, toughening it up, because it was just too easy for him.

Well, we won't hear that again for a while. "My swing just wasn't quite there this week," said Woods. "I got every ounce out of my game, squeezed the towel dry. I was proud of the way I hung in there. It was reminiscent of the way that guy (Nicklaus) used to do.

"Who knows, maybe I'll win another one in the future."

Nicklaus was asked if the emotion was stronger on this day than it was when he won in 1986 at the age of 46.

"It was emotional," he said, "but in a different way. There's nothing as emotional as coming down the stretch when you're winning. That's what I'm here for. That's why we do it.

"It would probably be stupid to say I wasn't thrilled, but it would be dishonest to say I wasn't disappointed."

To the end, the Golden Bear.

1999

The 1999 Masters was a story of a 19-year-old kid and a 44-year-old veteran, neither of whom won.

Sergio Garcia, nicknamed "El Nino," played in his first Masters. He was the most heralded newcomer to golf since Tiger Woods emerged, and he came with some of the same excitement Woods had brought.

Like Woods, Garcia had a long list of successes beside his name, and he had fellow countrymen Seve Ballesteros and Jose Maria Olazabal advising him and urging him along.

He fared only moderately well, but he had plenty of opportunities ahead of him.

Greg Norman got into contention again, and galleries that had suffered with him during his final-round collapse in 1996 pulled hard for him. He heard their cheers, felt their warmth, and this time, he held together. Olazabal won for the second time, but given the drama of Norman's quest, it seemed almost incidental.

AFTER A SHAKY START, EL NINO SETTLES INTO MASTERS CLOUD

On the first swing of his first Masters on Thursday, Sergio Garcia, a freckled, 19-year-old Spaniard known as El Nino—"Little Boy"—hooked his tee shot into some trees.

His playing partner, the old veteran Tiger Woods, 23, told him, "Don't worry. I hit it there in my first Masters."

Garcia bogeyed and left the green two shots behind Tiger. On the second hole, El Nino, so-named because he started winning golf bets off grown men when he was five years old, again did an unfortunate imitation of his spray—hitting mentor Seve Ballesteros.

He hooked his tee shot into a place Ben Crenshaw calls the "Delta ticket counter," because that's where you go to check out of the Masters in a hurry.

He had to take a drop out of a ditch, then went on to make a bogey and was three shots behind Woods.

Tiger told him, "Come on, don't worry. Just stay calm, it'll come."

Garcia would return the kindness. He said a few words of encouragement to Woods after El Tigre had triple-bogeyed the eighth hole. Garcia waited until the 10th to say it. "On the eighth, I didn't think it was the right time," he said, showing wisdom far beyond his years.

Both finally got it together on the back nine. Like a couple of kids out at the muni, they agreed they would shoot 32 or 33. Woods shot 34, Garcia 33, and when they walked off the 18th green, they were tied at par 72. It had been an excellent adventure. Garcia is the European version of Tiger Woods. He's a popular cover boy for magazines.

Equipment manufacturers are hovering around, waiting to sign him when he turns pro within the next short while. And he's a winner, always has been. All his life his playground has been the golf course where his father is pro. The great Ballesteros, who has tutored Garcia, toughened him up, readied him for anything, says, "He is, quite simply, the best player of his age I have seen."

Masters champion Mark O'Meara says, "Talent-wise, compared to Tiger Woods, I'd have to give the edge to Tiger. But when it comes to knowledge of the game and how to play it tee to green, Sergio is better than any young person I've been around. Thanks to the tutoring he has gotten from his father and Seve, he knows how to get the ball in the hole."

When he was 15, Garcia won the European Amateur. When he was 17, he won the Catalonia Open by five strokes over a decent field of pros, shooting three 64s.

Last year, he made the cut in all seven of his European Tour starts. He finished third in a Nike tournament in Greensboro. He won the British and Spanish amateurs and reached the semifinals in the U.S. Amateur.

Those are samples. He has played in so many events and won so many titles, he honestly can't remember how many he won last year.

No matter how much you've been around, playing in the Masters with Tiger Woods in front of a huge gallery can be a frightening thing, but after his jittery start, Garcia felt a curious calm come over him. "I got so relaxed," he said, "I couldn't imagine how relaxed I was. It surprised me a little. I told my dad (who was caddying for him) on the 10th tee, 'I don't know. I think I'm too relaxed.' I couldn't feel nothing. It was like I was on a cloud."

From time to time, he could hear family members or friends shouting to him, things like, "Vamos! Vamos!" (Let's go! Let's go!). He went. Birdies on the 10th, 11th, and 17th holes, all nasty par-fours, gave him his 33, and his 72, and earned him big, happy hugs from about a dozen relatives and friends waiting at the finish.

The Little Boy had played like a man. The Man.

NORMAN'S GRITTY PLAY ERASES
BAD MEMORIES

At the end, the squinting, tooth-grinding emotion was gone from Greg Norman's craggy features, and he could only pat the back of José Maria Olazabal, who was about to win the Masters with a final putt, and say, "Go do it."

This time, though, Norman still had his heart. It hadn't been ripped out by a once-in-a-lifetime chip shot or a great finish by a 46-year-old legend named Jack Nicklaus, or a final-round collapse that made everyone want to turn away.

This time, in defeat, Norman won. He played the toughest round of golf he's ever had to play, dogged every step of the way around the windswept Augusta National course by the ghost of 1996, when he blew a six-shot lead on Sunday and lost. This time he started out a shot behind and lost by three and he was disappointed, but this time he loved it and so did the thousands storming after him.

He lost, but his electricity had hearts pounding all afternoon. That is his greatest gift to the game. It is impossible not to be passionate about Greg Norman, one way or another. This time, he was an overwhelming favorite of the people.

Some poor play, some shoulder surgery, some time away from the game had made this one easier for him to take. He was finally back from all that, back in the thick of it on Sunday in Augusta.

"That's what you really miss," he said. "You really miss these moments. That's why you love to play."

Davis Love loved it, too, just being out there on the back nine thinking, as he did, "All I need is one good hole, an eagle or a birdie," and feeling the heat.

"Sometimes," he said, "it's hard to calm down."

He finished second by two shots, short again in his bid for a title that he seems born to win. Four times in the last five years, he has challenged.

Twice he's finished second, twice seventh.

But he said, "It was a great, great tournament because so many people had a chance to win. I was disappointed I didn't win, but I was pleased that I played another Masters when I had a chance to get nervous. There's no feeling like standing in the middle of the 11th fairway or on the 12th tee, no feeling as scary as that."

Love got past the perilous 11th and the devilishly tricky 12th all right, but he couldn't quite summon the surge it takes on a day like this. Great roars were erupting ahead of him and behind him, all telling him something wonderful had happened. He needed something to happen for him, and then it did.

On the par-three 16th, in a setting that Jack Nicklaus calls the most exciting in golf on a Masters Sunday afternoon, he missed the green but pitched in for a birdie, the ball going well to the left of the pin, then inching downhill into the cup.

"I just tried to hit it up the hill, let it do a U-turn, then beg it in," he said.

The greatest roars, though, were for Norman, and then, moments later, Olazabal. Norman came to the 13th hole one shot behind, but knifed a 198-yard four-iron 25 feet behind the cup and holed the putt for an eagle three. He was suddenly the leader.

But only for a minute, maybe two. The unflappable Olazabal rolled in a 21-foot putt for birdie that saved half of the lead for him. It was one of those great moments that invariably happen in this place on this day.

Norman fell on his own sword. He tried to hit his tee shots too far on the 14th and 15th, and it cost him bogeys. He couldn't go for the green in two on the par-five 15th from the trees and laid up short of the water. He hit a horrible sand wedge from there into a bunker, but said he had mud on his ball, and we're going to accept that this time.

As he said, "Don't make a mountain out of a molehill this time."

And then he made a mountain out of it. "I feel I climbed a pretty good mountain today," he said. "I feel good about that."

Everyone did.

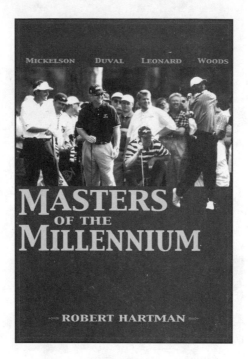

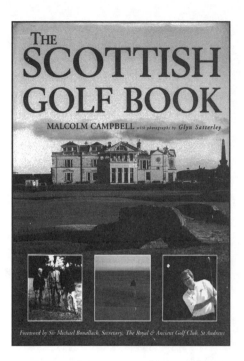

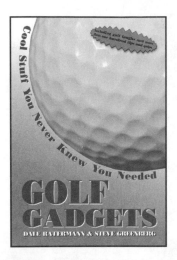
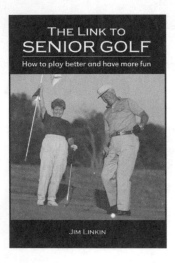

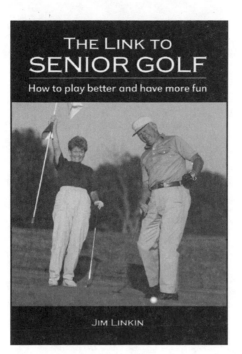